"*Latter Days* is a refreshing v⋯⋯⋯⋯⋯⋯⋯ an enthusiastic convert. I applaud Coke Newell and St. Martin's Press for presenting this innovative book."

—Susan Easton Black, professor of Church History and Doctrine, Brigham Young University, and author of *Impressions of a Prophet*

"Here the story of the Latter-day Saints, in the hands of a gifted writer and a great storyteller, takes its place among the most important nonfiction books of our day."

—L. Don LeFevre, former manager of Media Relations, The Church of Jesus Christ of Latter-day Saints

"I could not put this one down. Very well written and informative, *Latter Days* takes a valued place in my quick reference library on The Church of Jesus Christ of Latter-day Saints."

—Lee Groberg, award-winning documentary producer of *Trail of Hope: The Story of the Mormon Trail* (PBS, 1997) and *American Prophet: The Story of Joseph Smith* (PBS, 1999)

"Coke Newell has written the ideal introduction to Mormonism for the curious outsider. As a convert himself, he understands the misconceptions that have long distorted the public image of this distinctly American form of Christianity. More important, he also understands those modern perplexities for which Mormonism offers a timeless resolution.... Moving deftly from metaphysics to narrative, Newell draws from the Church's history of persecution and migration clear illustrations of the mortal-world meaning of transcendent beliefs, adducing compelling evidence that the historical trajectory of this dynamic faith ensures its increasing visibility in the decades ahead."

—Bryce Christensen, author of *Utopia Against the Family*

LATTER DAYS

An Insider's Guide to Mormonism,
The Church of Jesus Christ of Latter-day Saints

Coke Newell

St. Martin's Griffin
New York

To Elizabeth Louise Gehrig—you started it.

www.stmartins.com

Library of Congress Cataloging-in-Publication Data

Newell, Coke.
    Latter days : an insider's guide to Mormonism, the church of Jesus Christ of Latter-day Saints / by Coke Newell.
        p. cm.
    Includes bibliographical references.
    ISBN 0-312-24108-9 (hc)
    ISBN 0-312-28043-2 (pbk)
    1.Church of Jesus Christ of Latter-day Saints—History.   2. Church of Jesus Christ of Latter-day Saints—Doctrines.   I. Title
    BX8611.N49   2000
    289.3'09—dc21
                                                                00-027195
                                                                CIP

First St. Martin's Griffin Edition: May 2001

10 9 8 7 6 5 4 3 2 1

ACKNOWLEDGMENTS

Being a hermit both by nature and by nurture, I'm not a man of large networks. But the little one I relied upon for this book was a great one. My sincere appreciation goes to a number of people who assisted in the parturition of *Latter Days*.

First, to Michael Denneny at St. Martin's and Jim Hornfischer at Literary Group International, for seeing beyond the veil of convention. At the headquarters offices of The Church of Jesus Christ of Latter-day Saints: Brian D. Garner of the Church Educational System, and Ronald O. ("Omivorous") Barney of the Historical department for their close reading of the manuscript, sought for both to keep me accurate and to keep me employed; in the Public Affairs department: "Saint Louis" Don LeFevre (retired but never replaced) and Val N. Edwards, consummate scholars, perfect gentlemen, and valued friends; and to Arnie Augustin for opening the door.

Elsewhere: to Dan MacArthur for taking the chance; to Sid Price, Ray Beckham, Mark Scott, and Dean Tucker for going beyond the call; and to those who gave of their time to read and make comment on the book.

Finally, to my wife, Cindy, the most patient and precious partner a man ever had.

To all, thanks.

CONTENTS

In 1820 an obscure American farm boy went into the woods to pray
and came out with a message and mission that would challenge the
foundations of contemporary religion. But this new view of God, man,
and salvation proclaimed by Joseph Smith wasn't really new at all. It
was the plan from the very beginning.

Long before Eden, or T. Rex or even the Big Bang, billions of spirit
entities lived and learned in a premortal world, literal children of a
physical God. Individual intelligences imbued with motive and motion,
we exercised choice, initiative, and preference. But under our Father's
eye, and within his presence, we could only go so far. The Great Plan
of Happiness—the genetics within us—required that we leave our
heavenly home, take a physical body, and live by our spiritual wits in a
new world far away, a blue planet called Earth.

Set upon the earth as immortal beings, the first man and the first
woman soon understood that their eternal progress, or even happiness,
required that they pass through a mortal experience. But to get there,
they would have to die.

In contrast to the doctrine of most other Christian churches, Latter-day
Saints teach without reservation that the entire gospel plan—the Chris-

tian gospel—was known to and practiced by Adam and Eve, as were other advanced concepts of human learning and culture.

The Old Testament–era dispersion of the tribes of Israel sprinkled the blood of the covenant people throughout the lands of the earth. A fundamental focus of the Latter-day Saints is to find and gather those children of the covenant—with whom they share a literal heritage.

From his premortal stature as the most valiant of all spirit children of God, and following four millenia as the mighty God of the Old Testament, the Great Jehovah begins his turn on earth as the humblest of children, delivered in straw and diapered in rags. As Jesus of Nazareth he comes to full and early realization of his mission as the Savior of the world, a mission that will only be accomplished with the sacrifice of his life.

The Book of Mormon, like the Bible, is a compilation of the writings— historic and prophetic—of heaven-inspired men. Central to the book is an eyewitness account of the visit of the resurrected Savior to a group of people in ancient America.

With the Savior's return to heaven, the apostle Peter and his colleagues in the Judean ministry continue the work of Christ. But the seeds of rebellion are almost instantaneous. One by one, the apostles are killed, the converts hunted and driven, the pure truths changed. Centuries intervene, creeds rise, reformers rebel. Spiritual darkness covers the earth.

Following his vision of heaven in 1820, Joseph Smith faced the bitter scorn of neighbors and former friends for his continuing tales of heavenly visitors, Official and Exclusive Sanction, and new scripture. The creedal faiths of seventeen centuries, whatever else their differences, unitedly found such claims ludicrous at best, and blasphemous most likely. They determined to wipe Mormonism from the face of the earth.

From 1831 to 1844, the Latter-day Saints were driven from town to town, and state to state: New York, Pennsylvania, Ohio. In late 1838, thousands housed their children under tarps and trees, or in muddy caves carved into riverbanks spread out across far western Missouri. Then, Missouri's governor-elect Lilburn Boggs issued his famous decree: "exterminate [the Mormons] or drive them from the state." So through the winter of 1838–39, and across three hundred miles of frozen midwestern back country, ten thousand Latter-day Saints dragged all that hadn't been burned, abandoned, or killed three hundred miles to refuge in Illinois.

In Illinois, the Latter-day Saints founded a vibrant community that was the envy of the day. Named Nauvoo, it swelled toward twenty thousand residents by 1844. But if any among them were entertaining visions of taking their rightful and respected place in the mainstream of American society anytime soon, it wasn't Joseph Smith. In fact, his vision dictated exactly to the contrary: the Saints would suffer mightily and be driven once again. But this time, Joseph would not go with them.

Following the assassination of Joseph Smith and his brother, Hyrum, the world thought Mormonism had come to its end. Even the Latter-day Saints were in despondent disarray. But all they would need to carry on in strength had been well prepared for the people, including doctrine, policy—and Brigham Young.

Under Brigham Young's able leadership, the Latter-day Saints hung on in Nauvoo through the remainder of 1844 and much of 1845, continuing to build their city. But by the fall of 1845, their farms burning, mobs harassing them, and the leadership of both Illinois and the nation refusing to aid them, it was clear that their time in Illinois was coming to a close. But it was also clear that no place in America would take them next.

In the cold blue heart of winter, long before grass was growing or streams flowing to sustain their draft animals, twelve to fifteen thousand Latter-day Saints began their journey into the western wilderness, their eyes set on a remote basin in Mexican territory thirteen hundred miles away. It would be the largest forced migration in the history of America. Later scholars would see the experience as the single most important influence in molding the Latter-day Saints into a distinctive people.

What formed and cohered in the earliest days of the Mormon Trail to the west was a people apart: separate, unique, and alone, calling themselves the "Camp of Israel." Even journalists of the day were soon making comparisons to the ancient travels of Moses and his people: here was modern Israel, with its Prophet, its Exodus from bondage, and its sojourn toward the Promised Land.

Converging from three directions and a dozen lands, the Mormon pioneers moved toward their envisioned land of refuge—isolated, arid, unpeopled, and unwanted by the rest of humanity. The Valley of the Great Salt Lake would be just the right place.

Having established themselves in safety in the remote valley of the Salt Lake basin, the Latter-day Saints began a new era of settlement and expansion under the leadership of Brigham Young. Thousands of converts would flow into the valley from all over the world, and the next three decades would see the colonization of nearly four hundred communities across the American West.

Refuge from the long arm of intolerance and misunderstanding would grace the home base of the Latter-day Saints for only a few years. The

U.S. Army would march on Utah, and a prairie court would condemn their limited practice of polygamy. Though they would argue the latter issue all the way to the Supreme Court, thousands of fathers and husbands would be hunted and imprisoned. Seeing the future of the church on the verge of forfeit, the Mormon prophet would end the practice in 1890, paving the way for U.S. statehood.

More and more through the decades of the twentieth century, Latter-day Saint history would begin playing out in places like Adelaide and Johannesburg and Medellín. And it would play out prominently, setting a pace of international growth that would stun observers. In the words of one prominent sociologist, The Church of Jesus Christ of Latter-day Saints would enter the twenty-first century as "the first world religion since Islam."

Mormon doctrine corresponds with many concepts common to the larger body of Christian belief and practice: the world will end, Christ will return in glory, people will be judged. But from there the Latter-day Saints embrace an entirely divergent set of specifics regarding heaven, its purposes, and its eventual occupants.

How do you get a religion so precise, so comprehensive, and so radical to work—smoothly—in 165 nations of the world, attracting converts from all walks of life and faith? You speak to that engraved code, the DNA of deity. And then you explain it in an entirely new light, a light that goes all the way back. All the way to the beginning.

PREFACE

Students in an introductory college science course were instructed to collect water samples from a stream running close to their rural Colorado campus. For subsequent lab testing that would illustrate the varied dynamics of mountain stream biology, the instructor recommended as access points a number of eddies and oxbows sprinkled along the half-mile stretch just above the dorms. Seeing a simpler course, however, one team of students scooped water from under a footbridge that crossed the stream just below horse corrals a mere fifty feet from their classroom. When their sample was returned by the lab two days later, a handwritten note was paper-clipped to the results. It read: "Congratulations! Your horse is pregnant."

Dirty water produces questionable results.

Hundreds of books have been written on various aspects of the history, doctrine, or practice of The Church of Jesus Christ of Latter-day Saints, commonly, albeit mistakenly, called the "Mormon Church."[1] For over a century following its 1830 founding, the stated purpose of most such books was to expose the strange nature of this unique American religion whose followers were forced to flee "normal" American society in 1846, finding a place to practice their bizarre rituals only in the isolated wilderness of the Rocky Mountains of Utah. The last few decades, and particularly the final decade of the twentieth century, hosted a new list of titles, many from academic publishers. Most explored the complex nature of this vehemently Christian faith, which was exploding into mainstream modern culture as one of the fastest growing, most visible faiths in the world. (It is "a new world religion," said one prominent sociologist.)

---

[1]There is no "Mormon Church," and there never has been. Its correct name is The Church of Jesus Christ of Latter-day Saints. However, because the church accepts as scripture a volume known as the "Book of Mormon" it has often borne this nickname. One look at that correct nine-word title, however, will explain why I use *Latter-day Saint, Mormon,* and *"LDS"* interchangeably throughout this book.

Almost without exception, whether written in the nineteenth century or the twentieth, each of these books has fit into one of three categories:

1. the journalistic "outsider" view (including the dispassionate academic approach): one, controlling his malice, attempting to look in

2. the "dissident" or malicious view: former members or representatives of self-styled "rival" faiths attempting to topple the church or "redeem" its deluded masses

3. the "apologetic" view: the faithful insider attempting to strengthen the flock

Those books written by outsiders to the Latter-day Saints' faith and employing a reasonable range of objectivity vary widely in their ability to get it right, to really comprehend LDS thought and doctrine—Christian but *very* different. Those texts written by the dissidents, or even by objective outsiders who surrender to some odd compulsion to get their "research" from the mouths of such dissidents, continually end up with the same dirty water, contaminated and dangerously unreliable. (Would you study Catholicism at the knee of a rabbi?) Finally, those books written by the faithful are, almost without exception, written *to* the faithful, using language that only the faithful understand, and emanating from publishers and bookstores that only the faithful patronize.

With the publication of *Latter Days,* St. Martin's Press has opened the twenty-first century with a book unlike any other. I am fortunate to be the author they chose to write it.

Professionally, I'm on the inside of this tale: a card-holding Mormon high priest employed by the church as an international public relations officer at world headquarters in Salt Lake City, Utah. A returned missionary. Married in the temple. But historically and conceptually, I'm a convert to the faith, straight out of the rock-and-roll, vegetarian, whole earth, and homeschool, homeopathic Colorado mountains. And still into most of it.

*Faith*fully.

I can talk Lynyrd Skynyrd and Ram Dass and *Mother Earth News* with the best of 'em. Though I have a reserved seat four feet away from the Mormon Tabernacle Choir, my idea of sacred music tends more toward Loreena McKennitt and Nightnoise ("The Cricket's Wicket" will be playing when I enter heaven or I'm coming back for the CD).

Thus, while I will not claim absolute inerrancy throughout this volume, I don't hesitate to state right up front that you can trust what you read here. I won't ask you to accept, as in *believe,* the theology presented, and I can't be responsible for your interpretation of any of it. But I'll lay it right on the table: you're getting clean water.

From an internal perspective, Latter-day Saint message makers (e.g., PR guys, missionaries, your zealous neighbor) believe their greatest contribution to *your* life will be their religion's consummate capacity to answer three soul-gnawing questions common to the human experience:

1. Where did I come from?

2. Why am I here on earth?

3. What will become of me after this life is over?

Many of the pages that follow will examine Latter-day Saint doctrine that addresses these questions. It does so in the context of our version of the history of the universe, in chronological order. This is an approach that has never been used before. From my perspective, in order to comprehend Latter-day Saint beliefs and practices (e.g., large families), one must understand our chronology of earth and human existence (we lived elsewhere before coming to earth).

But are the answers to the three preceding questions the reason three hundred thousand people a year in 160 nations convert to The Church of Jesus Christ of Latter-day Saints? In my own case they broadly approximate, but certainly do not duplicate, the reasons I converted in 1976 at the culmination of a winding, yet upwardly inspiring—and to me, completely logical—journey from atheism to Native American thought to Zen.

At the beginning of the third post-Christian millennium, more than two-thirds of all eleven million Latter-day Saints worldwide are first-generation converts like myself. Their ancestors never heard church founder Joseph Smith preach before he was murdered, never fled the subsequent burnings in Nauvoo, never dragged all that was left to them across the frozen, windswept summits of the 1,300-mile Mormon Trail, and never carved subsistence dugouts into the dry, desert soil of Utah's remote Salt Lake basin. But they know the stories, they honor the people, and they feel privileged to accept the heritage. Most of us have walked bitter trails of our own, with our own reasons, our own questions, and our own summits to conquer on our way to faith.

Where I'm heading with this is right here: The story of Mormonism you are about to sample was drawn from above the horse pasture. The water is clean, fresh, usable.

But it wasn't bottled in Utah.

Crystal Lake, Colorado
August 15, 1999

Prologue: A Boy's Prayer

Contrary to the figure given in every other book on the faith, 1820 is not the beginning of Mormonism. That is, in fact, a very late date in the continuity of Mormon cosmology. But it serves as a fulcrum for so much of LDS thought and theology, it will here serve as our point of departure into a paradigm shift unlike any since Adam rearranged the molecules of man. It will be, for many, a trip through a parallel universe. So to help you keep your footing as we depart, we will begin as suggested by everyone else: in New York State in 1820. But from there we'll go places you haven't been in, oh, about six billion years.

He could have done something simple, like refuse to go to church or argue that the preacher was boring. After all, he was just a fourteen-year-old boy, and everyone would have understood.

He could have debated the interpretation of Bible verses, pitting Paul against Peter, or Presbyterians (his mother's faith) against Methodists (his personal favorite). Something common, ordinary. Understandable.

But no, young Joseph Smith had to go and turn religion on its head, making claims no one had ever made, pushing buttons no one had ever pushed. As he told his mother late that spring morning in 1820: "I have learned for myself that Presbyterianism is not true."[2]

In the emerging context of his own story, it would become the greatest understatement of his life. What happened to Joseph that clear spring day was, at once and for ever after, the turning point of his life and tens of millions of lives after him. It either happened or it didn't. Everything else would be subsidiary.

In all that Joseph Smith would do over the next twenty-four years, until the day of his death at the hands of a mob; in everything that would

---

[2]Although a number of things in peripheral Latter-day Saint doctrine suggest that this happened in April, the historical record merely says "spring."

happen in the growth of the church he would found ten years later, the events of this spring morning would remain the pivotal moment in time. And the foundation of Latter-day Saint thought.

It either happened or it didn't. No other perspective is of any relevance.

Here's the story. The time is early spring, 1820. The setting is the Finger Lakes region of western New York State, specifically, the village of Palmyra.

"There was in the place where we lived an unusual excitement on the subject of religion," wrote Joseph Smith in his 1838 *History*.

It commenced with the Methodists, but soon became general among all the sects in that region of country. Indeed, the whole district of country seemed affected by it, and great multitudes united themselves to the different religious parties, which created no small stir and division amongst the people, some crying, "Lo, here!" and others, "Lo, there!" Some were contending for the Methodist faith, some for the Presbyterian, and some for the Baptist.

For, notwithstanding the great love which the converts to the different faiths expressed at the time of their conversation, and the great zeal manifested by the respective clergy . . . , yet when the converts began to file off, some to one party and some to another, it was seen that the seemingly good feelings of both the priests and the converts were more pretended than real; for a scene of great confusion and bad feeling ensued—priest contending against priest, and convert against convert; so that all their good feelings one for another, if they ever had any, were entirely lost in a strife of words and a contest about opinions.

I was at this time in my fifteenth year. My father's family was proselyted to the Presbyterian faith, and four of them joined that church . . .

During this time of great excitement my mind was called up to serious reflection and great uneasiness; but though my feelings were deep and often poignant . . . it was impossible for a person young as I was, and so unacquainted with men and things, to come to any certain conclusion who was right and who was wrong.

In the midst of this war of words and tumult of opinions, I often said to myself: What is to be done? Who of all these parties are right;

or, are they all wrong together? If any one of them be right, which is it, and how shall I know it?

While I was laboring under the extreme difficulties caused by the contests of these parties of religionists, I was one day reading the Epistle of James, first chapter and fifth verse, which reads: If any of you lack wisdom, let him ask of God, that giveth to all men liberally, and upbraideth not; and it shall be given him.

Never did any passage of scripture come with more power to the heart of man than this did at this time to mine. It seemed to enter with great force into every feeling of my heart. I reflected on it again and again, knowing that if any person needed wisdom from God, I did; for how to act I did not know, and unless I could get more wisdom than I then had, I would never know; for the teachers of religion of the different sects understood the same passages of scripture so differently as to destroy all confidence in settling the question by an appeal to the Bible.

At length I came to the conclusion that I must either remain in darkness and confusion, or else I must do as James directs, that is, ask of God. So, in accordance with this, my determination to ask of God, I retired to the woods to make the attempt. It was on the morning of a beautiful, clear day, early in the spring of eighteen hundred and twenty. After I had retired to the place where I had previously designed to go, having looked around me, and finding myself alone, I kneeled down and began to offer up the desires of my heart to God. I had scarcely done so, when immediately I was seized upon by some power which entirely overcame me, and had such an astonishing influence over me as to bind my tongue so that I could not speak. Thick darkness gathered around me, and it seemed to me for a time as if I were doomed to sudden destruction.

But, exerting all my powers to call upon God to deliver me out of the power of this enemy which had seized upon me, and at the very moment when I was ready to sink into despair and abandon myself to destruction . . . I saw a pillar of light exactly over my head, above the brightness of the sun, which descended gradually until it fell upon me.

It no sooner appeared than I found myself delivered from the enemy which held me bound. When the light rested upon me I saw two Personages, whose brightness and glory defy all description, standing above me in the air. One of them spake unto me, calling me by name and said, pointing to the other—This is My Beloved Son. Hear Him!"[3]

And there lies the foundation of the Latter-day Saint story. Over the next ten years, when he would formally found The Church of Christ (modified to "The Church of Jesus Christ of Latter-day Saints" in 1838), Joseph Smith would earn the bitter scorn of neighbors and former friends for his continuing accounts of heavenly visitors (resurrected personages from beyond the mortal veil); official and exclusive sanction (in personal visits from ancient apostles Peter, James, and John, among others); and new scripture (the Book of Mormon and others).

Joseph Smith's announcement of what came to be known as his First Vision of God the Father and Jesus Christ the Son—separate, distinct, physical beings of human form—would launch a movement that would require Joseph's own life not many years hence and force some of the most engaging drama in American history. It would trigger the rise—slow at first, precipitous later—of a new world religion. Of its significance a later church president would say, "Our entire case, as members of The Church of Jesus Christ of Latter-day Saints, rests on the validity of this glorious First Vision. Nothing on which we base our doctrine, nothing we teach, nothing we live by, is of greater importance than this initial declaration."[4]

In the twenty-four years between Joseph's walk to the woods and his murder at the hands of an enraged mob in frontier Illinois would come the foundational framework for all the doctrine ever to be taught in The Church of Jesus Christ of Latter-day Saints. Although subsequent prophets would head the church, revelation would continue to flow, and patterns of practice would continue to evolve, the precedent or provision for each was established during the life of Joseph Smith. Like the U.S. Supreme Court recurring to the Constitution for legal meaning in an age more than two centuries removed, Mormon thought, doctrine, and policy—in a church of eleven million adherents—still finds its bearings in reference to "the Prophet," Joseph Smith.

But this new view of God, man and salvation proclaimed by Joseph Smith wasn't really new at all. It was the plan from the very beginning.

---

[3]Extract from "Joseph Smith History," *Pearl of Great Price*, The Church of Jesus Christ of Latter-day Saints.

[4]Gordon B. Hinckley, General Conference, October 1998.

PART 1

A New Heaven and a New Earth

Trailing clouds of glory do we come from God,
who is our home.
Heaven lies about us in our infancy.

WILLIAM WORDSWORTH
"Ode: Intimations of Immortality from
Recollections of Early Childhood"

CHAPTER 1

A Heavenly Start

"In the beginning" is a relative phrase. Latter-day Saint doctrine identifies no specific point on the cosmic ruler for the beginning of heaven, of earth, or of humanity. For the chronology of heaven—and of its God—we grant a very large ruler, one whose unit of measure is so vast as to render all calculations the nomenclature of eternity. As to the time of the creation of earth and its habitation by occupants we can begin a flirtation with numeracy, but the numbers are yet large, and unwieldy, and seemingly without inherent value.

Not so in regard to the purpose of that creation. To that there remains no question.

Far, far away—whether in physical distance or in metaphysical dimension, we make no claims[5]—and long, long ago, you and I were born as spirit children of God and, naturally, a Goddess, actual beings of glorified human form and substance. Our home and theirs was a brilliant orb, a crystalline sphere, where the pure light of the greatest of all stars, Kolob, shone endlessly (and yet does and will forever). Time on that planet-star, our Kolob-blessed home, was unmeasured and largely irrelevant. Irrelevant but for our date with destiny.

Thus, in *our* beginning, the great God and Goddess peopled their home in heaven with billions of spirit children, eternal intelligences clothed, through this spiritual birthing, with spiritual bodies; bodies complete of form: arms, legs, noses, ears, and so on. We were individual entities, male or female, like our parents, with personality and character. The children of the Gods looked liked the Gods: in the image of God created they us.

There, as children of God, we lived and moved and had our being

---

[5]"And there are many kingdoms; for there is no space in the which there is no kingdom; and there is no kingdom in which there is no space, either a greater or a lesser kingdom." (*Doctrine and Covenants* 88:37)

for untold millennia of time in "the regions of bliss."[6] We were accompanied by the spiritually created animals of all varieties, as "all things were first created in the spirit existence in heaven before they were placed upon this earth."[7]

Unlike our Father and Mother, we (the God-children; distinct species from the other life-forms) were spirit only, unadorned with the perfected, glorious bodies they had achieved through a process we would yet learn about. We were potential heirs, not equals. Our eternal progression required that we, like they had done successfully before us, leave our heavenly home, take a physical body, and pass through the memory-veiled testing grounds of a mortal probation.

Choice and accountability were the eternally paired principles upon which our progress would hinge: removed from their presence, how would we choose? Right and wrong were eternal verities and eternal opposites. Valiant obedience and willful rebellion were already apparent operatives in the premortal lives of each of us to varying degrees. Except for one.

The firstborn spirit son we knew as Jehovah was like our Father in every respect but that of having gained a physical, then glorified, body. Valiant was his every thought, obedient his every action. Great would be his course through eternity.

Thus after ages of time, in which our parents came to know us better than any mortal father or mother ever knows a child, a Grand Council was convened. There, with all of us present, the plan for our progression was presented: an earth, a mortal trial, and an evaluation.

The event, reopened in vision to a mighty and faithful prophet ages later, would tell it like this:

> Now the Lord had shown unto me, Abraham, the intelligences that were organized before the world was; and among all these there were many of the noble and great ones. And God saw these souls that they were good, and he stood in the midst of them, and he said: These I will make my rulers; for he stood among those that were spirits, and he saw that they were good; and he said unto me: Abraham, thou art one of them; thou wast chosen before thou wast born.

---

[6]Joseph Smith, *Evening and Morning Star*, August 1832.

[7]Joseph Fielding Smith Jr., *Doctrines of Salvation*, Vol. 1, p. 76.

And there stood one among them that was like unto God [this being the Great Jehovah] and he said unto those who were with him: We will go down, for there is space there, and we will take of these materials, and we will make an earth whereon these may dwell; And we will prove them herewith, to see if they will do all things whatsoever the Lord their God [our common Father] shall command them.[8]

The proposal then was this: from the elements of the universe and in space then existing, worlds were to be organized, then peopled by the spirit children of God. These noble and great ones, assisted, perhaps, by other valiant children who would people each planet, would help in the effort, designing and creating, through natural processes of time and function and according to natural-eternal law, the earth and other inhabitable globes. From those elements, human beings would be formed, gods in embryo, our immortal spirits to be clothed with the dust of the earth, and all memories of our former existence in the presence of God to be shut out. We would be left to face the trials of mortality and prove our mettle as gods-in-process. Choice, the eternal principle, would precede the effects of accountability, its essential companion.

It was made clear that none would pass through the trial unscathed, that none would remain clean. It was not so determined, it was simply known. Our tarnishment would come as the result not of another's transgression, but simply because the test would exceed the capacity of mortals.

How, then, asked our Father, knowing but seeking wisdom and initiative among his children, would any of us return? For no unclean thing would ever return to his presence following the mortal sojourn.

Quite simply, no one of us would measure up.

At that, another son of God arose, this one also a "son of the morning" (one of the eldest, among the firstborn in that premortal sphere). Forever rebellious, and outrageous in his arrogance, this brother we called Lucifer proposed to save us all, to bring home every mortal sojourner, regardless of merit or effort. He would merely and simply abrogate the law and open the gates of eternity.[9]

---

[8]Abraham 3:24–25.

[9]See Robert J. Mathews, *New Testament Sydney B. Sperry Symposium*, January 29, 1983, p. 159. Lucifer would later use this very approach with great success, but not in heaven. (See 2 Nephi 28:21–23, Book of Mormon.)

Such a proposal was immediately recognized by most for its ignorance, for the immutable nature of agency and accountability—eternal laws of existence—had long been known and experienced by all of us. The only question remaining to most was how, following the surely less-than-spotless mortal trial of our moral agency, would any return to the presence of God without blemish? Force was clearly not an option, nor was the suspension of law, for such, even if possible, would make of heaven a hell.

The Great Jehovah arose and continued. Of course, these humans would be granted agency, the right and the power to choose. Certainly, some would choose poorly. Two things would strengthen our chances. First, an enlightening voice, a whisper in our minds, would speak to us as the voice of conscience; obedient response to it would earn us the right to an even greater enlightenment, the directing presence or power of another Son of God, the Holy Ghost, who would lead the progressively obedient back to a full knowledge, even a lifting of the veil of memory. Second, Jehovah himself would come to earth, clothed in a mortal frame, and live a sinless life in our behalf. As all broken laws—the natural and immutable laws of heaven—bore a just and natural and immutable penalty, he would suffer himself to bear all things, even death, to work out the recompense, to make up the difference between our efforts and the requirements of heaven, in behalf of each of us.

If the Father would accept such an expiation, such atonement, both justice and mercy could be satisfied—in fact, perfected.

A shout of joy for this magnanimity coursed in waves through the heaven (see Job 38:7).

But Lucifer bellowed once again, protesting this acquiescent offer. "I will bring them all," he bragged to the Father, bring them all back regardless of their personal effort or any shade of personal valiance developed. (Perhaps he wanted peers.) But then, "Here am I, send me, I will be thy son, and I will redeem all mankind, that one soul shall not be lost. And surely I will do it; wherefore *give me thine honor*".[10]

He wanted to reign.

Such bald-faced presumption had yet to be uttered in our heavenly home, and the stir it caused was ferocious. Some of our brothers and

---

[10]Moses 4: 1, *The Pearl of Great Price*. (italics mine).

sisters yelled it was the only way, the only guarantee that this earth existence would not become instead a sure road to their ruination.

In the midst of commotion, the Great Jehovah stood once again. He waited. The heavens stilled. The law of heaven, of the universe, he reminded us, required such a course as he had endorsed, a course that allowed agency and demanded accountability. It was the course of gods, the very path our parents had trod in a similar way ages before. And he would do all we couldn't, within the demands of justice. He would build that bridge back to eternity, if only we would let him.

At that, the rancor resumed, and the heavens shook with an unknown murmur. Quietly, Jehovah turned to the Father, acknowledging his right to decide:

"Father, thy will be done," he said, "and the glory be thine forever."[11]

And the Father said: " 'I will send the first.' And the second was angry, and kept not his first estate; and, at that day, many followed after him."[12]

And all hell broke loose in heaven. The Book of Revelation calls it very plainly "war" (Rev. 12: 9–12). Lucifer and a full one-third of the children in heaven fought the valiant, led by one known as Michael, who both Jude and Paul would ages later refer to as the "Archangel."

Having defied the laws of the universe, the rebellious clearly and effectively lost the contest, and "neither was their place found any more in heaven."[13] They were cast out, disinherited. Their "father" (ruler) from then on would be Lucifer, and their dominion outer darkness. Thus did Lucifer become Satan, the devil, the tempter. Having rejected the eternal plan of heaven, these objectors selected the alternative: never would they take upon themselves a mortal body or complete the course toward Godhood. By their rebellion they had, in fact, rejected the opportunity for eternal progression before even having attempted it. Their role would yet play out on the earth, but it would be a role of darkness and eternal misery. Precisely, they would *become* agents of adversity for others: the spirits whispering of greed, lust, ire, and hatred. They had exercised their agency and borne the effect.

---

[11]Moses 4: 2.

[12]Abraham 3:27–28.

[13]Rev. 12:9–12.

"Wherefore, because that Satan rebelled against me, and sought to destroy the agency of man, which I, the Lord God, had given him, and also, that I should give unto him mine own power; by the power of mine Only Begotten, I caused that he should be cast down; and he became Satan, yea, even the devil, the father of all lies, to deceive and to blind men, and to lead them captive at his will, even as many as would not hearken unto my voice."[14]

And what of those who remained in heaven? Many wept over their fallen kin, their unfaithful brothers and sisters.

To the obedient son, the firstborn among spirits, the faithful and true—Jehovah—the Father then granted full power and authority to effectuate the creation of the earth (and innumerable others). It would be his to rule, his to redeem, and following the successful completion of his own mortal sojourn upon it, his to inherit. Due to his perfect obedience to the will of the Father (which was itself one and the same with the eternal law of the universe), Jehovah was, in fact, granted a premortal measure of Godhood, as was the Holy Ghost (we do not know the premortal name of this individual). In all things, through eons of time, they had shown themselves unfailingly faithful to and allied with the Father's every thought, act, and design.

Jehovah, now introduced to all of us as the presiding God of the coming world, organized from among his siblings the manpower sufficient to create it. Certainly the "noble and great ones" filled responsible positions in that effort. Michael, subordinate in honor and obedience only to Jehovah, and who would at a future stage take up residence on this planet as its first mortal flesh, played a principal role, even as "the chief manager in that operation."[15]

Jehovah and his selected hands would now begin the physical creation of the earth. It would be a magnificent creation, worthy of the children of God.

---

[14]Moses 4:3–4.

[15]Brigham Young, *Journal of Discourses*, Vol. 3, p. 319, April 20, 1856.

CHAPTER 2

The Choice

About the time Joseph Smith was adjusting for good his concept of deity, an Italian excavator working in Egypt uncovered eleven well-preserved mummies in a large tomb on the west bank of the Nile River. By 1835, the four mummies that had not yet been sold to collectors in the eastern United States found their way in a traveling exhibit to Kirtland, Ohio, where Joseph, twenty-nine years old and married, was then living.

Believing the mummies were worth owning (and they were definitely for sale), Joseph engaged the assistance of a number of church members in Kirtland to purchase them on behalf of the church. Through a process of study and inspiration similar to that with which he had previously translated the Book of Mormon, he shortly thereafter announced that portions of papyrus found within the mummies contained some writings of the patriarch Abraham, and another those of Joseph, both of whom had lived in Egypt. From those papyri descended, in 1842, The Book of Abraham, from which much of the foregoing Latter-day Saint doctrine regarding the creation is known.[16]

Details, yes, but not everything.

For instance, no rigid standard is annunciated by Latter-day Saint doctrine regarding the period required for the creation of the earth, nor does faithful orthodoxy insist on a particular viewpoint. Throughout the process, however long, Latter-day scripture merely says that "the Gods watched those things which they had ordered until they obeyed."[17] And such obeisance may well have taken the 4.5 billion years suggested by most modern science texts. Or more. The gods were not in a hurry.

Though individual church authorities have over time held divergent

---

[16]See *Documentary History of the Church*, 2:236, 238, 286; other writings, including an inspired revision of the early chapters of Genesis known as "Selections from the Book of Moses," would join the Book of Abraham in 1851. Collectively, they are called *The Pearl of Great Price* and accepted as among the "standard works" of The Church of Jesus Christ of Latter-day Saints.

[17]Abraham 4:18.

views on the specific clicks of the creation clock, none has ever exceeded nor argued the written statement of The First Presidency of the church given in April 1931: "Upon the fundamental doctrines of the Church we are all agreed. Our mission is to bear the message of the restored gospel to the world. Leave geology, biology, archaeology, and anthropology, no one of which has to do with the salvation of the souls of mankind, to scientific research, while we magnify our calling in the realm of the Church. . . ." In conclusion they said: "Neither side of the controversy [creationism versus science] has been accepted as a doctrine at all."[18]

An official church position on the age of the earth (or the processes by which it was created) does not exist. And in abeyance to these words found in *Doctrine and Covenants,* one of the volumes of scripture accepted by Latter-day Saints, one likely won't exist for a long time: "Verily I say unto you, in that day when the Lord shall come [the Second Coming], he shall reveal all things; Things which have passed, and hidden things which no man knew, things of the earth, by which it was made, and the purpose and the end thereof; Things most precious, things that are above, and things that are beneath, things that are in the earth, and upon the earth, and in heaven."[19]

And "until that day comes," says another official church publication, "we must rely on what we are taught in the scriptures and what we assume to be true based on the evidence gathered and examined by science."[20]

Perhaps the bottom line in all creation discussion by Latter-day Saints is this: God did it, and he knew what he was doing.

And here's what he did:"And the Gods[21] organized the earth to bring forth grass from its own seed, and the herb to bring forth herb from its own

---

[18]First Presidency Minutes, April 7, 1931; also *Doctrine and Covenants* 101: 25, 32–34.

[19]*Doctrine and Covenants* 101:32–34.

[20]"Fossils and the Scriptures" by Brigham Young University geologist Morris Petersen, in *Ensign* (the official church magazine for adults), September 1987: 28–29.

[21]That Latter-day Saint doctrine allows for the existence of many more gods than the two likely referenced here—Jehovah and the Father—will become much clearer in later chapters. But as stated by the ancient apostle Paul, though "there be gods many, and lords many, but to us there is but one God" (1 Cor. 8:5–6), one God alone "with whom we have to do" (Heb. 4:13). That God is, ultimately, the Father of our immortal spirits; but by extension it includes all within the Godhead: the Father; Jehovah/Christ, the God over this earth and its inhabitants, our Savior; and the Holy Ghost, three individuals perfectly unified in singularity of purpose. We have nothing to do with any other gods, nor they with us.

seed, yielding seed after his kind; and the earth to bring forth the tree from its own seed, yielding fruit, whose seed could only bring forth the same in itself, after his kind; and the Gods saw that they were obeyed."[22]

This process of planning, organization, and patient waiting on the self-directing and self-correcting entrenchment of innately programmed natural processes describes the Latter-day Saint view of the creation of the earth and of its self-management today. To Latter-day Saints, the earth is a living being whose very voice has been heard by the great prophet Enoch. It entered the mortal creation (having, like everything else, undergone a previous spiritual creation), received its baptism at the Flood, and will yet pass through a final cleansing and be redeemed to "paradisaical glory" as the eternal abode of the righteous.

Which brings us to Adam.

At some point, seeing that the processes of earth were obeying, the time became ripe for humans to take up their mortal habitation. "So the Gods went down to organize man in their own image, in the image of the Gods to form they him, male and female to form they them."[23]

We know nothing of the details, nor does such knowledge have any bearing on our ultimate salvation. In some way the premortal spirits of Adam and Eve came to earth, clothed upon now by the "dust" or elements of the temporal creation. Humans, and on this there is no speculation, are the direct and lineal offspring of God, formed in God's image and endowed with divine attributes. That, very simply, is our heritage and potential: a premortal existence, the brief mortal probation, and a postmortal eternity. It lends a chronological perspective to J. R. R. Tolkien's term *middle earth*.

From the elements of earth, Michael, now to be called Adam, the "first man,"[24] took up residence on the blue planet with his wife, to whom he was married at some point "by the hand of God" (Jehovah) in "a garden of beauty and peace."[25] For what length of time we do not know, Adam and Eve walked in the presence of the Gods (Jehovah and the Father), conversed with them, received instruction from them. As the instruction progressed, choice was offered. Before Adam were brought all "the beast[s] of

---

[22]Abraham 4:12.

[23]Abraham 4:27.

[24]Bruce R. McConkie, *The Mortal Messiah*, Vol. 1, p. 295.

[25]Ibid.

the field, and every fowl of the air" and all the other creatures "to see what he would call them; and whatsoever Adam called every living creature, that should be the name thereof."[26] At some point following physical maturity, they were commanded to "multiply and replenish the earth."

That, however, was an impossibility.

They were not yet mortal, and the autonomous expansion of their species was out of their reach. Spirit, not blood, a substance not subject to the normal vicissitudes of mortality, coursed through their veins. Subsequently, the fuller breadth of the reality and purpose of Adam and Eve's challenge was introduced: having learned of choice, they were presented with accountability. It would change eternity.

"And I, the Lord God, commanded the man, saying: Of every tree of the garden thou mayest freely eat, but of the tree of the knowledge of good and evil, thou shalt not eat of it, nevertheless, thou mayest choose for thyself, for it is given unto thee; but, remember that I forbid it, for in the day thou eatest thereof thou shalt surely die."[27]

Thus was introduced the great dilemma: Adam and Eve had been commanded to produce and bear children, thus fulfilling one step of their own creation and enabling a critical component in the creation of the earth. Yet as immortal beings—some pure essence flowing through veins of earthly element—they could not reproduce. In their current state, offspring was impossible.

To add complexity to perplexity, that old nemesis Lucifer then came to them, convincing a serpent to allow the forever disembodied rascal to speak through him, and tempted Eve, saying:

Hath God said—Ye shall not eat of every tree of the garden?

And the woman said unto the serpent: We may eat of the fruit of the trees of the garden; But of the fruit of the tree which thou beholdest in the midst of the garden, God hath said—Ye shall not eat of it, neither shall ye touch it, lest ye die.

And the serpent said unto the woman: Ye shall not surely die [a lie] For God doth know that in the day ye eat thereof, then your eyes shall be opened [a truth], and ye shall be as gods, knowing good and evil [an egregious deceit: they would not at all be as Gods, merely fallen mortals].

---

[26]Abraham 5:20.

[27]Moses 3:16–17.

And when the woman saw that the tree was good for food, and that it became pleasant to the eyes, and a tree to be desired to make her wise, she took of the fruit thereof, and did eat, and also gave unto her husband with her, and he did eat."[28]

And thus came the Fall, mortality, the earthly portion of the eternal play—act 2 of a three-act structure.

While the opinion has been expressed in Latter-day Saint literature that the Fall of Man—the opening of mortality—came as the result of "the eating of things unfit, the taking, into the body of the things that made of that body a thing of earth."[29] (which is technically accurate), the simple fact exists that Eve disobeyed a direct commandment of God, an action precipitating the Fall all on its own. A change was wrought on the bodies of Adam and Eve, or more accurately, on the substance coursing through their veins: it turned to blood, the life-source of mortality. It made it a thing of the earth.

So was it a sin? After all, weren't Adam and Eve commanded "not to partake" of the fruit of the tree?

To the contrary, the "transgression" of Adam and Eve was in fact a brilliant move, a bit of prescient genius (on the part of Eve primarily). The *first* command they were given was to multiply, to engender earth-offspring. In their immortal state, such was impossible. Yet God, being God, an immortal, perfect being, could not tell his creation to enact a fall from immortality. The created would have to see the wisdom of pursuing such a course on their own. And they did.

They saw beyond Satan's lies and remembered the commandment. And the plan: "Adam fell that men might be; and men are, that they might have joy."[30]

All was well. Mortality was planned, initiated, and underway.

There, in a garden named Eden, act 2 began.

---

[28]Moses 4:7–13.

[29]James E. Talmage, Conference Report, October 1913, p. 119. Talmage continued: "I take this occasion to raise my voice against the false interpretation of scripture . . . that the fall of man consisted in some offense against the laws of chastity and of virtue. Such a doctrine is an abomination. It is not true; the human race is not born of fornication. Let it not be said that the patriarch of the race, who stood with the gods before he came here upon the earth, and his equally royal consort, were guilty of any such foul offense."

[30]2 Nephi 2:25.

CHAPTER 3

The Place Where Adam Dwelt

Having wisely and selflessly chosen to introduce mortality to the earth, a state that affected not just the two humans but all earth-creation and even the earth itself, Adam and his wife (married for eternity previous to the introduction of mortality) were, naturally, evicted from the garden. That the cradle of man remained on the earth for an unspecified period of time, the scriptures affirm,[31] but it remained out of reach, forbidden, unpeopled.

Instead, Adam and his wife wandered north by northeast approximately 40 miles to a place that would, at some point, gain the name "Adam-ondi-ahman," or "the place where Adam dwelt" in the Adamic language.

Joseph Smith referred to Jackson County, Missouri, as the ancient site of Eden as early as 1832. Specifically named was an area within today's Kansas City suburb of Independence. Quietly chastised for such a claim by even some members of the church, Joseph clarified enough of his position over the next few years that by 1838 it was comfortable doctrine. That was the year he discovered Adam's sacrificial altar.

Led by associates to an ancient stone structure hidden deep in some woods about 22 miles northeast of the boundaries of Jackson County, Joseph announced that it was an altar, built by Adam himself in the place he and Eve settled after being banished from the Garden of Eden.[32]

From *The Pearl of Great Price:*

And Adam and Eve, his wife, called upon the name of the Lord, and they heard the voice of the Lord from the way toward the Garden of Eden, speaking unto them, and they saw him not; for they were shut out from his presence. And he gave unto them commandments, that

---

[31]Certain later passages of scripture, like the one mentioning where Cain lived in Genesis 4:16, give land locations in reference to Eden.

[32]Letters of Heber C. Kimball, cited in Otten and Caldwell, *Sacred Truths of the Doctrine and Covenants*, Vol. 2, p. 279.

they should worship the Lord their God, and should offer the firstlings of their flocks, for an offering unto the Lord. And Adam was obedient unto the commandments of the Lord. And after many days an angel of the Lord appeared unto Adam, saying: Why dost thou offer sacrifices unto the Lord? And Adam said unto him: I know not, save the Lord commanded me. And then the angel spake, saying: This thing is a similitude of the sacrifice of the Only Begotten of the Father, which is full of grace and truth. Wherefore, thou shalt do all that thou doest in the name of the Son, and thou shalt repent and call upon God in the name of the Son forevermore.[33]

In contrast to the doctrine of most, if not all, other Christian churches, Latter-day Saints teach without reservation that the entire gospel plan—the Christian gospel—was known to and practiced by Adam and Eve.

And thus the Gospel began to be preached, from the beginning, being declared by holy angels sent forth from the presence of God, and by his own voice, and by the gift of the Holy Ghost.[34]

And he [God] called upon our father Adam by his own voice, saying: I am God; I made the world, and men before they were in the flesh.

If thou wilt turn unto me, and hearken unto my voice, and believe, and repent of all thy transgressions, and be baptized, even in water, in the name of mine Only Begotten Son, who is full of grace and truth, which is Jesus Christ, the only name which shall be given under heaven, whereby salvation shall come unto the children of men, ye shall receive the gift of the Holy Ghost, asking all things in his name, and whatsoever ye shall ask, it shall be given you.

And our father Adam spake unto the Lord, and said: Why is it that men must repent and be baptized in water? And the Lord said

---

[33]Moses 5:4–8. Joseph named the place Adam-ondi-Ahman, meaning, "Valley of God, where Adam dwelt," and prophesied that this was the place where Adam would one day return to sit in council with his righteous progeny. For some few months in 1838, until Joseph was imprisoned and his people driven out by mob action, nearly a thousand Latter-day Saints lived in the area.

[34]Moses 5:58.

unto Adam: Behold I have forgiven thee thy transgression in the Garden of Eden.

Hence came the saying abroad among the people, that the Son of God hath atoned for original guilt, wherein the sins of the parents cannot be answered upon the heads of the children, for they are whole from the foundation of the world.

And the Lord spake unto Adam, saying: Inasmuch as thy children are conceived in sin [meaning, into a world where sin exists], even so when they begin to grow up, sin conceiveth in their hearts, and they taste the bitter, that they may know to prize the good.[35]

Thus, from the beginning, Adam knew, and taught to his children:

1. A Savior, Jesus Christ, would come to earth in "the meridian of time"[36] to

2. declare the gospel of repentance and salvation

3. establish an earthly organization (church) in which was vested the power to administer the ordinances of salvation

4. break the bands of this mortal death (through the Resurrection)

5. and to work out an atonement for the mistakes wrought by every man and woman throughout the course of earth's history (and that of the innumerable other earths like this one over which Christ had jurisdiction). Such atonement would be available to all, but of effect only for those who would repent of their sins and come to God through specific heaven-ordained ordinances and consecrations administered by those holding the authority (item 3).

Among those ordinances was baptism by immersion in water, which Adam and Eve both received at the hands of "the spirit of the Lord." An-

---

[35]Moses 6:51–55.

[36]Moses 5:57. This is the earliest instance of this terminology in Latter-day Saint scripture. It establishes the mortal birth and ministry of Christ as the center point of the earth's temporal, or mortal, existence.

other was Adam's ordination, under the hands of God, to "the priesthood after the order of the Son of God," the very power and authority of God now given to man to act in his name on the earth. "Now this same Priesthood, which was in the beginning, shall be in the end of the world also."[37]

With time, and angelic tutoring, they came to understand even more confidently the wisdom of Eve's transgression.

> And in that day Adam blessed God and was filled, and began to prophesy concerning all the families of the earth, saying: Blessed be the name of God, for because of my transgression my eyes are opened, and in this life I shall have joy, and again in the flesh I shall see God.
>
> And Eve, his wife, heard all these things and was glad, saying: Were it not for our transgression we never should have had seed, and never should have known good and evil, and the joy of our redemption, and the eternal life which God giveth unto all the obedient.[38]
>
> And Adam and Eve blessed the name of God, and they made all things known unto their sons and their daughters.[39]

But many rebelled. Lucifer, now known as Satan, tempted the children of Adam and Eve, and many gave heed to his enticements.

How did he do it? How does he do it today?

These truths are self-evident in Latter-day Saint doctrine: evil exists; opposites are essential; the right to choose, and the eternal nature of that principle, is paramount. Choice, however, does not mean freedom from consequences. Consequence, the immutable companion of choice, is of the essence of eternal law. God the Father knew (understanding perfectly the eternal law) that given their moral agency, some of his children would choose goodness, fairness, kindness, even godliness, and some would not, to varying degrees. From this testing, he would pick his own jewels, those who would become like him and fulfill the inherent destiny of their race.

Thus the rebellious Lucifer, or Satan, was allowed to tempt the mortal spirits in any way he could think of. The temptation toward sexual promiscuity and license was [and remains] a favorite. Anger is popular. Lust for

---

[37]Moses 6:7.

[38]Moses 5:10–11.

[39]Moses 5:12.

riches or power. Jealousy. Upon any who would begin to respond to Satan's whisperings for any or each of these, he would gain a gradual hold.

Though Satan mistakenly thinks he is the god of this world, the Creator nevertheless grants him a significant segment of wiggle room. This arrangement is made readily apparent in the biblical Book of Job, although it is clear in a number of Latter-day Saint references. He works through other people (as does the true God), through whisperings in the spiritual ear (as does the true God), through film and television and books (ditto), through pride, poverty, and faithless promises (uniquely his).

Which is how he got Cain.

Probably from the very beginning, though taught otherwise by faithful parents on earth, Cain loved the paths of Satan more than those of God. That he would have chosen to come to earth in the first place suggests, with other Latter-day Saint scripture,[40] that a wide range of valiancy existed in the premortal realm, some barely making the cut. Quick to reject counsel, arrogant and vile, Cain sought his own way. Eventually, knowing he had a willing victim, Satan spoke directly to Cain, promising to deliver his brother Abel, with all his numerous flocks and herds, into Cain's hands. Quickly Cain realized an opportunity to profit and rid himself of a brother he despised.[41]

So he killed him.

And Cain, for the last time ever, heard the voice of the Lord, saying. "What hast thou done? The voice of thy brother's blood cries unto me from the ground. And now thou shalt be cursed from the earth which hath opened her mouth to receive thy brother's blood from thy hand. When thou tillest the ground it shall not henceforth yield unto thee her strength. A fugitive and a vagabond shalt thou be in the earth."[42]

Following his great sin, the first earth-death that we know of, Cain was shut out entirely from the presence of God—a presence he had known. For him, the light of heaven's memory went out.

Among Adam's posterity, however, were many righteous sons and daughters. (Latter-day Saints take literally the 930 years given as Adam's

---

[40]*Doctrine and Covenants* 93:38: "Every spirit of man was innocent in the beginning [of time]; and God having redeemed man from the fall, men became again, in their infant [mortal] state, innocent before God."

[41]As noted, Latter-day scriptures make it clear that Adam and Eve had many sons and daughters precedent to Cain and Abel.

[42]Moses 5:35–38.

post-Fall—that is, mortal—life span.) And "a book of remembrance was kept . . . and by them [Adam and Eve] their children were taught to read and write, having a language which was pure and undefiled."[43] Here, in text written down some twenty-five hundred years later by Moses, is presented a foundational tenet of Latter-day Saint theology that defies much of modern learning, and does so without flinching: an advanced body of knowledge was common among the children of Adam and Eve. In addition to the reading and writing of a "perfect" language, at least some among these ancient peoples had vast wisdom in regard to astronomy, mathematics, physics, and other fields of knowledge, perhaps more than we have today.

Ancient prophets had detailed visions of the universe that remain unequaled, and telescopes were not needed. At the basest level, Latter-day Saint scriptures originating on two continents point out, for instance, that prophets of God living long before Galileo were well aware that the earth was round and that it revolved around the sun, itself but a minor star in a much larger cosmos. It was, for instance, Abraham and his great-grandson Joseph who taught the Egyptians their astronomy, the Hebrew prophets having learned it from their predecessor, Enoch, the seventh generation from Adam. (This Enoch preached and taught so effectively that an entire city—the "City of Holiness," or "Zion"—and its inhabitants were taken up to heaven, to return with Christ at his Second Coming.)[44]

In general, Latter-day Saint doctrine in regard to "primitive societies" is that they are the degenerated *remnants* of higher cultures, not the exploratory beginnings of them.

"And Adam knew his wife again, and she bare a son, and he called his name Seth. And Adam glorified the name of God; for he said: God hath appointed me another seed, instead of Abel, whom Cain slew.

"And the days of Adam, after he had begotten Seth, were eight hundred years, and he begat many sons and daughters; And all the days that Adam lived were nine hundred and thirty years, and he died."[45]

He had fulfilled his mission, and fulfilled it well. He would yet return to the earth in glory.

---

[43]Moses 6:4–6.

[44]The Bible states only that "Enoch walked with God: and he was not; for God took him." (See Gen. 5 :21–24 for the context; Luke merely mentions his genealogy).

[45]Moses 6:2, 10–11.

CHAPTER 4

Oh, Israel

Latter-day Saints accept the Old Testament record as scripture, the authorized record of God's dealing with a certain people of the ancient Middle East, those eventually known as Israelites. That the same God—as Jehovah—dealt with and inspired people not included in the Old Testament story is certain. God's inspiration to his children has never been limited to the members of a certain faith or genealogy. "The great religious leaders of the world such as Mohammed, Confucius, and the Reformers, as well as philosophers including Socrates, Plato, and others, received a portion of God's light. Moral truths were given to them by God to enlighten whole nations and to bring a higher level of understanding to individuals. . . . We believe that God has given and will give to all peoples sufficient knowledge to help them on their way to eternal salvation."[46]

I may well be the only man on the planet who ever came to Mormonism by way of Jack Kerouac and the Tao Te Ching but the *logic* of such a maneuver is well accepted by Latter-day Saints. (Okay, not by all of them.)

The key to *saving* faith, *ultimate* faith on what may be an otherwise circuitous journey is authority: who has God set to be his authoritative ministers? In the Old Testament era of earth's history, it became the Israelites, and in fact only certain men among them (and only men).[47] Such authority would be called, as we've seen revealed to Adam, the "priesthood."

One of its great administrators would be Noah.

Ten generations from Adam, the valiant premortal spirit known as

---

[46]Statement of the First Presidency regarding God's Love for All Mankind, February 15, 1978.

[47]This man/woman thing is simply the order of a universe that operates according to immutable law; it has absolutely nothing to do with capability or intelligence or comparative worth of the two sexes. To faithful Latter-day Saints the suggestion that one can give the priesthood to whomever one likes is absurd: valid authority of the true priesthood of God is not ours to hand out.

Gabriel was born into mortality. As the earthly son of Lamech (grandson of Enoch), who named him Noah, he was instructed in the ways of the gospel and ordained to the priesthood by a father who had heard the words from the lips of Adam himself only a century and a quarter before. A follower of righteousness, he would preserve the seed of Adam on the earth even though the rest of humanity would die in his day, destroyed by a deluge that would cover the earth and drown all other living things.

Did water really cover the earth? Why?

Latter-day Saints do indeed believe in the literal covering of the earth by water. "[We] look upon the earth as a living organism,"[48] wrote LDS apostle John A. Widstoe, "one which is gloriously filling 'the measure of its creation.' [We] look upon the flood as a baptism of the earth, symbolizing a cleansing of the impurities of the past, and the beginning of a new life. This has been repeatedly taught by the leaders of the church. The deluge was an immersion of the earth in water."[49] Even if only by a millimeter of it.

Widstoe continues: "The fact remains that the exact nature of the flood is not known. We set up assumptions, based upon our best knowledge, but can go on further. In fact, the details of the flood are not known to us."

What Latter-day Saints do accept is the following:

1. A great flood did occur.

2. It covered the earth completely for at least a moment of time (immersion).

3. All "flesh" besides that residing with Noah on the ark did perish.

4. All living beings on the earth after the flood, including humans, descend from the representatives of their respective species present on that ark (postdeluge mutants and new species are allowed).

---

[48]The great prophet Enoch even heard its voice! (See *Pearl of Great Price,* Moses 7:48).

[49]John A. Widtsoe, *Evidences and Reconciliations,* pp. 127–128.

Perhaps the most unique thing Latter-day Saint doctrine adds to the Noah story is that it at least began on the American continent, probably somewhere within the Mississippi River basin. As to where the ark landed five months later, we are largely silent. The populations descended from Noah clearly began to people the area of today's Middle East, but according to the Bible it was not until the time of Peleg, the fifth generation from Noah, that the earth was divided into continents and islands.[50]

One of the most significant characters in all of Latter-day Saint doctrine would be born ten generations later; his name would be called Abram, later Abraham.

To illustrate his significance to Latter-day Saints, consider this: a computer word search of the King James Version of the Old Testament, that used by most[51] Latter-days Saints, turns up 193 references to Abraham. Latter-day Saint scriptures outside of the Bible show 196. In my standard issue KJV, he is named or referred to on fifty-three pages of text; fifty-six in the non-Bible LDS scriptures. There are 66 references to Abraham in the writings of New Testament authors; 58 in the Book of Mormon and *Doctrine and Covenants*.

But in the Latter-day Saint scriptures, as mentioned earlier, he has his own book. Let's consider the expanded Abraham from the Latter-day Saint perspective.

From the Book of Abraham: "Now the Lord had shown unto me, Abraham, the intelligences that were organized before the world was; and among all these there were many of the noble and great ones; And God saw these souls that they were good, and he stood in the midst of them, and he said: These I will make my rulers; for he stood among those that were spirits, and he saw that they were good; and he said unto me: Abraham, thou art one of them: thou wast chosen before thou wast born."[52]

The language here is reminiscent of that used by the Lord in telling the Prophet Jeremiah of his own premortal existence: "Then the word of the Lord came unto me, saying, Before I formed thee in the belly I knew thee; and before thou camest forth out of the womb I sanctified thee, [and] I ordained thee a prophet unto the nations." (Jer. 1:4–5)

---

[50]See Gen. 10:25.

[51]In English-speaking nations, or where available in translation, it is the standard.

[52]Abraham 3:22–23, *The Pearl of Great Price*.

Yet Abraham would become one of the greatest of the "great ones." Due to his faithfulness, even at the risk of his life,[53] he would become the father of whole nations and the patriarch through whose loins the Savior himself would descend. Due to his great faithfulness he would be party to a covenant with God that would make him the man through whom "all the families of the earth [would] be blessed."[54]

This is how it happened. Abraham's father Terah having gone astray after gods who were not gods, Abraham would seek and receive the high priesthood under the hands of its valid high priest, Melchizedek, the King of Salem (later named Jerusalem) and one of the most righteous men who ever lived. According to Joseph Smith, "Melchizedek was a man of faith, who wrought righteousness; and when a child he feared God, and stopped the mouths of lions, and quenched the violence of fire."[55] So great a man was he that the high priesthood itself was called after his name. "Before his day it was called the Holy Priesthood after the Order of the Son of God," wrote Joseph Smith in 1835. "But out of respect or reverence to the name of the supreme Being, to avoid the too frequent repetition of his name, they, the Church, in ancient days called that priesthood after Melchizedek, or the Melchizedek Priesthood."[56]

Some of that covenant would be available to future heirs by bloodline, giving perceived boast to certain Jews in Jesus' day that "we have Abraham to our father" (Matt. 3:9). But it would also descend by way of priesthood ordination. Said the Lord to Abraham: "And I will make of thee a great nation, and I will bless thee above measure, and make thy name great among all nations, and thou shalt be a blessing unto thy seed after thee, that in their hands they shall bear this ministry and Priesthood unto all nations."[57]

With the dispersion of the tribes of Israel in the eighth and sixth centuries B.C. and again in 70 A.D., the blood of Abraham was scattered through the lands of the earth as the peoples migrated and intermarried.

For instance, in approximately 600 B.C., a prophet in Jerusalem

---

[53]An occasion detailed in the Book of Abraham.

[54]Abraham 2:11

[55]Inspired Version (Joseph Smith translation) of the Bible (Gen, 14: 26).

[56]*Doctrine and Covenants* 107:2–4.

[57]Abraham 2:9.

named Lehi (a contemporary of Jeremiah), warned by the Lord of the coming destruction of the city, led his family away and into the wilderness. Taking with them the sacred records of their people (Israelites, through Joseph the eleventh son), they followed the Lord's instruction in building a ship and floating the seas to a new land remote and distant. A record kept by successive generations of their own prophets would a thousand years later be abridged by one of the last of them, taking for its title his own name: the Book of Mormon. A thousand years after that, the remnant of their people would become known as the "American Indians."

So it is in part through this literal "seed" of Abraham's body that millions upon millions in future nations far from Israel would be blessed, as valid inheritors of the Abrahamic covenant. But the priesthood would continue as well, although not in such a linear fashion.

Bottom line: Members of The Church of Jesus Christ of Latter-day Saints are children of Israel. The majority descend from Joseph, the eleventh son, and most of those through his second-born, Ephraim. Prevailing LDS thought is that even those joining the church in the most disparate of places are in fact literal blood descendants or they never would have responded to the message of the gospel in the first place: "My sheep hear my voice." (John 10:27)

Thus one may hear Latter-day Saints in Utah—more there than anywhere else, but less so today than in the past—refer to non–Latter-day Saints as "Gentiles." (One Utah town even hosts a "Gentile Street," named for a resident of a former day. It intersects with Church Street and Angel Street just west of Main.)

This theology paints a family portrait not readily kosher to many Jews: Joseph and Judah, arm in arm. The concept is fundamental theology to Latter-day Saints, however. Unlike many other Christian societies (and non-Christian ones), Latter-day Saints feel not only a strong kinship with their kin descendants, the Jews, they feel, as individuals and as a church, a covenantal obligation to them. A primary purpose of the Book of Mormon, that record of the American offshoot of Israel, is "the convincing of the Jew and Gentile that JESUS is the CHRIST, the ETERNAL GOD, manifesting himself unto all nations."[58]

---

[58] From the Title Page, *Book of Mormon*; emphasis in the original.

An aspiring challenge.

But another is to praise them: "[Nations of the earth] shall have a Bible; and it shall proceed forth from the Jews, mine ancient covenant people. And what thank they the Jews for the Bible which they receive from them? Do they remember the travails, and the labors, and the pains of the Jews, and their diligence unto me, in bringing forth salvation unto the Gentiles? O ye Gentiles, have ye remembered the Jews, mine ancient covenant people? Nay; but ye have cursed them, and have hated them, and have not sought to recover them. But behold, I will return all these things upon your own heads; for I the Lord have not forgotten my people."[59]

So Abraham's son Isaac would receive this priesthood under his father's hand. He in turn would ordain his son Jacob, later to be called Israel, whose twelve sons would likewise be ordained. The eleventh son, Joseph, would inherit the birthright and be instrumental in the temporal salvation of Israel in his own day (feeding them in Egypt). Just as Joseph had been long separated from his brethren, a branch of his progeny would likewise "run over the wall" and find inheritance among "the utmost bound of the everlasting hills" (Gen. 49:22–26), interpreted by Latter-day Saints to mean the ancient ramparts of the American topographical spine: the Rockies/Andes. The third son of Jacob/Israel, named Levi, would be the great-grandfather of Moses. Moses would receive the priesthood from his father-in-law Jethro, who was not a descendant of Jacob/Israel but *was* a descendant of Abraham through some other line.

But Moses would be the last to hold it for some time. With his sojourn toward the Promised Land accomplished, and as the children of Israel continued to rebel against the Lord in the wilderness of Sinai, the Lord God "took Moses out of their midst, and the Holy Priesthood also,"[60] meaning the High, or Melchizedek priesthood.[61] Only the lesser Aaronic or Levitical priesthood, that priesthood capable of administering the outward or temporal matters of worship—the "Mosaic law"—remained.

---

[59]Nephi 29:3–5. Nor did Joseph Smith forget his people. By his assignment, modern church apostle Orson Hyde (having Jewish lineage) traveled to Palestine and, in a prayer offered privately on Sunday morning, October 24, 1841, from the Mount of Olives, dedicated the land of Palestine for the return of the Jews to their homeland and for the preaching of the Christian gospel. Within the decade European Jews were migrating back to Palestine.

[60]*Doctrine and Covenants* 84:22–25.

[61]Meaning, as well, that Moses was never buried because he never died; he was translated, or taken to heaven without tasting of death.

Through the remainder of the pre-Christian administration, each of the successive prophets in the Old Testament record would be ordained to this higher priesthood, not in successive lineage, but by personal and individual ordination under the hands of Jehovah himself,[62] down to Malachi, "the last of the prophets of note . . . before the opening of the dispensation of Christ."[63]

But in time Moses would return to earth, as would a number of other Old Testament prophets, all with a purpose and all with their priesthood intact.

The first to return would be the father, after Adam, of them all: one Gabriel, who had already served his mortal probation—and served it well, as Noah—would announce the coming miraculous births of the rightful soon-to-preside heir of the Aaronic priesthood ("he shall be called John"[64]) and of his earthly cousin, to be named Jesus, the Messiah, the Christ.

Jehovah himself would take his turn on earth.

---

[62]*Teachings of the Prophet Joseph Smith*, pp. 180–81.

[63]James E. Talmage, *Articles of Faith*, Ch. 13, pp. 240–241.

[64]Luke 1:60.

PART 2

The First Coming and a Falling Away

In listening to [the Latter-day Saints] I discovered, as I think, the great secret of their success in making converts. They speak to a common feeling; they minister to a universal want. They contrast strongly the miraculous power of the gospel in the apostolic time with the present state of our nominal Christianity. They ask for the signs of divine power . . . [and] any declaration in the scriptures that this miraculous power of faith was to be confined to the first confessors of Christianity.

JOHN GREENLEAF WHITTIER
Among the Mormons

CHAPTER 5

The Fulcrum of Time

At some point in the spring of the Palestinian year,[65] the Son of the Morning, the firstborn in the premortal realm, Jehovah of the Old Testament record, and the God and Creator of this earth, condescended toward his sojourn upon it, foreordained to be the Savior of all created. He was born of a choice mortal woman, sired by an immortal man, even a God. *The* God. The Father. Thus he was the Son of God, a being possessed of both mortal appetites and godly powers, earthly passions and supernal potential. He came subject to thirst, fatigue, pain, and anguish both physical and emotional. He was the "only begotten in the flesh"—the only human being ever to share mortal and immortal parentage.

Whatever the exact circumstances of the procreative act, about which the church takes no official public stance, two firm attestations remain: Jesus was the Son of God (not of Joseph, not of the Holy Ghost), and Mary was in fact a virgin both before and following Jesus' conception within her womb. (She would give birth to children of Joseph, her future husband, later.)

At this point, one clarification is required. When Adam and Eve fell in the garden, they brought mortality into the world—that is, death. As an aftereffect of the mortal Fall, their progeny became subject to the weaknesses of the flesh, but each, tempted individually by the enticements of a fallen world, would sin on his or her own; Adam cursed none of them with original sin. Says an LDS Article of Faith: "We believe that men will be punished for their own sins, and not for Adam's transgression."[66] We don't even call it a sin, and he certainly didn't burden us with any. The only effect of his act was to introduce mortality.

Latter-day Saints believe Mary was unquestionably "one of the no-

---

[65]Probably in April; see James E. Talmage, *Jesus the Christ*, Ch. 8, p. 104, and *Doctrine and Covenants* 20:1.

[66]Articles of Faith 1:2.

blest and greatest of all the spirit offspring of the Father,"[67] trailing, if anyone at all, perhaps only Eve in her spiritual standing. Of her, a Book of Mormon prophet nearly ninety years before Christ's birth saw "a precious and chosen vessel."[68] Like her betrothed, Joseph (a first cousin), she was of the royal line descended from David. And although Christ carried in his veins blood only from Mary (and not of Joseph), the conclusion is clear: "Had Judah been a free and independent nation, ruled by her rightful sovereign, Joseph the carpenter would have been her crowned king; and his lawful successor to the throne would have been Jesus of Nazareth, the King of the Jews."[69]

The existing Old Testament record provides plenty of prophecy regarding the advent of a messiah, and a smattering of detail. The Book of Mormon record, on the other hand, contains extensive and detailed prebirth prophecy of the Messiah, including the name by which he would be known in mortality. Several specific entries follow.

From 592 B.C.:

Yea, even six hundred years from the time that my father left Jerusalem, a prophet would the Lord God raise up among the Jews— even a Messiah, or, in other words, a Savior of the world.[70]

And my father said he [John the Baptist] should baptize in Bethabara, beyond Jordan; and he also said he should baptize with water; even that he should baptize the Messiah with water. And after he had baptized the Messiah with water, he should behold and bear record that he had baptized the Lamb of God, who should take away the sins of the world.[71]

---

[67]Bruce R. McConkie, *Mormon Doctrine*, p. 471, s.v. "Mary."

[68]Alma 7:10.

[69]Talmage, *Jesus the Christ*, p. 87.

[70]1 Nephi 10:4. Book of Mormon dates are the accepted approximations.

[71]1 Nephi 10:9–10.

From 588 B.C.:

Behold, he offereth himself a sacrifice for sin, to answer the ends of the law, unto all those who have a broken heart and a contrite spirit; and unto none else can the ends of the law be answered.[72]

And behold it shall come to pass that after the Messiah hath risen from the dead, and hath manifested himself unto his people, unto as many as will believe on his name, behold, Jerusalem shall be destroyed again; for woe unto them that fight against God and the people of his church. Wherefore, the Jews shall be scattered among all nations; yea, and also Babylon shall be destroyed: wherefore, the Jews shall be scattered by other nations.[73]

For according to the words of the prophets, the Messiah cometh in six hundred years from the time that my father left Jerusalem; and according to the words of the prophets, and also the word of the angel of God, his name shall be Jesus Christ, the Son of God.[74]

And after the Messiah shall come there shall be signs given unto my people of his birth, and also of his death and resurrection; and great and terrible shall that day be unto the wicked, for they shall perish; and they perish because they cast out the prophets, and the saints, and stone them, and slay them; wherefore the cry of the blood of the saints shall ascend up to God from the ground against them.[75]

From 124 B.C.

And he shall be called Jesus Christ, the Son of God, the Father of heaven and earth, the Creator of all things from the beginning; and his mother shall be called Mary. And lo, he cometh unto his own, that salvation might come unto the children of men even through faith on

---

[72] 2 Nephi 2:7.

[73] 2 Nephi 25: 14–15.

[74] 2 Nephi 25:19.

[75] 2 Nephi 26:3.

his name; and even after all this they shall consider him a man, and say that he hath a devil, and shall scourge him, and shall crucify him. And he shall rise the third day from the dead; and behold, he standeth to judge the world; and behold, all these things are done that a righteous judgment might come upon the children of men.[76]

From 83 B.C.:

I say unto you, that I know of myself that whatsoever I shall say unto you, concerning that which is to come, is true; and I say unto you, that I know that Jesus Christ shall come, yea, the Son, the Only Begotten of the Father, full of grace, and mercy, and truth. And behold, it is he that cometh to take away the sins of the world, yea, the sins of every man who steadfastly believeth on his name.[77]

30 B.C.:

O remember, remember, my sons, the words which King Benjamin spake unto his people; yea, remember that there is no other way nor means whereby man can be saved, only through the atoning blood of Jesus Christ, who shall come; yea, remember that he cometh to redeem the world.[78]

And:

Behold, I say unto you that none of the prophets have written, nor prophesied, save they have spoken concerning this Christ.[79]

Of Jesus' mortal ministry we rely primarily upon, and are grateful for, the New Testament writers. To each of the gospels we concede the traditional eponymic authorship: Matthew his, Mark his, Luke and John in their turn. The written record seems clear enough and nothing in the

---

[76]Mosiah 3:8–10.

[77]Alma 5:48.

[78]Helaman 5:9.

[79]Jacob 7:11.

unique "Mormon canon" has suggested otherwise. With other Christians, we accept the matters reported in the New Testament—the life of Christ—as the culminating years of authorized Judaism.

Of his early years, the record is quiet. Beyond the inimitable record of his humble birth in a stable, delivered in straw and diapered in rags, we add but little. Perhaps most significant is that we claim, with many other biblical scholars, that he was born not in December but in the springtime of the year, most likely in April (the Hebrew month *Nisan*). Specifically, April 6, 1830, was the day The Church of Jesus Christ of Latter-day Saints (its initial eight years as variably "The Church of the Latter-day Saints" or "The Church of Christ") was officially organized; that date, according to the prophet Joseph Smith, "being one thousand eight hundred and thirty years since the coming of our Lord and Savior Jesus Christ in the flesh."[80] It is not rigid doctrine, certainly not as to the exact year. Nevertheless, we celebrate Christmas with all Christendom on December 25.

We accept without pause the New Testament claim that Jesus had half-brothers and half-sisters, children of Joseph and Mary born subsequent to his birth, and wonder at the logic of those who would impute some shade of shame to this fact.

Rising by merit of righteousness through the mists of veiled memory, Jesus comes to full and early realization of his mission as the Savior of the world, a mission that will be accomplished only with the sacrifice of his life.

Reaching the years of legal and ecclesiastical majority in Palestine,[81] he seeks baptism by full-body immersion in the waters of the river Jordan at the hands of his second cousin, John; in fact, he insists upon it so as to "fulfill all righteousness."

It is important to note that John was more than just a "voice in the wilderness," and likely a much more affable guy than Hollywood directors have been wont to paint him. As a rightful agent of the Aaronic priesthood, he could appropriately baptize others for the remission of sins. Yet due to his ordination to that power under the hands of an angel when John was a mere eight days old, he held the keys of that authority. In the

---

[80]*Doctrine and Covenants* 20:1.

[81]According to Numbers 4:47, priests of the Levitical order were to begin their official duties at this age; as Jesus was not a Levite, we can only assume that he began his ministry at a similar age so as to not arouse even greater ire among the people.

words of Mormon apostle Joseph Fielding Smith, "he was the rightful presiding priest of the Aaronic order in Israel"[82] and great was his mission. Latter-day Saint doctrine holds with the pronouncement of Jesus some-time later that "Among those that are born of women there is not a greater prophet than John the Baptist."[83]

Thus Christ begins his formal ministry, and as his gains momentum, the Baptist's wanes, ending eventually in this latter's death. But John's ministration among men would by no means end with his mere death.

Christ chooses twelve men to help establish his church, an author-itative organization charged with preaching the gospel and administering the ordinances of salvation. Missionaries are sent forth, both from among the Twelve and from among the "other seventy." His own selection posed a direct contradistinction to the seventy Jewish elders who comprised the Sanhedrin, itself the descendant of the body of seventy "elders of Israel" who Moses was commanded to call to service.[84] The sick are healed by the laying-on of hands. Miracles are performed.

Having all authority in earth and in heaven, yet deferring to the pro-cess he himself had set in motion, Christ takes three of the Twelve to the top of a "high mountain apart," likely that called Mount Hermon. There appear to the four of them at least two beings from the eternal world. To the amazement of these faithful Jews, one is the great lawgiver, Moses, who fifteen centuries before had been taken from the earth yet holding the keys of the Melchizedek priesthood. But with him is another great immortal being holding keys, Elias.[85] Upon the three apostles these beings confer the rights and powers of their respective ministries, Simon Peter being named the senior holder of the keys of presidency (latent while Jesus remained on the earth).

---

[82] Joseph Fielding Smith Jr., *Doctrines of Salvation,* Vol. 3, pp. 88–89. Also, it is well known in biblical scholarship that those holding the "official" office of high priest (of the Aaronic priesthood) in Judea during the lifetime of Christ, including the condemnatory Joseph Cai-aphas, were often political appointees more than rightful heirs.

[83]Luke 7:28.

[84]Exod. 24:1.

[85]It is not clearly known who this "Elias" might have been. In Latter-day Saint theology "Elias is both a name and a title. . . . The name Elias may refer to a preparer, a forerunner, a restorer, to Elias himself, or to Elijah." (*Encyclopedia of Mormonism*), Vol. 2, s.v. "Elias." Other candidates for the identity of this particular Elias include Noah and John the Baptist. (See also note 165.)

Toward the end of Jesus' mortal days—these apostles having been especial witnesses to the raising of the dead; the healing of lepers, the blind, and cripples; and the stilling of mountainous ocean waves—he engages Peter in a heart-probing discussion that will in no small measure define the future of Christianity.

> When Jesus came into the coasts of Caesarea Philippi, he asked his disciples, saying, Whom do men say that I the Son of man am?
>
> And they said, Some, John the Baptist: some, Elias; and others, Jeremias, or one of the prophets.
>
> He saith unto them, But whom say ye that I am?
>
> And Simon Peter answered and said, Thou art the Christ, the Son of the living God.
>
> And Jesus answered and said unto him, Blessed art thou, Simon Barjona: for flesh and blood hath not revealed [it] unto thee, but my Father which is in heaven.
>
> And I say also unto thee, That thou art Peter, and upon this rock I will build my church; and the gates of hell shall not prevail against it.[86]

Upon which rock? Peter?

Why on earth (or heaven) would the Son of God establish his church on the foundation of another man, as the Roman church would interpret it three centuries later?

Latter-day Saint doctrine ascribes a tripartite explanation for this statement of the Savior's. First, in the fullest sense, Christ himself is the only rock upon which his church would be established. Second, Peter's ecclesiastical stature as the head apostle, the one upon whom earthly governance of the church and all its ordinances would fall at Christ's death, would in fact be a rock of foundation. And third, revelation from God, that miraculous spiritual mechanism by which Peter recognized fully who stood before him, is a foundation of the church and the only manner sufficient to run it. We thus recognize Peter as the Prophet, the presiding high priest of the Melchizedek priesthood, and the only mortal being holding the keys of its use and administration. Following the bestowal of divine authority on the Mount of Transfiguration, such keys were also

---

[86]Matt. 16:13–18.

vested in James and John, brothers "surnamed Boanerges," but only in the sense of remission. In fact, Peter would be the last man to exercise the keys of presidency of the high priesthood for eighteen centuries.

But what of these faithful Jews—Peter, James, John, and the rest— as their lives changed before their eyes? Was the history of Judaism of no purpose? The Law of Moses vain? Had it all been false? Misguided?

In one sense, it had all been perfect. As given by the Lord Jehovah and administered or taught righteously by his prophets, it was as it was supposed to be. Yet erring men had frequently frustrated the effort and, by time of the Lord's ministry, strayed far in many cases from the true course. For instance, for nearly two hundred years, the "official" high priest (of the Aaronic priesthood) in Palestine had been a political appointee, whether or not he was a rightful descendant of Aaron.[87] Jesus would often rebuke, sharply, those of the priestly class who could not (or would not) see, in him, the fulfillment of their entire careers. Instead, he scoured them as "hypocrites" who "devour widow's houses"; as "blind guides, which strain at a gnat, and swallow a camel"; and as "whited sepulchres, which indeed appear beautiful outward, but are within full of dead [men's] bones, and of all uncleanness."[88]

The Lord Jehovah—*their* Lord Jehovah—was here now, in the flesh. Yet although Old Testament prophecies of the coming messiah were abundantly familiar to his contemporaries—his descent from the Davidic line, his birth to a virgin in the tiny village of Bethlehem, his rejection by the house of Israel, and even the specific ignominies of his final hours—few of them, even among the rabbinical scholars, could see what was happening before their eyes.

When overwhelmed by the appearance of the great lawgiver of Israel on the Mount, Peter struggled to say something intelligent, appropriate. "Lord, it is good for us to be here," he offered. "If thou wilt, let us make here three tabernacles; one for thee, and one for Moses, and one for Elias. While he yet spake, behold, a bright cloud overshadowed them: and behold a voice out of the cloud, which said, This is my beloved Son, in whom I am well pleased; hear ye him. And when the disciples heard

---

[87]See 2 Macc. 4:7–9.

[88]Matt. 23: various.

[it], they fell on their face, and were sore afraid. And when they had lifted up their eyes, they saw no man, save Jesus only."[89]

Peter and his companions now understood very well: the promised Messiah stood before them.

As for the law of Moses, the words they had earlier heard Jesus speak were likely now clearly understood: "Think not that I am come to destroy the law, or the prophets," he pronounced on the Mount of Olives. "I am not come to destroy, but to fulfil. For verily I say unto you, Till heaven and earth pass, one jot or one tittle shall in no wise pass from the law, till all be fulfilled."[90]

To his chosen prophets following his resurrection he would explain: "Behold, I say unto you that the law is [now] fulfilled that was given unto Moses. Behold, I am he that gave the law, and I am he who covenanted with my people Israel; therefore, the law in me is fulfilled . . . therefore it hath an end."[91]

He had established his church, an organization comprised of specific and essential components—an identified and traceable (to the Lord) authority; with specific priesthood offices held by apostles, prophets, seventy, bishops, evangelists, and others (see Eph. 4:11–13); a standard doctrine and the commission to promulgate it. Now he prepared for his awesome culminating task, the atonement for the sins of all who would ever inhabit this earth. It would be the reason for which he was born, the fulfillment of that premortal pledge before God the Father and all his assembled children, including those who would later reject him. It would be the most important event in the history of the world, the zenith of mortal purpose and experience, the fulcrum of time.

Jesus alone could complete this journey. Prophets could teach doctrine; angels could visit the earth and give authority. But only the Son of God, the sinless Only Begotten Messiah could atone for the sins of all who would ever live. Like the lambs without blemish that had given their lives on the altars of Israel for four thousand years in similitude of this final and infinite sacrifice, Jesus would die so that others might live.

---

[89]Matt. 17: 4–8.

[90]Matt. 5:17–18.

[91]3 Nephi 15:4–9.

To those familiar with traditional Christian theology, this Atonement, from the Latter-day Saint perspective, is mostly the same, although somewhat expanded: one, being perfect, although "in all points tempted like as we are, yet without sin,"[92] would offer himself the expiation for the demands of eternal justice, a justice required by the law of heaven wherever eternal laws had been broken. Because of his redeeming sacrifice, his ransom, each of us could return to the presence of God. But Latter-day Saint doctrine diverges right there from the traditional view in one very significant way, that denoted by the word *could*.

The expansion goes as follows: the Atonement for the sins of mankind was effectuated primarily in the Garden of Gethsemane, some eighteen hours before its concluding act on the cross. It was there that Jesus' "sweat was as it were great drops of blood falling down to the ground,"[93] an agony so unfathomable, so unparalleled as to remain, through all time, indescribable and incomprehensible. Of that experience Jesus would later explain that he had "suffered these things for all, that they might not suffer if they would repent . . . which suffering caused myself, even God, the greatest of all, to tremble because of pain, and to bleed at every pore, and to suffer both body and spirit. . . ."[94]

Nailed to a cross the following afternoon, an exquisite agony to be sure and one we recognize with the utmost of reverence and recoil, the Savior of the world completed the atonement but initiated the final step of his mortal mission. Quite simply, he agreed to die. Because he was the Son of God, imbued with all power, a son of woman yet Son of God, he could make that choice. He knew the course, although, as his final exclamations witness, he did not entirely know the magnitude of its anguish, and he followed it. And by so doing he "broke the bands of death," for all time, and for all creatures human and otherwise. All things granted living souls in the days of creation—all creatures great and small[95]—would again rise from

---

[92]Heb. 4:15.

[93]Luke 22:44.

[94]*Doctrine and Covenants* 19:16, 18.

[95]That animals, fishes, birds, and the like have living souls, having been created as we were in a premortal realm, is solid and accepted Mormon doctrine, and their continuance in the eternal worlds is certain. Of them no "obedience" has been required; rather, they have "filled the measure of their creation" by merely passing through mortality and gaining a body. A similar destiny for plant life is assumed, although less is known about their exact

the grave, the teeming mold or the fissiparous winds of earth to live forever, embodied, complete, and perfected. All living things, having become mortal or subject to aging and death at the Fall of Adam, would follow that course and come to their mortal end. But then, the bands of death having been burst forever by the Son of God, they would rise once again from that interlude, "corruption [would] put on incorruption."[96] Being the author and initiator of the event, Jesus would be "the first fruits of them that slept."[97] Others would follow him, some almost immediately.

But universal *resurrection* is not synonymous with universal *salvation*. Not all who die go to the same place.

The process can be best explained by the events of the next three days, and here Latter-day scripture fills in several enormous gaps in the traditional Christian account.

At the point of Christ's physical death, an event granted of his own volition once all things were accomplished (completed, fulfilled), his premortal spirit—his mental, emotional self once known to all Israel and, previous to that, by all heaven, as Jehovah—went to a world of spirits. In his own words to one of two fellow sufferers on the cross (both, as far as we know, duly convicted criminals) only hours before, he had referred to it thus: "Verily I say unto thee, To day shalt thou be with me in paradise."[98] This gracious promise has engendered in much of Christian theology the idea that a deathbed repentance is sufficient to land one in heaven alongside Christ.

This idea is unsupportably ambitious, if not downright silly.

While pondering verses written by the apostle Peter nearly nineteen centuries before, sixth LDS church president Joseph F. Smith had, and then recorded, the following "Vision of the Redemption of the Dead."[99]

On the third of October, in the year nineteen hundred and eighteen.
I sat in my room pondering over the scriptures, and reflecting upon the

---

spiritual makeup. I, for one, fully expect to find limber pines and golden lupine in eternity, even if I have to make my own.

[96]Mosiah 16:10, The Book of Mormon.

[97]1 Cor. 15:20.

[98]Luke 23:43.

[99]*Doctrine and Covenants*, Section 138, recorded October 3, 1918.

great atoning sacrifice that was made by the Son of God, for the redemption of the world . . . that through his atonement, and by obedience to the principles of the gospel, mankind might be saved.

While I was thus engaged, my mind reverted to the writings of the
apostle Peter, to the primitive saints scattered abroad throughout Pon-
tus, Galatia, Cappadocia, and other parts of Asia, where the gospel had
been preached after the crucifixion of the Lord.

I opened the Bible and read the third and fourth chapters of the
first epistle of Peter, and as I read I was greatly impressed, more than
I had ever been before, with the following passages:

For Christ also hath once suffered for sins, the just for the unjust, that
he might bring us to God, being put to death in the flesh, but quick-
ened by the Spirit: By which also he went and preached unto the spirits
in prison. . . . (I Peter 3:18–20)

For for this cause was the gospel preached also to them that are
dead, that they might be judged according to men in the flesh, but live
according to God in the spirit. (1 Peter 4:6)

As I pondered over these things which are written, the eyes of my
understanding were opened, and the Spirit of the Lord rested upon me,
and I saw the hosts of the dead, both small and great. And there were
gathered together in one place an innumerable company of the spirits
of [men]. . . .

President Smith goes on to relate that these spirits

were assembled awaiting the advent of the Son of God into the spirit
world, to declare their redemption from the bands of death. Their sleeping dust was to be restored unto its perfect frame, bone to his bone,
and the sinews and the flesh upon them, the spirit and the body to be
united never again to be divided, that they might receive a fulness of
joy (for the dead had looked upon the long absence of their spirits from
their bodies as a bondage).

While this vast multitude waited and conversed, rejoicing in the
hour of their deliverance from the chains of death, the Son of God
appeared declaring liberty to the captives who had been faithful. And
there he preached to them the everlasting gospel, the doctrine of the

resurrection and the redemption of mankind from the fall, and from individual sins on conditions of repentance.

Here, then, was Paradise: a spirit world inhabited by innumerable beings who had lived honorable lives, or lives of some conscious effort toward good. For some it may have been a concerted and lifelong effort: for others—perhaps the thief on the cross, although we know little else about the merits of his life—a late-blooming cognizance. In any case, it was—is—a place of learning, of opportunity, of progress. Not of easy guarantees. The fullness of the gospel plan was presented to those inhabiting it then, and to all who have inhabited it since. Clearly, millions in the history of the earth have never heard the specifics of Christian theology nor been afforded the chance to fulfill its covenantal obligations, such as baptism. They will, even though they be "dead." And they will be accorded the opportunity to accept it or reject it.

To what end?

Let us continue the vision.

But unto the wicked [Christ] did not go, and among the ungodly and the unrepentant who had defiled themselves while in the flesh, his voice was not raised; neither did the rebellious who rejected the testimonies and the warnings of the ancient prophets behold his presence, nor look upon his face. Where these were, darkness reigned, but among the righteous there was peace.

Clearly two different places.

As for any postmortal ministry among the disobedient, President Smith saw that such did in fact happen—all were given complete opportunity—but it did not happen at the hands of the Savior.

But behold, from among the righteous, he [Christ] organized his forces and appointed messengers, clothed with power and authority, and commissioned them to go forth and carry the light of the gospel to them that were in darkness [a realm since referred to by Latter-day Saints as "spirit prison"].

And thus was the gospel preached to the dead.

With this context established, then, let me make very clear one point.

Dead is just a word; like *sour* or *awesome* or *perfect*, it conjures various meanings to various people. To many, even within Christian cultures where the Christian alternative should make every soul at least hope for its truth, some take *dead* to mean the end. Final. Oblivion.

To the Latter-day Saints it means much less, and much more. *Dead* is a valid viewpoint only to those who are still "alive." It is a moment, a passing, a portage into the next stage of life, postmortality, where there is a continuation of the very unique and complete individuality of every soul. Were you to encounter your deceased mother or your forfeited child (and many have), you would know them immediately. The Resurrection, whose specifics we will shortly discuss, would have tendered each individual a body free of defects, deformities, and scars, but the person would be the same, only now with a sureness of knowledge of things divine.

Of this we have no question. The "dead," when commissioned to do so, have returned; our prophets and many others have seen them, conversed with them, made inquiry into detail and purpose and process. We have no doubts.

We, the remaining, miss them; we mourn, and appropriately so, for we are bereft of their companionship for some years. But we need not suffer. "If in this life only we have hope . . . we are of all men most miserable."[100]

Life, for each of us, goes on. It is a central pillar of Latter-day Saint belief.

It was of this process that the apostle Paul would write his query, so baffling to the uninspired religions of the next eighteen centuries: "Else what shall they do which are baptized for the dead, if the dead rise not at all? why are they then baptized for the dead?"[101]

Those in the spirit world, whether Paradise or prison, would hear the gospel of the Son of God; they would be given opportunity to accept it. Ordinances of earth would one day be performed vicariously in their behalf: baptism, marriage, the eternal linking of family ties. But, as in mortality, they would be free to choose or reject such efforts. (This "work for the dead" and its outcomes will be discussed in greater detail in chapter 19.)

---

[100] 1 Cor. 15:19.

[101] 1 Cor. 15:29.

Christ's labors in the spirit world consumed much of three "earth days." During that time, in which his physical body lay in the quiet tomb, he preached to the worthy spirits and he organized and commissioned his missionary forces among them. Upon the completion of this labor, he returned triumphant to his Father, there to receive his body once again, now glorified, perfected, and immutably eternal. He became an exalted man: a God.

He returned to the earth, showing himself unto many (over five hundred people) on at least eleven different occasions and for up to forty days in the vicinity of Palestine. Visible to his believers were the wounds in his hands and his feet, marks on an otherwise perfect body given to serve for some unknown period of time as proof or validation of who he was and what he had done. But the risen Messiah's body was not merely visible; it was palpable. "Handle me and see," he told his disciples on the beach, "for a spirit hath not flesh and bones, as ye see me have."[102]

A real, tangible, physical (although glorified and perfect) body of flesh and bones (no longer coursing with blood, but spirit) is the real, promised effect of the Resurrection, not just on Christ but, because of him, on each of us. It is its whole purpose, the completing of a circle begun with our inhabiting of a physical body sometime before birth.

A Book of Mormon prophet put it this way: "The soul shall be restored to the body, and the body to the soul; yea, and every limb and joint shall be restored to its body: yea, even a hair of the head shall not be lost; but all things shall be restored to their proper and perfect frame."[103]

All will be restored to wholeness, their physical form conforming to the shape, fullness, and features of their premortal spirit, like a glove upon a hand. Only now and forever more, the resurrected spirit-body will be beyond the effects of sickness, injury, or aging. The crippled, the blind, the mentally handicapped will each assume a perfected eternal form.

With his own perfected body, this Jesus then visited the American continent.[104] As the apostle John would testify in his record, "other sheep" would soon see the glory of the Resurrected Son of God with their own eyes.

---

[102]Luke 24:39.

[103]Alma 40:23.

[104]It would not, of course, be called *America* for another 1,474 years. The term is here used merely to simplify the context for the reader; further references to *America* and *American* are used with this in mind.

CHAPTER 6

Christ in America

The Book of Mormon has placed The Church of Jesus Christ of Latter-day Saints, its prophets and members, into the critic's sights and the antagonist's rhetoric as much as any other matter, both in 1830 and today. And twenty, fifty, or two hundred years will not see that change. Then, as now, the primary attack is directed against the Book of Mormon and against Joseph Smith upon, ultimately, one and the same basic matter: the claim of new scripture, new revelations from God, and new prophets.

And from one perspective, the attack is a robust one: nobody has ever proved the Book of Mormon to be historically and geographically accurate, nor has anyone ever proved that Joseph Smith actually saw God and Jesus Christ. At first counterthrust, one could say the critics likewise have no proof to the contrary, merely an empirical void.

But this misses the point entirely. To the well-grounded Latter-day Saint, such arguments (advanced by either side) are captious and irrelevant. This is religion, not accounting. It functions at a plane far above, beyond, and divergent from historiography and radiometric dating, and it is "proved" in other ways. In the Latter-day Saint view, it will *all* be proved someday by those very methods, but such means used for that end will remain even then substandard and irrelevant.

These are matters of faith, and the only appropriate proving grounds are personal and internal; one man, one woman at a time; between each and the God he or she seeks to know. My personal experience with the Book of Mormon, thirteen chapters in and seven hours after first hearing about it, remains one of the most sublime and inexplicable experiences of my life. It was undeniable.

Hours later, two clean-cut[105] Mormon missionaries challenged me to put to a test a promise given by the final prophet in the Book of Mormon:

---

[105]I mention this only because it stood in such contrast to my own standard of grooming at the time.

"I would exhort you that when ye shall read these things . . . that ye would ask God, the Eternal Father, in the name of Christ, if these things are not true; and if ye shall ask with a sincere heart, with real intent, having faith in Christ, he will manifest the truth of it unto you by the power of the Holy Ghost."[106]

I told them that wouldn't be necessary, it had already happened, and I asked them how I could join their church. The missionary to my right, the new kid fresh off a Utah farm (the other was from West Virginia), fell backward out of his chair, hitting his head on the corner of my closet.

And that, with a few variations, is how it happens for three hundred thousand people a year.

We're not worried about the Book of Mormon; it will accomplish its own work in its own way.

As recorded by the Prophet Joseph Smith in 1841: "I told the brethren that the Book of Mormon was the most correct of any book on earth, and the keystone of our religion, and a man would get nearer to God by abiding by its precepts, than by any other book."[107]

The Book of Mormon, like the Bible, is a compilation of the writings—historic and prophetic—of heaven-inspired men; specifically, the heaven-authorized ones known as prophets. In the case of the Book of Mormon, a number of things distinguish it from the Hebrew record.

1. It is a history and spiritual testament of two separate groups of people who crossed the ocean by sea and settled in the ancient Americas; one group from approximately 2200 B.C. to 300 B.C., and the other (most being descendants of Joseph who was sold into Egypt) from 592 B.C. to A.D. 421.[108]

2. Unlike many versions of the Bible,[109] it was source-translated only once, from its original "reformed Egyptian" into English. That trans-

---

[106]Moroni 10:3–4.

[107]November 28, 1841, DHC 4:461.

[108]We do not claim that Book of Mormon peoples were the first to occupy the American continent, nor do we deny the probability of migrations over the Bering land bridge.

[109]Believing it the best commonly available translation, Latter-day Saints use primarily the King James Version (KJV) of the Bible.

lation was done by Joseph Smith through "the gift and power of God" and some ancient interpreters known as the Urim and Thummim.[110] (Subsequent translations into more than ninety languages have all been precisely controlled renderings from the English.)

3. Unlike the Bible, extractions and abridgments of the numerous documents (plates, papyri, etc.) that make it up were compiled entirely by one man, an ancient American prophet named Mormon.

4. The abridgment was engraved on thin plates, or rectangular sheets, of gold, bound with metal rings (a codex), and placed with the Urim and Thummim in a stone box and buried in a hillside.

Central to the Book of Mormon, in both message and drama, is the eyewitness account given in the Book of Third Nephi of the visit of the resurrected Savior to a huge group of people in ancient America. According to this record, more than twenty-five hundred individuals witnessed a voice speaking from the heavens, a voice they did not understand until they "did open their ears to hear it."

And it came to pass, as they understood they cast their eyes up again towards heaven; and behold, they saw a Man descending out of heaven; and he was clothed in a white robe; and he came down and stood in the midst of them; and the eyes of the whole multitude were turned upon him, and they durst not open their mouths, even one to another, and wist not what it meant, for they thought it was an angel that had appeared unto them.

And it came to pass that he stretched forth his hand and spake unto the people, saying, "Behold, I am Jesus Christ, whom the prophets testified shall come into the world. And behold, I am the light and the life of the the world; and I have drunk out of that bitter cup which the Father hath given me, and have glorified the Father in taking upon me the sins of the world, in the which I have suffered the will of the Father in all things from the beginning."

And it came to pass that when Jesus had spoken these words the

---

[110]This tool is mentioned once in the Bible (Exod. 28:30) and numerous times in Latter-day scripture.

whole multitude fell to the earth; for they remembered that it had been prophesied among them that Christ should show himself unto them after his ascension into heaven.[111]

Of central importance to Latter-day Saints, the account of this visit is often referred to as the "fifth gospel" (joining Matthew, Mark, Luke, and John). Its early portions parallel very closely the Sermon on the Mount as rendered in Matthew. Later material describes the institution of the sacrament (the taking of bread and wine in remembrance of the Savior), the ordination of twelve ministers (whose ecclesiastical jurisdiction was limited to the people among whom they served, unlike the Twelve in Jerusalem, whose jurisdiction is global), and the miraculous healing of hundreds of blind, lame, and sick.

Direction is given; authority is conferred. Explication is made of their separation from the land of their forefathers six hundred years before ("ye were separated from among them because of their iniquity"), and reference is made to a comment recorded in the New Testament only by John that "other sheep" would soon "hear [his] voice"[112] "And verily I say unto you, that ye are they of whom I said: Other sheep I have which are not of this fold; them also I must bring, and they shall hear my voice; and there shall be one fold, and one shepherd."[113]

But then the Savior makes a promise that has become a key focus in Latter-day Saint endeavor: "And verily, verily, I say unto you that I have other sheep, which are not of this land, neither of the land of Jerusalem, neither in any parts of that land round about whither I have been to minister. For they of whom I speak are they who have not as yet heard my voice; neither have I at any time manifested myself unto them. But I have received a commandment of the Father that I shall go unto them, and that they shall hear my voice, and shall be numbered among my sheep, that there may be one fold and one shepherd; therefore I go to show myself unto them."[114]

Although the thought of other (non-Bible) scriptures and other (non-

---

[111]3 Nephi 11:8–12.

[112]John 10:16.

[113]3 Nephi 15:21.

[114]3 Nephi 16:1–3.

Bible) ministrations by the Savior today causes inimitable indigestion for most (only-Bible) Christian sects, it was a matter of clear understanding to Book of Mormon peoples. "For behold, I shall speak unto the Jews and they shall write it; and I shall also speak unto the Nephites [Book of Mormon people] and they shall write it; and I shall also speak unto the other tribes of the house of Israel, which I have led away, and they shall write it; and I shall also speak unto all nations of the earth and they shall write it. And it shall come to pass that the Jews shall have the words of the Nephites, and the Nephites shall have the words of the Jews; and the Nephites and the Jews shall have the words of the lost tribes of Israel; and the lost tribes of Israel shall have the words of the Nephites and the Jews."[115]

Although Latter-day Saints have been maligned from the beginning due to our acceptance of this American volume of extrabiblical scripture, the Book of Mormon isn't the end of it, and we have never claimed it would be. "Wherefore, because that ye have a Bible ye need not suppose that it contains all my words; neither need ye suppose that I have not caused more to be written. For I command all men, both in the east and in the west, and in the north, and in the south, and in the islands of the sea, that they shall write the words which I speak unto them: for out of the books which shall be written I will judge the world, every man according to their works, according to that which is written."[116]

And according to that which is written in this fifth gospel, the Savior clarifies a number of points now obscure in or missing from the New Testament, among them:

1. Not one to either offer or recommend memorized prayers, but rather ones spoken freely from the heart, Christ nevertheless stipulated that two particular ordinance-prayers[117] were to follow his exact wording: that offered by the officiator when baptizing another and those offered over the sacramental emblems of the bread and wine.

---

[115] 3 Nephi 29:12–13.

[116] 3 Nephi 29:10–11.

[117] The exact wording for the sacramental prayers was first entered in the Book of Mormon record nearly four hundred years later, but it was likely given at this time.

And for each of these ordinances—integrally intertwined—he clarified both purposes and procedures.

Baptism, the essential portal through which one officially enters the pathway that leads to eternal life (it does nothing to guarantee it), is to be a requirement only of those capable of being accountable for their own sins, which it utterly remits (covers, washes away) if, and only if, one has repented beforehand. In other words, "little children are whole, for they are not capable of committing sin. Wherefore . . . it is solemn mockery before God, that ye should baptize little children."[118] Consequently, no one is accepted for baptism into The Church of Jesus Christ of Latter-day Saints before the age of eight years, which was revealed in 1831 as the age at which the Lord will begin to hold children, and not their parents, responsible for their actions. Likewise, individuals with severe mental disabilities neither should be baptized nor need to be. They, with children who die in their early years, are automatically "alive in Christ,"[119] inheritors of heaven without a single further effort.

Among these ancient Americans, as among their counterparts in Palestine, the Savior instituted the blessing and partaking of the sacramental emblems: bread, in likeness of his body; and wine, in likeness of his surrendered blood. Unlike baptism, which had been practiced since the time of Adam, the sacrament was a new ordinance, part of the new covenant established with Christ's sacrifice on the cross. Although wine was used for this ordinance in the early days of The Church of Jesus Christ of Latter-day Saints, water was substituted beginning as early as the late summer of 1830. That year, in a revelation to Joseph Smith, the Lord clarified: "It mattereth not what ye shall eat or what ye shall drink when ye partake of the sacrament, if it so be that ye do it with an eye single to my glory."[120] And in counterpoint to the theology behind the sacrament in certain other Christian churches, the bread and water change into no other substance upon ingestion, such as the very body and blood of Christ. To Latter-day Saints, this transubstantiation of the elements serves

---

[118]Moroni 8:8–9.

[119]Moroni 8:12.

[120]*Doctrine and Covenants* 27:2.

no purpose and in fact masks the purpose for which the sacrament is taken: as a covenant to remember the Lord's sacrifice and live accordingly. Further, such a dogma—essentially crucifying the Lord anew each time one partakes—denies the very essence and capacity of the one-time–and–forever infinite atonement.

2. The essentiality of proper authority for administering his church, its ordinance, and teachings was made very clear. Twelve individuals chosen and set apart under the Lord's hand for directing the ministry among this particular people (their authority lay subordinate to that of the twelve apostles in Palestine) were then baptized, and they subsequently baptized the others, although many, if not most, had already been previously baptized. The Lord's word in this regard lend themselves to no misunderstanding: "Wherefore, although a man should be baptized an hundred times [by one not holding proper authority], it availeth him nothing, for you cannot enter in at the strait gate by the law of Moses, neither by your dead works."[121]

3. During his ministry among them, certain of the American disciples asked the Risen Lord how they might hence refer to themselves and the church he was commanding them to establish. His answer, once heard, must have embarrassed the questioner, so elementary it was: "Have they not read the scriptures, which say ye must take upon you the name of Christ, which is my name? For by this name shall ye be called at the last day; how be it my church save it be called in my name? For if a church be called in Moses' name then it be Moses' church; or if it be called in the name of a man then it be the church of a man; but if it be called in my name then it is my church, if it so be that they are built upon my gospel."[122]

Simplicity itself: the church of Jesus Christ. Its adherents would be known as "Christians" or "saints," as they were just then learning as well in Palestine.[123]

---

[121]*Doctrine and Covenants* 22:2, April 1830.

[122]3 Nephi 27:5–8.

[123]The Pauline epistles make this clear in the New Testament. Latter-day revelation makes it even clearer: "saints" are not perfect people, merely committed, baptized believers.

Yet the same question, and the same answer, would be repeated eighteen hundred years later. In this later instance the Lord would expand the logic somewhat, explaining that the "saints" of the later generation could properly distinguish themselves from those of the earlier with that simple aggregation: The Church of Jesus Christ *of Latter-day Saints.*

4. The Lord then recited to the ancient Americans the revelation to the prophet Malachi that is also recorded in the third and fourth chapters of that Old Testament book, reiterating the law of tithing and the future coming of Elijah, to "turn the heart of the fathers to the children, and the heart of the children to their fathers, lest I come and smite the earth with a curse."[124] This prophesied return of Elijah in his mission to turn hearts would be a significant event in the early years of the latter-day faith.

5. In expounding a theme his American prophets had written of for more than two thousand years (a theme that pervades the Book of Mormon), the Savior laid out the future of the land upon which he now stood and the people he presently addressed: their descendants would eventually reject him, and their present society would cease to exist; a culturally and spiritually degraded remnant would live to see another people inhabit, then control, the land; by these they would be "scattered and smitten," becoming a "hiss and a byword," driven into submission; through these newcomers (European "Gentiles"), the remnant (who would be scattered among the "native" peoples of North and South America) would once again come to a knowledge of the Savior and their true ancestry, once again becoming "a pure and a delightsome people."

Coloring the entire Third Nephi account is the recurrent ministry of compassion exercised by the Lord: innumerable healings, unspeakable prayers on the people's behalf, his supernal tenderness toward children. Elder Bruce R. McConkie has written: "The words he spoke and the deeds he did among the Nephites are a crowning capstone to his earthly

---

[124]3 Nephi 25:6.

ministry. Many of the passages far excel anything in the biblical accounts; they reveal his grandeur and greatness in a way not otherwise known, and they round out our knowledge of the nature and kind of life that he lived among men."[125]

But as in Palestine, where he remained among his faithful disciples for a full forty days after his Resurrection, strengthening them, he would also leave these Nephites, fully capable. The doctrine had been given and recorded; authorized servants had been ordained and prepared. The real, intended, and equitable course would now be to leave them on their own to rely on the inspiration and direction that would come from the third member of the "Godhead," the Holy Ghost, to see how they would conduct their lives in his absence.

The Book of Mormon peoples would enjoy an almost unanimous peace and generous brotherhood for nearly two hundred years before most would reject and fall away from the truth, plunging the nation into a turmoil that would end in the utter destruction of their civilization.

In Palestine, a similar course would prevail. But there it would only take a handful of decades.

---

[125]*The Mortal Messiah*, Vol. 4, p. 307.

CHAPTER 7

Of Peter, Popes, and Prophets

With the Savior's return to heaven—now an embodied, plenary God like his father—Peter and his ordained, legitimate colleagues in the apostleship pushed forward with the work Jesus had set them to. That work, simply enough, was to build Christ's kingdom on the earth by preaching the new gospel. A similar work would proceed in the Americas and, as revealed in the Book of Mormon, elsewhere among other sheep of the fold.

As shown previously, prophets in both the old and new worlds had long taught the gospel of the coming Messiah, including that he himself would one day come to earth to establish his church or kingdom. The record shows that the faithful in the Americas, separated physically and spiritually from the ubiquitous influence of strident societal Judaism, had been living the law of Moses while acknowledging it as the precursor of a higher gospel for hundreds of years before Christ's birth and ministry.

"For we labor diligently to write, to persuade our children, and also our brethren, to believe in Christ, and to be reconciled to God. . . . [Yet] notwithstanding we believe in Christ, we keep the law of Moses, and look forward with steadfastness unto Christ, until the law shall be fulfilled. For, for this end was the [Mosaic] law given; wherefore the law hath become dead unto us, and we are made alive in Christ because of our faith; yet we keep the law because of the commandments."[126]

In Palestine, however, the remaining and overwhelmingly contiguous influence of the Mosaic religion—Judaism—prevailed in the hearts and minds of the people. It is impossible to know with accuracy how many Christian converts were gained in those early years, but neither is it very important. Both the historical and the scriptural record show that most of the Jews continued to wait for a messiah who would come in temporal power and temporal glory to save them from their temporal challenges.

---

[126]2 Nephi 25:23–25.

This Jesus story, this "carpenter's son," this illegitimate usurper who was not even a proper Levite—this was a tale and an episode to forget and erase quickly.

"His blood be on us, and on our children,"[127] insisted the Jews before Pilate.

Therefore, within a short period of time, the "chief apostle" and newest prophet, Peter, was instructed by the Lord to take the gospel to those not of the house of Israel, among whom he found and baptized, first of all, the worthy convert Cornelius. Suddenly, Jews who disregarded the Christian message in any case took offended notice of this action. To his detractors Peter spoke: "It was necessary that the word of God should first have been spoken to you: but seeing ye put it from you, and judge yourselves unworthy of everlasting life, lo, we turn to the Gentiles. For so hath the Lord commanded us, saying, I have set thee—meaning the God of Israel—to be a light of the Gentiles, that thou shouldest be for salvation unto the ends of the earth."[128]

Yet even many of the converts were offended: although this Christian movement, this Christian gospel, was a new one, were not the Israelites the people for whom it had been designed, as an extension of the Mosaic heritage and the Abrahamic covenant? Peter himself had at first resisted the promptings, even arguing with the angel who led him through the vision that would teach him the principle and take him to Cornelius. Having learned and accepted the truth, however, Peter was quick to establish the underlying doctrine for the body of the church: God had his reasons for choosing a particular people from among all others to bear his name. For twenty centuries it had been the children of Abraham. Now he had spoken again: the gospel was to go to the Gentiles as well. (The episode would be repeated in uncanny parallel almost exactly twenty centuries later.)

Two fundamental doctrines were thus clarified:

1. "The Lord God will do nothing but he revealeth his secret unto his servants the prophets."[129] God makes the decisions and notifies

---

[127]Matt. 27:25.

[128]Acts. 13:46–47.

[129]Amos. 3:7.

his prophet, who notifies the people. No other course of action is authentic or authorized.

2. The verses describing this event now found in the New Testament Book of Acts are scripture, and that's exactly how it happens: "Holy men of God [speak] as . . . moved by the Holy Ghost" (2 Peter 1:21) and "whatsoever they shall speak when moved upon by the Holy Ghost shall be scripture, shall be the will of the Lord, shall be the mind of the Lord, shall be the word of the Lord, shall be the voice of the Lord, and the power of God unto salvation" (*Doctrine and Covenants* 68:4).

As long as there are prophets on the earth, the Lord will continue to reveal his mind and will unto them, and they, in turn, will be obligated to pass along the information as commanded. And it would *all* be scripture. Inexplicably, the exact same process by which the New Testament record was written would, eighteen centuries later, be rejected by the extant Christian remnants. But such a "turning of things upside down"[130] would afflict the Christian church long before then.

Peter, the prophet, and various apostles, including Paul, who would be one of four eventual replacements in the Twelve that we have record of, would see clear signs of disharmony in the church within a short time. Perhaps reflecting on a warning given by the Messiah himself that "false Christs and false prophets" would "deceive the very elect,"[131] they warned the church members (referred to as "saints" more than sixty times in the King James version of the New Testament, as in all of Paul's letters) of "grievous wolves" who would enter among them, "not sparing the flock;"[132] of "divisions" and "heresies"[133] and "seducing spirits and doctrines of devils,"[134] and of baptized Christians who would "not endure sound doctrine"

---

[130]Isa. 29:16.

[131]Matt. 24:24.

[132]Acts. 20:29.

[133]I Cor. 11:18,19.

[134]I Tim. 4:1.

but rather "turn away their ears from the truth and . . . be turned unto fables."[135]

But such a "falling away"[136] from sound doctrine and authorized principles was only the half of it. Very soon, the authorized ministers themselves would all, except one, be killed.

"According to tradition Peter, Andrew, Simon, and Philip were crucified [Peter upside down]; James and Paul were beheaded; Bartholomew was flayed alive; Matthew was slain with a battle-ax; Thomas was run through with a lance; James was beaten to death; Thaddeus was shot through with arrows; Barnabas was stoned; Mark was dragged to death in the streets of Alexandria; and John, the one surviving apostle, was banished to that rocky little island in the Aegean Sea called Patmos."[137]

Among scholars and theologians, these martyrdoms are hardly disputed. What it all means is another matter entirely. To Latter-day Saints, it means the church established by the Savior ceased to exist as an authoritative body well before the end of the first century, a course fully expected by the premortal Jehovah and mentioned by his prophets for centuries preceding. Stragglers, some of them competent, many of them devout, surely remained. But they had no keys and little authority. With Peter's death, known to have occurred sometime between A.D. 64 and 68, revelation for the body of saints ceased. Most of them scattered. By the time of the fall and occupation of Jerusalem in A.D. 70, the plenary Christian church no longer existed.

Only one apostle remained, one man endowed with the keys of authority, one who had been promised that he would never die. Whether John the Beloved could have continued to preside following Peter's death (his brother James had died under Herod's sword in A.D. 42) is discussionable, but moot. No one has ever claimed their authority descends from him. For instance, in the list of popes between Peter and the end of the first century, the Roman Catholic church contains four names—Linus, Anacletus, Clement I, and Evaristus—while the apostle John,

---

[135] 2 Tim. 4:3–4.

[136] 2 Thess. 2:3.

[137] This particular accounting is as stated by LDS general authority Sterling W. Sill in April 1956, but as researched and understood by most Christian historians based on a number of ancient records.

clearly the only remaining possibility for exercising the keys of authority, is never mentioned.

Was John still around? The historical record makes clear that indeed he was.

Having escaped miraculously an attempt on his life in a cauldron of burning oil, this final eyewitness of the life and Resurrection of the Son of God was banished to an eight-year exile on the remote isle of Patmos in about A.D. 91 by the Roman emperor Domitian. It is there he received the vision now known to all Christendom as the "Revelation" or the "Apocalypse,"[138] a symbolic vision of the final days of earth.

But following that exile, an era of legally supported persecution of all remaining Christians, John, now about 88 years old, returned to Ephesus and wrote his three New Testament epistles and possibly his gospel testimony (the Book of John).

Clearly, Christians remained. Some, including very likely a few holding priesthood authority that could be traced directly to Peter or other apostles, may have continued to minister among the faithful. But the keys of apostleship, of presidency, either ceased with Peter or remained with John.

So what of John? The Lord's own promise given to him nearly seventy years before was that he would "tarry until I come in my glory, and shalt prophesy before nations, kindreds, tongues and people."[139]

Yet following John's final few utterances after the release from Patmos, we have nothing. Centuries intervene. Creeds bearing no real resemblance to the original Christian simplicity are dictated in Nicaea and Constantinople. Political rule and religious practice both based on false principles become so intertwined that everything they touch for the next twelve centuries founders within an era known as the Dark Ages. The words of the Old Testament prophet Amos suddenly seem the scriptural signature of the day: "Behold, the days come, saith the Lord God, that I will send a famine in the land, not a famine of bread, nor a thirst for water, but of hearing the words of the Lord: And they shall wander from

---

[138]Although typically positioned as the final book in the New Testament, most biblical scholars and historians insist Revelation was written before John's three epistles, and perhaps even before his gospel.

[139]*Doctrine and Covenants* 7:3.

sea to sea, and from the north even to the east, they shall run to and fro
to seek the word of the Lord, and shall not find it."[140]

And in the apostle Paul's words: "Now we beseech you, brethren . . .
That ye be not soon shaken in mind, or be troubled, neither by spirit,
nor by word, nor by letter as from us, as that the day of Christ is at hand.
Let no man deceive you by any means: for that day shall not come, except
there come a falling away first, and that man of sin be revealed, the son
of perdition. . . ."[141]

Following centuries of convoluted doctrine-making, forced confes-
sion, and enforced ignorance, heaven-inspired men such as Erasmus,
Martin Luther, John Calvin, and John Wesley launch their courageous
bids for a return to the ancient doctrines as taught by Christ. (With many
others, Latter-day Saints add Johannes Gutenberg to the list of heaven-
inspired men.) In their day, and in great measure due to their efforts, the
writings of the ancient apostles and prophets are once again made available to the common people in the common tongues then being employed.

A new dawn appears imminent. The famine nears an end.

Through it all, no John. But his turn was coming. And he would not
come alone.

---

[140]Amos 8:11–12.

[141]2 Thess. 2:1–3.

PART 3

Beyond the First Vision

If God spare me, I will one day make the boy that drives the plow . . . to know more of scripture than the Pope does.[142]

BIBLE TRANSLATOR WILLIAM TYNDALE (1494–1536)

---

[142]Quoted in J. Paterson Smyth, *How We Got Our Bible* (1928), 85.

CHAPTER 8

Angels on the Earth

Latter-day Saint youth learn it like this: there are only two possibilities for the existence of an authorized, legal Christian church today: one descended through an unbroken papal line from Peter, the prophet of God, or one reemergent from the ground up, which would, of course, require heavenly authorization. In the case the Catholics have it wrong, by assuming an authorized descendancy they can't appropriately claim, no reformation would cut the cake, leaving all the Protestants without a legal leg to stand on. And in either case, "authorized" would be a tough claim to carry.

Any claims to authorized ministration, either through descendancy or new ordination, would seem to require that either (1) Christ himself or (2) Peter, the man entrusted by Christ with the keys of the earthly kingdom, or even possibly (3) John, who held those same keys and outlived Peter, come back from the dead to name a successor.

Which is, of course (1, 2, and 3), exactly what happened.

It may appear from the last chapter that Latter-day Saint belief holds the Catholic Church and its protestant stepchildren in something less than high regard. Such a stance has in fact been aggressively promoted by certain LDS church leaders in the past, and it made the final edit in influential books authored by them. It is not heard today. A softening of the rhetoric may have initially come simply in an effort to more effectively acclimate the large volume of incoming converts from those faiths. Preeminent today, however, is the more doctrinal view that we are to be about the business of increasing faith in Christ by building upon foundations already developed, not decreasing it by destroying them.

Yes, we disagree with some of Protestant and Catholic doctrine. But no, we do not disregard their principles, their effectiveness in lifting the souls of people, nor their selfless work throughout the earth in the name of the same God we worship.

But God has returned, and he returned for a reason: the postapostolic dilution, dissolution, and disarray we call "The Great Apostasy," a rapid and near total departure from the eternal gospel as taught by Christ; an era of theological invention, subversion, and atrocity by men (frequently not the bona fide clergy, but rather mere political despots) who knew not God nor even how to describe him.

As intimated previously we hold a number of the Reformers in high esteem; their efforts were laudable, and their vision was inspired: the true gospel as taught by Christ and the ancients was *not* being practiced. But efforts to reform, to realign with scripture, would be ineffectual. Luther himself, even though excommunicated from the "mother church," never intended to launch a new one: "I am deeply interested in so purifying every church that all men may worship God as they see fit," he wrote, "[but] as to organizing a new church, I have neither the desire nor the authority to do so."[143]

And there was the real problem: no authority from heaven. Zip. Nada. None.

Luther may have in fact been referring to his personal loss of authority from the Catholic Church following his excommunication, or he may not have, yet his statement is valid in either case: he had no authority. Ironically, descendants of the Protestant tradition rejected the authority of Rome and of the Roman church, and then proceeded to carry on despite their illegitimate lineage. So the doctrine was changed to fit the practice: authority by ordination was no longer needed; believers were entitled to simply claim authority from the scriptures now available to them.

That such a practice is not what those very scriptures taught, nor how it had worked anciently—in other words, variant understanding of the scriptural record—is really a secondary consideration for Latter-day Saints. Varying interpretations of the same verses of scripture can go on and on and have for centuries. That's entirely what led to the formation of hundreds of Christian sects both in former and present days, all of them protesting the existing interpretation of the existing text. It's the very same thing that, according to his own record, drove Joseph Smith into the woods that misty morning in 1820. But an accurate understanding of the Latter-day Saint message at its core—something that even

---

[143]Cited by Joseph L. Wirthlin, Conference Report, April 1943, p. 118.

many spiritually immature LDS missionaries have trouble grasping—means that interpretations are irrelevant.

Following the personal return of God and Jesus Christ to the earth in April 1820, the guesswork was over.

Wrote Joseph Smith in 1838:

> My object in going to inquire of the Lord was to know which of all the sects was right, that I might know which to join. No sooner, therefore, did I get possession of myself, so as to be able to speak, than I asked the Personages who stood above me in the light, which of all the sects was right (for at this time it had never entered into my heart that all were wrong)—and which I should join.
>
> I was answered that I must join none of them, for they were all wrong; and the Personage who addressed me said that all their creeds were an abomination in his sight; that those professors were all corrupt; that: "they draw near to me with their lips, but their hearts are far from me, they teach for doctrines the commandments of men, having a form of godliness, but they deny the power thereof."
>
> He again forbade me to join with any of them; and many other things did he say unto me, which I cannot write at this time. When I came to myself again, I found myself lying on my back, looking up into heaven. When the light had departed, I had no strength; but soon recovering in some degree, I went home. And as I leaned up to the fireplace, mother inquired what the matter was. I replied, "Never mind, all is well—I am well enough off." I then said to my mother, "I have learned for myself that Presbyterianism is not true."[144]

The chronological duration of Joseph's visitation, whether measured in minutes or hours, is not known. But the identity of the messengers was made very clear to him: God the Eternal Father and Jesus Christ the Son, the Messiah, had stood before him and spoken "as one man speaks to another." In fact, following the Father's introduction, the Son had done all the speaking and perhaps even been left to complete the pronouncement by himself; he was and had been for millions of years, after all, the

---

[144]*History of the Church*, Vol. 1, Ch. 1, p. 6.

God given charge of this world.[145] There could be no greater messenger and no clearer message: the authorized Church of Jesus Christ was not to be found on the earth.

It would be absurd to think that fourteen-year-old Joseph broadcast to the four winds of murmur and gossip the account of his visitation; this was a profound, soul-wrenching experience. He shared it with his parents and family and with a minister to whom he had felt some spiritual companionability. "I was greatly surprised at his behavior," wrote Joseph. "He treated my communication not only lightly, but with great contempt, saying it was all of the devil, that there were no such things as visions or revelations in these days; that all such things had ceased with the apostles, and that there would never be any more of them."

The minister then noised the thing abroad, bringing derision and ridicule on the entire Smith family, a ridicule that would never abate. But Joseph remained firm.

> I had actually seen a light, and in the midst of that light I saw two Personages, and they did in reality speak to me; and though I was hated and persecuted for saying that I had seen a vision, yet it was true; and while they were persecuting me, reviling me, and speaking all manner of evil against me for so saying, I was led to say in my heart: Why persecute me for telling the truth? I have actually seen a vision; and who am I that I can withstand God, or why does the world think to make me deny what I have actually seen? For I had seen a vision; I knew it, and I knew that God knew it, and I could not deny it, neither dared I do it; at least I knew that by so doing I would offend God, and come under condemnation.[146]

What Joseph was not at all sure of, however, was what he was supposed to do next. The response to his specific offered prayer—which of all the churches is true?—had been given, certainly not in the way he had expected but given certainly enough. The extent of his commission at this point was "to continue as I was until further directed."

---

[145]As an effect of the Fall of Adam, people on earth forfeited the Father's presence, except for rare instances such as this where, for some moments, one is redeemed from that exclusion.

[146]Joseph Smith History 1:25.

"I had found the testimony of James to be true," he later wrote, "that a man who lacked wisdom might ask of God, and obtain, and not be upbraided."

He would ask the further questions three years later.

"I continued to pursue my common vocations in life until the twenty-first of September, one thousand eight hundred and twenty-three," he wrote, "all the time suffering severe persecution at the hands of all classes of men, both religious and irreligious, because I continued to affirm that I had seen a vision."[147]

This was only the beginning.

On the night just mentioned, he "betook [him]self to prayer," seeking further light and knowledge as to what specific course he should be pursuing. At some point in his prayer, a light began gathering in his room, illuminating it as if at midday. The light appeared to reach like a conduit straight up through the ceiling of his room and into the night sky. Then the light concentrated itself at the foot of his bed, where a being of light suddenly appeared. The individual was in the form of a man, "standing in the air, for his feet did not touch the floor."

He had on a loose robe of most exquisite whiteness. It was a whiteness beyond anything earthly I had ever seen; nor do I believe that any earthly thing could be made to appear so exceedingly white and brilliant. His hands were naked, and his arms also, a little above the wrist; so, also, were his feet naked, as were his legs, a little above the ankles. His head and neck were also bare. I could discover that he had no other clothing on but this robe, as it was open, so that I could see into his bosom.[148]

Not only was his robe exceedingly white, but his whole person was glorious beyond description, and his countenance truly like lightning. The room was exceedingly light, but not so very bright as immediately around his person. When I first looked upon him, I was afraid; but the fear soon left me.

In the strong voice of a man, which he clearly was, the personage called Joseph by name and introduced himself as Moroni [More-OWN-eye].

---

[147]Joseph Smith History 1:27.

[148]And there were no wings; he was human, not a bird.

He said there was a book deposited, written upon gold plates, giving an account of the former inhabitants of this continent, and the source from whence they sprang. He also said that the fullness of the everlasting gospel was contained in it, as delivered by the Savior to the ancient inhabitants; also, that there were two stones in silver bows— and these stones, fastened to a breastplate, constituted what is called the Urim and Thummim—deposited with the plates; and the possession and use of these stones were what constituted "seers" in ancient or former times; and that God had prepared them for the purpose of translating the book.[149]

The book, of course, extracted from its burial place in the hill four years later, would be translated into English, (from what Mormon called "reformed Egyptian") and published in 1830 as the Book of Mormon.[150] The entire translation of the Book of Mormon record would take fewer than ninety days. A minimum of fourteen individuals besides Joseph Smith would see, and most would handle, the plates it was written on before Joseph finished his work and returned them to Moroni. Eleven witnesses testified in print that they had "seen and hefted" the plates, jeopardizing friendships and livelihood with their testimony. Although six would eventually leave the church over other matters, not one would ever retract this testimony.

The Book of Mormon process would catalyze a number of events, all of them bearing directly on biblical doctrines so long debated, twisted, and tossed.

While translating a portion of the plates now rendered as 3 Nephi 11 in the Book of Mormon, Joseph Smith and his scribe, a former schoolteacher named Oliver Cowdery, read of the Savior's personal in-the-flesh instructions to his American disciples regarding baptism. The manner of baptism described there, following which there were to be no further "disputations" among them, was by full-body immersion in water.

Full-immersion baptism was being practiced by some in Joseph's day, but to others—then as now—a ritual sprinkling was deemed sufficient. While sprinkling appears a rather creative interpretation of the process as described in the New Testament, the point was at least an arguable

---

[149]*History of the Church*, Vol. 1, Ch. 2, pp. 10–11.

[150]The hill Cumorah lies about four miles south of Palmyra, New York.

one needing clarification. So Joseph and Oliver headed into the woods to seek divine guidance. It would be Oliver's first visit with an angel.[151]

The date was May 15, 1829. Kneeling in prayer near the banks of the Susquehanna River in northeastern Pennsylvania, Joseph and Oliver quickly sensed a presence accompanying them and looked up to see a glorious being standing above them in the air. It was a man, but it was not Moroni. "The messenger who visited us on this occasion . . . said that his name was John, the same that is called John the Baptist in the New Testament, and that he acted under the direction of Peter, James and John, who held the keys of the Priesthood of Melchizedek, which Priesthood, he said, would in due time be conferred on us."[152]

With little ado that we know of, the resurrected key-holding high priest of the Levitical order laid his hands upon the two and said, "Upon you my fellow servants, in the name of Messiah, I confer the Priesthood of Aaron, which holds the keys of the ministering of angels, and of the Gospel of repentance, and of baptism by immersion for the remission of sins; and this shall never be taken again from the earth, until the sons of Levi do offer again an offering unto the Lord in righteousness."

Joseph records: "He said this Aaronic Priesthood had not the power of laying on hands for the gift of the Holy Ghost, but that this should be conferred on us hereafter; and he commanded us to go and be baptized, and gave us directions that I should baptize Oliver Cowdery, and afterwards that he should baptize me. Accordingly we went and were baptized. I baptized him first, and afterwards he baptized me, after which I laid my hands upon his head and ordained him to the Aaronic Priesthood, and afterwards he laid his hands on me and ordained me to the same Priesthood, for so we were commanded."[153]

Thus Joseph and Oliver were now authorized to do exactly as the messenger who ordained them had anciently done: preach repentance, baptize, call for the blessing of angels—and wait. They were forerunners, preparers; John had recognized the limits of his authority 1,799 years before, and his successors were clearly apprised of it now. Joseph and Oliver would soon baptize others, including Joseph's younger brother

---

[151]He would see Moroni and the gold plates one month later.

[152]*History of the Church,* Vol. 1, Ch. 5, p. 40

[153]Ibid., pp. 39–40.

Samuel Harrison Smith. Samuel would prove his worth to the church in the few years remaining to him and die within weeks of Joseph's murder.

Almost immediately upon returning to their translation labors, says Joseph, "we began to have the Scriptures laid open to our understandings, and the true meaning and intention of their more mysterious passages revealed unto us in a manner which we never could attain to previously, nor ever before had thought of. In the meantime we were forced to keep secret the circumstances of having received the Priesthood and our having been baptized, owing to a spirit of persecution which had already manifested itself in the neighborhood. We had been threatened with being mobbed from time to time, and this, too, by professors of religion."[154]

And then, approximately two weeks later,[155] the long-promised and long-awaited happened: in a secluded woods on the Susquehanna River somewhere south of Colesville, New York, the ancient apostles Peter, James, and John the Beloved, the first two now glorious resurrected beings (and John still in an immortal yet preresurrection state), appeared in the flesh before Joseph and Oliver and conferred upon them the Melchizedek priesthood, the keys of presidency, and ordained them to the holy apostleship, with Peter acting as voice.

Following the visitation of these ancient apostles, having held in reserve the keys of their ministry for nearly eighteen centuries; of John the Baptist, holding likewise the keys of his; and of Moroni, who over the course of six years would visit Joseph more than twenty times,[156] Joseph Smith would proclaim the opening of a new and comprehensive gospel era. It was the dawning of the "dispensation of the fulness of times," said Joseph, "a whole and complete and perfect union, and welding together of dispensations, and keys, and powers, and glories . . . revealed from the days of Adam even to the present time. And not only this, but those things which never have been revealed from the foundation of the world, but have been kept hid from the wise and prudent, shall be revealed unto babes and sucklings in this, the dispensation of the fulness of times."[157]

---

[154]*History of the Church*, Vol. 1, Ch. 5, p. 43.

[155]The exact date was not recorded, but the latest scholarship suggests this date. See *Brigham Young University Studies*, Vol. 38, No. 1, 1999, p. 28.

[156]See *Encyclopedia of Mormonism*, Vol. 2, (s.v. "Moroni, Visitations of," and Vol. 4, s.v. "Visions of Joseph Smith.")

[157]*Doctrine and Covenants* 128:18.

Some of that revelation would come direct from heaven, as Joseph's journey with angels was far from over, but much of it would come straight from the ancient manuscript now in his possession. In the six years between Moroni's first visit in 1823 and his final (possibly the twenty-fourth) in 1829, Joseph would learn much more than doctrine. According to his mother, Lucy, Moroni and at least one additional Book of Mormon prophet functioned as private tutors: "Joseph continued to receive instructions . . . and we continued to get the children together every evening for the purpose of listening while he gave us a relation of the same. . . . He would describe the ancient inhabitants of this continent, their dress, mode of traveling, and the animals upon which they rode; their cities, their buildings, with every particular; their mode of warfare; and also their religious worship. This he would do with as much ease, seemingly, as if he had spent his whole life among them."[158]

Joseph's early reputation as a visionary, a "seer," would in fact extend far beyond the borders of his home or the devotional or theological confines of Mormonism. He would once be sought out and employed for a time by a man living more than one hundred miles away who was seeking old Spanish treasure. In his need to make a living, in a way that was not uncommon among the rural poor of New York, Joseph obliged the man for a time, but soon talked him out of the venture and into the church. A handful of such episodes led to Joseph's being called a "money digger" and a "glass looker."

David Whitmer, hired by Oliver Cowdery in 1829 to move Joseph and his belongings to Fayette, New York, first encountered Joseph walking toward him on the road, fully expecting him at that moment, although Whitmer had just covered a distance of a hundred miles and had been on the road for nearly three days.

"Oliver told me," said Whitmer later, "that Joseph had informed him when I started from home, where I had stopped the first night, how I read the sign at the tavern, where I stopped the next night, etc., and that I would be there that day before dinner, and this was why they had come out to meet me; all of which was exactly as Joseph had told Oliver, at which I was greatly astonished."[159]

---

[158]Smith, Lucy Mack. *History of Joseph Smith.* Preston Nibley, ed. Salt Lake City, 1958, p. 83.

[159]Lyndon W. Cook, ed., *David Whitmer Interviews: A Restoration Witness,* p. 27.

When Cowdery had first contacted Whitmer regarding the urgent need for his services, Whitmer "did not know what to do, I was pressed with my work. I had some twenty acres to plow, so I concluded I would finish plowing and then go. I got up one morning to go to work as usual, and on going to the field, found between five and seven acres of my ground had been plowed during the night. I don't know who did it; but it was done just as I would have done it myself, and the plow was left standing in the furrow."[160]

Then: "The day following this circumstance he went out to spread plaster over a field, according to the custom of the farmers in that locality, when, to his surprise, he found the work had been done, and well done. David Whitmer's sister, who lived near the field, told him that three strangers had appeared in the field the day before and spread the plaster with remarkable skill. She at the time presumed that they were men whom David had hired to do the work."[161]

The first five thousand copies of the Book of Mormon were offered for sale on March 26, 1830. Eleven days later, Tuesday, April 6, "being one thousand eight hundred and thirty years since the coming of our Lord and Savior Jesus Christ in the flesh," Joseph and five others, fulfilling the requirements of the state of New York, formally organized the Church of the Latter-day Saints in a small log home near Fayette, New York. Among the five was Joseph's younger brother, Samuel, and his oldest brother, Hyrum.[162]

Although various converts—both before and following their baptisms—had proselyted with manuscript pages of the Book of Mormon for a number of months, in late June Joseph set apart his younger brother Samuel as the first "official" missionary of the church. Leaving on June 30, Samuel traveled more than four thousand miles "from Maine to Missouri" over the next fifteen months, returning occasionally only to fill his knapsack with more books and depart anew. Besides the books, he traveled light: sleeping wherever he found himself at night, eating whatever he was offered or could beg. Although he met with much resistance, he organized four branches of the church. Thrilled with the labor, he re-

---

[160]Ibid.

[161]George Q. Cannon, *Life of Joseph Smith*, pp. 67, 68.

[162]The firstborn Smith son, Alvin, had died in 1823.

turned nevertheless discouraged, thinking all too few believed and accepted what he thought to be the most magnificent message in two thousand years. Clearly the most significant achievement of his mission he would learn of months later. But the full significance of the matter he would never live to witness.

Early in his journey, Samuel left a copy of the Book of Mormon at the home of one John P. Greene, a Methodist preacher, who, on learning of the book's claimed origin, said he was not interested but would nevertheless take a subscription paper on his preaching circuit. Should he find anyone who wanted a copy he would give his name to Samuel when he got back. Samuel tells the story from there.

When I arrived [back] at Mr. Greene's, Mrs. Greene informed me that her husband was absent from home, that there was no prospect of selling my books, and even the one which I had left with them, she expected I would have to take away, as Mr. Greene had no disposition to purchase it, although she had read it herself and was much pleased with it.

I made her a present of it, and told her that the Spirit forbade my taking it away. She burst into tears, and requested me to pray with her. I did so, and afterwards explained to her the most profitable manner of reading the book which I had left with her; which was, to ask God, when she read it, for a testimony of the truth of what she had read, and she would receive the Spirit of God, which would enable her to discern the things of God. I then left her, and returned home.

According to Mrs. Smith, when Mr. Greene returned home, he was told what Samuel had said about reading the book. Mrs. Greene asked him to read it so.

This, he for a while refused to do, but finally yielded to her persuasions, and took the book, and commenced perusing the same, calling upon God for the testimony of his Spirit. The result of which was, that he and Mrs. Greene were in a short time baptized. They gave the book to Phineas Young, Mrs. Greene's brother, who read it, and commenced preaching it forthwith. It was next handed to [Phineas's brother], and from him to Mrs. Murray, his sister.[163]

"It was not uncommon in the earliest days of the movement," wrote a later commentator, "for a man to hear Mormonism preached one day, be baptized the next, be ordained an elder on the following day and the day after that to be out preaching Mormonism."[164]

For this particular brother of Phineas Young, the process took a little longer. Reading the book nine times over the next year and a half, studying it from every angle and with mighty prayer, he eventually requested baptism. But this was no ordinary man. Within two decades he would be the most famous Latter-day Saint in the world and, within another, one of the most widely known Americans. To the Latter-day Saints he would be known simply as "Brother Brigham."

Although spiritual manifestations such as healings and visions would accompany the rapidly swelling number of Latter-day Saints often enough to make it seem an era of open pentecost, the foundational tenet made crystal clear in the ordinations under the hands of the ancients was that the house of God was a house of order: one man received revelations for the church as a whole. Through that man, Joseph Smith, Oliver Cowdery would receive the following counsel in that fall of 1830: "Behold, verily, verily, I say unto thee, no one shall be appointed to receive commandments and revelations in this church excepting my servant Joseph Smith, Jun., for he receiveth them even as Moses. And thou shalt be obedient unto the things which I shall give unto him, even as Aaron, to declare faithfully the commandments and the revelations. . . . Thou shalt not command him who is at thy head, and at the head of the church; For I have given him the keys of the mysteries, and the revelations which are sealed, until I shall appoint unto them another in his stead."[165]

That one man, and one only, would be recognized as qualified to say "thus saith the Lord" is a foundational tenet of Mormonism, and Joseph Smith's vision-packed tenure would serve to establish that doctrine more

---

[163]Franklin S. Harris, Jr., *The Book of Mormon: Messages and Evidences*, p. 174.

[164]Richard Shelton Williams, "The Missionary Movements of the LDS Church in New England, 1830–1850" (master's thesis, Brigham Young University, 1969), p. 10.

[165]*Doctrine and Covenants* 28:2–7.

than anything else. For nearly fifteen years, it appeared to the Latter-day Saints that he would be *the* prophet, the *only* prophet, and the *last* prophet before the Second Coming of Christ, which event was expected at any time. Both perceptions would soon face some rather significant modification.

What sounds in that preceding scriptural verse like a thesis statement for tyranny must be taken in context: a single individual would in fact preside over the church and be the ultimate authority in determining matters of doctrine or policy. But he would rarely act alone. The establishment of a First Presidency (typically two assistants or "counselors" to the Prophet) in March 1832, the Quorum of the Twelve (February 1835), and the Seventy (late February 1835)[166] created a broad body of general church leadership, all drawn from among the common members. Formalized theological training was neither required nor countenanced. ("We believe that a man must be called of God, by prophecy, and by the laying on of hands by those who are in authority, to preach the Gospel and administer in the ordinances thereof."[167] "And no man taketh this honour unto himself, but he that is called of God, as was Aaron."[168]) In very few instances of formative church history was Joseph Smith alone, and in fewer still was he dogmatic.

In one of the most pivotal moments in church history, he was, once again, with Oliver Cowdery.

Sunday, April 3, 1836
Kirtland, Ohio

In the afternoon, I assisted the other Presidents in distributing the Lord's Supper to the Church, receiving it from the Twelve, whose privilege it was to officiate at the sacred desk this day. After having performed this service to my brethren, I retired to the pulpit, the veils

---

[166]Certain members of the Seventy were named to "general authority" status in August 1835, although many "other seventy" served with local ecclesiastical jurisdiction until 1986, when ordination as a Seventy became strictly a General (churchwide jurisdiction) Authority calling. In April 1997, "Area Authority Seventies" (jurisdiction limited to specific world regions) were named for the first time.

[167]Articles of Faith 1:5.

[168]Heb. 5:4.

being dropped, and bowed myself, with Oliver Cowdery, in solemn and silent prayer. After rising from prayer, the following vision was opened to both of us.

The veil was taken from our minds, and the eyes of our understanding were opened. We saw the Lord standing upon the breastwork of the pulpit, before us; and under his feet was a paved work of pure gold, in color like amber. His eyes were as a flame of fire; the hair of his head was white like the pure snow; his countenance shone above the brightness of the sun; and his voice was as the sound of the rushing of great waters, even the voice of Jehovah, saying: "I am the first and the last; I am he who liveth, I am he who was slain; I am your advocate with the Father. Behold, your sins are forgiven you; you are clean before me; therefore, lift up your heads and rejoice."[169]

This initial vision having closed, serving in some sense as an introduction, three more heavenly beings next appeared to Joseph and Oliver.

Moses appeared before us, and committed unto us the keys of the gathering of Israel from the four parts of the earth, and the leading of the ten tribes from the land of the north.

After this, Elias appeared, and committed the dispensation of the gospel of Abraham, saying that in us and our seed all generations after us should be blessed.

After this vision had closed, another great and glorious vision burst upon us; for Elijah the prophet, who was taken to heaven without tasting death, stood before us, and said: "Behold, the time has fully come, which was spoken of by the mouth of Malachi, testifying that [I] should be sent, before the great and dreadful day of the Lord come, to turn the hearts of the fathers to the children, and the children to the fathers, lest the whole earth be smitten with a curse; therefore, the keys of this dispensation are committed into your hands; and by this ye may know that the great and dreadful day of the Lord is near, even at the doors."

---

[169]*History of the Church*, Vol. 2, pp. 434–435; Elder John Murdock, a close companion of the Prophet, further described the Savior's eyes as a "keen penetrating blue." (See John Murdock journal, typescript, Brigham Young University Archives, p. 13.

Moses, Elias, and Elijah? To the Mormons?

"It is interesting to know," wrote Joseph's grandnephew more than a century later, "that on the third day of April 1836, the Jews were celebrating the feast of the Passover, and were leaving the doors of their homes open for the coming of Elijah. On that day Elijah came, but not to the Jewish homes, but to the temple in the village of Kirtland near the banks of Lake Erie, to two humble servants of the Lord who were appointed by divine decree to receive him."[170]

For what purpose such an epiphany? If, as the Latter-day Saints claim, the lower and higher priesthoods had already been restored at the hands of angels, why were these additional visits necessary? It could be suggested that each visitation imprinted firmly on the Prophet's mind the specific functions he was to soon pursue as part and portion of the "restitution of all things"[171]—the gathering of Israel, the turning of hearts to the fathers (i.e., ancestral generations), the dispensation of Abraham.

It was more fundamental than that. Of the three immortal beings who came, two—Moses and Elias—had come in like manner and with identical purpose to Peter, James, John, and the Savior on the Mount of Transfiguration (Mark 9). And like in that transcendent visit, the expediency of heaven required that something much greater than impressing the recipients was involved. These beings from the eternal worlds came to a new prophet, he who stood at the head of the final dispensation, each "declaring their dispensation, their rights, their keys, their honors, their majesty and glory, and the power of their priesthood."[172] They held their own keys, meaning "the privilege and authority to administer in the ordinances of the gospel of Jesus Christ,"[173] from their own ministrations upon the earth.

With the keys long held, and now bestowed by Elias, Joseph could rightfully extend the covenant blessings of Abraham,[174] whose seed now numbers as the sands of the seashore. With those conferred by Moses,

---

[170]Joseph Fielding Smith, *Church History and Modern-day Revelation*, Vol. 3, pp. 78, 84.

[171]Acts 3:21.

[172]Bruce R. McConkie, *Doctrinal New Testament Commentary*, Vol. 3, p. 531.

[173]Joseph F. Smith, *Gospel Doctrine*, 5th ed., p. 142.

[174]This is most likely the man actually named "Elias," about whom very little is known in biblical scripture or otherwise. He clearly "lived in the days of Abraham and . . . held the keys of that dispensation." (Joseph Fielding Smith Jr., *Doctrines of Salvation*, Vol. 3, p. 127)

that great prophet of Israel, Joseph could begin gathering those of the covenant long since scattered like wayward sheep to all quarters of the globe. And with those bestowed by Elijah, who as a translated being (immortal but not resurrected) had a unique relationship to both the living and the dead, he could begin the work of salvation for the dead.

Whoa. Stop.

In my brief experience with "my own" Mormon missionaries years ago, only three things stand apart from the otherwise vague and muddled memory of that week with crystal clarity. One is my experience with the Book of Mormon, which I've already mentioned. Another is the senior missionary quoting this question of Paul's in the New Testament: "Else what shall they do which are baptized for the dead, if the dead rise not at all? why are they then baptized for the dead?" (1 Cor. 15:29)

Part of the impact was the mere hearing of King James old English, a style of language with which I was mostly unfamiliar, having listened to plenty of Steeleye Span but very little Shakespeare. Part was the concept itself: the performing of ordinances of salvation for those who were already dead.

That in fact is the doctrine, and Elijah came restoring the keys to begin it anew for the first time since Paul's era in which it was a functioning but fading effort among the saints of his day.

Other visitations would yet occur.

The long period of apostasy and darkness was over; the Restoration was largely complete. The return to the ancient doctrines and practices sought by Luther and Calvin and Wesley was a reality. Two years before his death, Joseph would exclaim with great vigor:

Now, what do we hear in the gospel which we have received? A voice of gladness! A voice of mercy from heaven; and a voice of truth out of the earth; glad tidings for the dead; a voice of gladness for the living and the dead; glad tidings of great joy. Moroni, an angel from heaven, declaring the fulfilment of the prophets—the book to be revealed. The voice of Peter, James, and John in the wilderness . . . on the Susquehanna river, declaring themselves as possessing the keys of the kingdom, and of the dispensation of the fulness of times!

And again, the voice of God . . . at sundry times, and in divers places through all the travels and tribulations of this Church of Jesus Christ of Latter-day Saints! And the voice of Michael, the archangel;

the voice of Gabriel, and of Raphael, and of divers angels, from Michael or Adam down to the present time, all declaring their dispensation, their rights, their keys, their honors, their majesty and glory, and the power of their priesthood; giving line upon line, precept upon precept; here a little, and there a little; giving us consolation by holding forth that which is to come, confirming our hope!

Brethren, shall we not go on in so great a cause? Go forward and not backward. Courage, brethren; and on, on to the victory! Let your hearts rejoice, and be exceedingly glad.[175]

This restored Christianity had come at the hands of the authorized servants who had last administered it. But its effects would very soon catalyze an episode that would much more resemble the time of Moses. The new Camp of Israel was about to be expelled from Egypt, forced into a mass Exodus for which there is no parallel in American history.

Joseph's pep talk would help. But they would need Brother Brigham.

---

[175]*Doctrine and Covenants* 128:18–22.

CHAPTER 9

The Untold Story

I spent the morning of Wednesday, July 9, 1997, in the back of a horse-drawn wagon banging its way slowly up the almost imperceptible rise of one of the West's most historic and notable nonfeatures: South Pass, Wyoming. It was through this broad draw that nearly a quarter of a million wanderers, a good chunk of them Mormon pioneers, crossed the spine of the continent in the mid-1800s.

With me in the back of the wagon was a television producer from Los Angeles, jotting down notes about why my people had come this way. The event being commemorated was the 150th anniversary of the blazing of the Mormon Trail, the wilderness road that led nearly seventy thousand perse-cuted and driven Christian pilgrims from the familiarity of their homelands to the remote and desolate vastness of the Great Salt Lake basin 1,350 miles to the west. Between April 20, 1997, and trail's end ninety-three days later, July 24, an estimated ten thousand participants and 330 media outlets joined in for some portion of the reenactment trek. Around four hundred people went all the way, about sixty of them on foot.

In fact, my people never walked this trail, which I told the producer. My people were likely part of the reason the Latter-day Saints were on it in the first place, which I didn't tell her.

But I'm getting ahead of myself. Why the Latter-day Saints were out here in the first place is one of the most disturbing episodes in American history. As I unfolded it for the producer, she asked me why she'd never heard this story in her American history classes. Nor had I, and I had no answer for her. In pondering it since, the only thing that ever seemed likely was that, until we were big enough to be unavoidable, Christian America simply never found the Mormon story much to its taste.

So here's the story you never heard.

Everywhere that Joseph went, travail was sure to go. Bowing to some persecution (to which he was ever subject), but in large measure inde-pendent of that, Joseph Smith and his wife Emma moved to the Kirtland,

Ohio, area in February 1831. Missionaries in that district were experiencing great success, having converted nearly one hundred and fifty to the church in a month, including most of the Campbellite congregation and their pastor, Sidney Rigdon. Joseph felt such fertile ground would not be unkind to his growing flock.

He was wrong.

In the early morning hours of March 24, 1832,[176] Joseph was awakened by Emma's screams. A dozen men grabbed Joseph and carried him from the house and to a nearby meadow, where they stripped him of his clothes, gouged his flesh with their fingernails, and pasted him with hot tar and chicken feathers, breaking one of his front teeth as they tried to force some of the hot tar into his mouth. Nearby lay Sidney Rigdon, similarly treated but, to Joseph's knowledge, either dead or unconscious, having been dragged by the heels, his head bouncing, over the threshold of his cabin, across the woodpile, and for nearly a hundred yards over the frozen ground.

Joseph soon made his way back to his house,[177] where Emma saw him and fainted, thinking that he had been "mashed all to pieces."[178] His wife and friends used hot water and lard to peel the tar from his skin and hair, and the following day, a Sunday, he preached a sermon and baptized three people. In the listening crowd was Simonds Ryder, the man who had replaced Rigdon as pastor of the Campbellite congregation, then converted to Mormonism, and then exited that faith and functioned as ringleader of the previous night's mob.

Rigdon was worse off. He was found wandering naked and delirious, his head swollen, lacerated and bleeding. Owing to a similar dragging behind a horse when he was seven years old, Rigdon would suffer

---

[176]Some records give the date as March 25.

[177]In March 1832 Joseph and Emma were boarding at the home of John Johnson in nearby Hiram. The previous April, Emma had given birth to twins who died within hours. (Her first child, Alvin, had also died within hours of his birth.) A friend, Julia Murdock, who gave birth to twins the same day as Emma, died following their birth, and Joseph and Emma were allowed to adopt the motherless babies. On the night here named, Joseph and Emma had been up most of the night tending these two, who were severely afflicted with measles. In the rush and chaos of the house invasion, one of the twins, eleven-month-old Joseph, was exposed to the bitter weather and died five days later. Thus in her first five years of marriage Emma had lost four children; only the surviving adopted twin remained.

[178]*History of Joseph Smith,* Millennial Star, Vol. 14, p. 148.

from violent moodswings and bouts of prolonged sickness for the rest of his life.

Yet even in the midst of such tension (Joseph was quite sure it would accompany the Latter-day Saints anywhere they went), the doctrine of a physical gathering was rapidly emerging, and Kirtland served as one of its hubs. Mormon settlers would triple the town's population over the next few years and gain relative control over regional commerce and politics.

But by the summer of 1831, Joseph Smith had designated Jackson County, Missouri, as Zion, the true gathering place, where they would build up the New Jerusalem and establish "the land of [our] inheritance."[179] Hundreds of converts began flowing toward that western frontier.

Although church leaders would occasionally travel to Missouri, a distance of more than 900 miles, Joseph and a number of other Latter-day Saints would retain their residences in Kirtland, where they would labor to complete a temple by 1836.[180] Many of the early and fundamental doctrines of the church were established in Kirtland.

By 1833, Latter-day Saint converts were flowing into rural western Missouri, establishing frontier settlements in the regions surrounding Independence. This was the last bus stop in America, the embarkation point for Santa Fe and the Rocky Mountains: frontier, wild and wholly woolly. The last thing the locals wanted was a bunch of heretical do-gooders peopling their plains. Especially abolitionists. In July 1833, the Mormons went so far as to publish in their monthly newspaper an article entitled, "Free People of Color." In Missouri.

"It requires no gift of prophecy," stated one irate citizens' committee, "to tell that the day is not far distant when the civil government of the county will be in their hands; when the sheriff, the justices, and the county judges will be Mormons."[181] Subsequently, the committee issued its proclamation of intent.

---

[179]*Doctrine and Covenants* 57:3.

[180]It was to this temple that Moses, Elijah, and Elias came, as noted in chapter 7. Although the building still stands, it is no longer owned by the church.

[181]"A meeting of the citizens of Jackson county, Missouri, called for the purpose of adopting measures to rid themselves of the sect of fanatics, called Mormons, held at Independence on the 20th day of July, 1833," in *Western Monitor*, Fayette, Missouri, August 2, 1833, as cited in *History of the Church*, Vol. 1, Ch. 28, p. 396.

We the undersigned, citizens of Jackson county, believing that an important crisis is at hand, as regards our civil society, in consequence of a pretended religious society of people that have settled and are still settling in our county, styling themselves Mormons; and intending as we do, to rid our society, peaceably if we can, forcibly if we must, and believing as we do, that the arm of the civil law does not afford us a guarantee, or at least, a sufficient one against the evils which are now inflicted on us, and seem to be increasing by the said religious sect, deem it expedient and of the highest importance to form ourselves into a company for the better and easier accomplishment of our purpose, which we deem it almost superfluous to say, is justified as well by the law of nature, as by the law of self defence.[182]

By the fall of that year, the Latter-day Saints in Missouri—now a third of the population in that region—were being driven from their homes by gun-toting neighbors and at least one, Bishop Edward Partridge, was hot-tarred and feathered.

Messengers hurried news of the usurpation to church headquarters, reaching Kirtland in February. By May 1834, Joseph was on the march west with "Zion's Camp," a contingent of somewhat more than one hundred men. By the time they entered Missouri in early June, there were about two hundred men, eleven women, and seven children, all armed. About that time, the Missourians burned down every remaining Mormon home and shop in Jackson County.

Although Joseph had received an earlier pledge from Missouri Governor Daniel Dunklin that state militia would assist the Latter-day Saints in reoccupying their settlements, that pledge now came to naught as Dunklin feared civil war should he appear to favor the Mormons. A suggestion was offered by church leaders that the state purchase the abandoned properties from the evicted, who would then go elsewhere. That, too, came to nothing.

On June 22, Joseph Smith abandoned the militaristic designs of Zion's Camp, reasoning nothing beneficial could come from a resumption of living arrangements amidst obvious enemies. He instructed the Saints to start anew, and most received charitable treatment from residents of

---

[182]Cited in *Times and Seasons*, Vol. 5, p. 419.

Clay County, to the north. By the end of June, the remaining supplies had been distributed to the refugees, and Zion's Camp broke up, most of its members returning to Ohio. Eight months later, nine of the first twelve apostles and all of the first Quorum of Seventy would be called from the ranks of Camp members.

The settlement in Clay County was understood to be a temporary arrangement, and efforts were launched to find a new home. Throughout 1835 and 1836, however, the Mormon ranks swelled with converts, mostly eastern immigrants and nearly all living in destitute conditions. Old slave shacks were purchased; dugouts were dug; lean-tos were leaned. And tensions rose. The temporary sick camp on Crooked River was threatened with violence.

By fall 1836, most of the Latter-day Saints were removing to a remote grass prairie in far northern Ray County, which they soon named Far West. Again, crude shelters began to rise. In December, a Missouri state legislator who had befriended the Saints, Alexander W. Doniphan, introduced a bill to create two new small counties from northern Ray. He proposed naming the new counties Daviess and Caldwell after two famous Kentucky Indian fighters. These would be exclusively for settlement by the Latter-day Saints, who would have their own militia and their own representation in the state legislature. Although the militia angle was hotly debated, most considered this segregation of the Latter-day Saints an excellent solution, and the bill was signed into law. Included was a six-mile-wide buffer zone between the "Mormon counties" and the "Missouri counties" where no one was permitted to settle.

In March 1838, Joseph Smith led a general migration of the eastern Saints to Far West. By July, approximately five thousand Latter-day Saints were occupying the region, and Joseph oversaw the establishment of several new communities. As they had done previously in Jackson County, a temple site was selected and dedicated in Far West. Also in Far West, Joseph received a revelation in which he was given the formal name of the church, "even The Church of Jesus Christ of Latter-day Saints."[183]

But by midsummer, the threats to the church were not only external but internal. Four church officers, including the second elder of the church, Joseph's "assistant president" Oliver Cowdery, were found prof-

---

[183]*Doctrine and Covenants* 115:4.

iting from funds designated for helping the poor incoming settlers, and excommunicated. In his own way, each began to retaliate. In a fiery speech on June 19, church presidency first counselor Sidney Rigdon publicly threatened the dissenters, suggesting in his "Salt Sermon"[184] that they leave Far West or suffer harm. A subsequent speech given publicly on Independence Day proclaimed the Latter-day Saints would no longer stand passive in the face of "mobocracy."

Sometime in the summer of 1838, the First Presidency oversaw the creation of a community network that would undertake the full range of community-building activities, organized so that "in this time of alarm no family or person might be neglected."[185] Employing a biblical model of a covenant community (Exod. 18:21) that established a successive and accountable hierarchy of captains over tens, fifties, and hundreds, the various squadrons of the organization assumed responsibility for the securing or production of provisions, construction of dwellings, and protection of the community. On the heels of the Salt sermon and the Independence Day speech, and in light of the growing threat to life and property, the latter squadron soon gained an emotional if not numerical life of its own.

Encouraged at least in part by the tenor of those speeches, one Sampson Avard began directing a covert renegade band that made a number of hit-and-run or openly aggressive moves within the region. Known as *Danites*,[186] from a similar role played by the militant tribe of Dan in the Old Testament, Avard and his accomplices were soon defying even church leaders in their quest for revenge. Joseph suspended Avard's official sanction, but the band continued. Soon he was excommunicated, and his aggression turned toward the church. In court testimony offered only a few months later, he revealed himself a complete traitor to the Latter-day Saints and any honorable enterprise. Yet the myth of the Danites as "avenging angels" was born.

"By 1900," writes Brigham Young University historian David J. Whit-

---

[184]From: "Ye are the salt of the earth: but if the salt have lost his savour, wherewith shall it be salted? it is thenceforth good for nothing, but to be cast out, and to be trodden under foot of men." (Matt. 5:13)

[185]*History of the Church, Period I,* Vol. iii, pp. 178–181.

[186]*Danites* was the term given to the community-building organization as a whole, but as at that time self-defense held a prominent position in the needs of the people, it very quickly attached itself in the minds of most to the military component.

taker, "at least fifty novels had been published in English using the Avard-type Danite to develop story lines of murder, pillage, and conspiracy against common citizens." Among them were tales by Arthur Conan Doyle (*A Study in Scarlet*), Zane Grey (*Riders of the Purple Sage*), and Robert Louis Stevenson (*The Dynamiter*). "The image became so pervasive that few reader were willing to question the accuracy of such portrayals."[187]

The image in no way died out in 1900, however. As recently as 1995, a made-for-television film perpetuated the old stereotype in living color.[188]

On August 8, election day, mobs in Gallatin, Missouri, prohibited the Latter-day Saints from voting, to which Joseph responded with a call to the resident militia to protect their fellows. Instantly, the region was inflamed, and soon there was open conflict. Latter-day Saint settlements came under siege, and by October 1838, thousands were housing their children under tarps and under trees, or in muddy caves carved into riverbanks spread out across far western Missouri. Houses and fields began to burn.

On Wednesday, October 24, 1838, a band of marauding locals dropped by a secluded Mormon homestead and abducted the three occupants at gunpoint. Alerted to the crime, church apostle David W. Patten took a contingent of men and pursued them. At dawn the following morning, as they approached the banks of Crooked Creek (also known as Crooked River) from the east, a teenager named Patrick O'Banion was shot from his saddle without warning. Silhouetted against the pale light of morning, the Mormons were easy targets. Rushing the river, where the Missouri mobbers lay hidden beneath the banks of the stream, they opened fire. Minutes later, one Missourian and three Latter-day Saints lay dead. A dozen were wounded. The mobbers took flight for the woods, leaving their prisoners. A number of them were later heard to state that each was the only survivor of the "Mormon" aggression.

Apostle Patten, badly gut-shot, was transported by litter to a cabin three miles away where his wife arrived under guard just before he died at about 10 P.M.

Rumors fueled by mobocratic paranoia soon reached the ears of newly elected governor Lilburn W. Boggs, who as a lawyer in Jackson County had previously heard entreaties from the Latter-day Saints. And

---

[187]*Encyclopedia of Mormonism*, Vol. 1, S. V. "Danites."

[188]Naturally, *The Avenging Angel*, Turner Broadcasting Corporation.

denied them. Inflamed with his own vanity and eager to light off some show of political potency, he issued his infamous "Extermination Order." The entire text is illuminating.[189]

Military Order by the Governor of Missouri
Head Quarters, Militia
City of Jefferson, Oct. 27, 1838

To Gen. [John B.] Clark
　　Sir: Since the order of the morning to you, directing you to cause four hundred mounted men to be raised with your division, I have received by Amos Rees, Esq. and Wiley E. Williams Esq., one of my aids, information of the most appaling [sic] character, which changes the whole face of things, and places the Mormons in the attitude of an open and avowed defiance of the laws, and of having made open war upon the people of this State. Your orders are, therefore, to hasten your operations and endeavour to reach Richmond, in Ray county, with all possible speed. The Mormons must be treated as enemies, and must be exterminated or driven from the State, if necessary, for the public good. Their outrages are beyond all description. If you can increase your force, you are authorized to do so to any extent you may think necessary. I have just issued orders to Maj. Gen. Wallock, of Marion county, to raise 500 men and to march them to the northern part of Davies, and there united with Gen. Doniph[a]n of Clay, who has been ordered with 500 men to proceed to the same point, for the purpose of intercepting the retreat of the Mormons to the North. They have been directed to communicate with you by express. You can also communicate with them if you find it necessary. Instead, therefore, of proceeding, as at first directed, to re-instate the citizens of Davies in their homes, you will proceed immediately to Richmond, and there operate against the Mormons. Brig. Gen Parks, of Ray, has been ordered to have four hundred men in his brigade in readiness to join you at Richmond. The whole force will be placed under your command.

L. [Lilburn] W. Boggs, Gov.
And Commander-in-chief

---

[189]*Mormon Redress Petitions: Documents of the 1833–1838 Missouri Conflict*, Clark V. Johnson, ed., Religious Studies Center, Brigham Young University, 1992.

Feeling justified by the orders of his own governor, on October 30, Colonel William O. Jennings of the Missouri state militia took 240 men and attacked the tiny LDS settlement of Haun's Mill on Shoal Creek in remote eastern Caldwell County. Having been forced to surrender all weapons in the settlement five days before as part of a "truce," Joseph Smith had in fact counseled Jacob Haun to desert the settlement and bring his people to Far West. Assuming the truce was authentic, and thinking it cowardly to abandon the settlement, Haun instead told his fellows it was the Prophet's counsel that they endeavor to maintain the place. Thus most of the settlers were waiting quietly at the doors of their homes when Jennings's men rode into view. When three horsemen lurched forward, guns blazing, the women and children fled south across a frozen stream into the woods. Mary Stedwell was one of the first hit, in the hand, but she fell over a log into which the horsemen sent more than a dozen lead balls. Another dozen women and children were hit as they ran. But Jennings wanted the men, most of whom had rushed for position inside the blacksmith shop. The mobbers thrust their muskets through the cracks in the widely spaced logs and fired, killing seventeen men and small boys.

Although the massacre was over within minutes, many wounded lay dying. Sixty-two-year-old Thomas McBride was on his back in the dirt, his gun laying at his side. A militiaman named Jacob Rogers came up to him and demanded it. Unable to move, the old man said simply, "Take it." Rogers grabbed the weapon, turned it around, and shot the old man in the chest. He then pulled a harvesting knife from his saddle and hacked up McBride, who was still alive. Another militiaman, William Reynolds, entered the blacksmith shop where he discovered ten-year-old Sardius Smith and his little brother Alma hiding beneath the bellows, whimpering at the side of their dead father. Sardius begged for their lives, but Reynolds grinned at his associates, saying, "Nits make lice," and blew the child's brains out, splattering his little brother.[190] He then sent another ball into six-year-old Alma, destroying most of his hip.[191]

---

[190]Historical sources vary on who killed little Sardius (or Sardis) Smith; it seems a half dozen men thought the brave deed worthy of personal claim. (See Baugh, "Massacre at Haun's Mill," *Brigham Young University Studies*, Vol. 38, No. 1.)

[191]Amanda Barnes Smith writes of a vision from God in which she was told in detail how to save her little boy's leg. She would later write: "It is now nearly forty years ago, but Alma has never been the least crippled during his life, and he has traveled quite a long period of the time as a missionary of the gospel and a living miracle of the power of God" (Amanda

After plundering the settlement, even stripping clothes off many of the dead, the militiamen scattered. Late that evening, from their hiding places in the woods, widows and orphans crept into the carnage and, still fearing a return, anxiously interred most of the seventeen corpses in a deep hole they had hoped to make into a well.

Thinking it their only chance at staying alive, they bid farewell to their dead, gathered their wounded, and fled to the settlement of Far West twelve miles away.

In the early morning hours of October 31, twenty-five hundred state militia troops under the command of Major General Samuel D. Lucas, an avowed and notorious "Mormon hater," descended upon the village, where approximately one hundred and fifty Latter-day Saint men had assembled their wives and families. The stench of Crooked River and Haun's Mill yet warm in the air, the settlers had torn down a number of their own homes in order to erect a breastwork of the timbers.

The Mormon militiaman in charge, Colonel George M. Hinkle, raised a flag of truce and approached the general. Fearing for his own life, he there struck a bargain egregious to the welfare of the Saints. That deal, as later read to the assembled Saints by General John Clark, follows.[192]

Far West, Missouri
October 31, 1838

Gentlemen—You whose names are not attached to this list of names, will now have the privilege of going to your fields to obtain corn for your families, wood, etc. Those that are now taken, will go from thence to prison—be tried, and receive the due demerit of their crimes.

It now devolves upon you to fulfill the treaty that you have entered into, the leading items of which I now lay before you. The first of these you have already complied with, which is, that you deliver up your leading men to be tried according to law [Joseph and Hyrum Smith and about eighty associates]. Second, that you deliver up your arms—

Barnes Smith journal, cited in *LDS Biographical Encyclopedia*, Andrew Jenson, Vol. 2, p. 796).

[192]*History of Caldwell County*, pp. 140–141.

this has been attended to. The third is, that you sign over your properties to defray the expenses of the war—this you have also done. Another thing remains for you to comply with, that is that you leave the State forthwith, and whatever your feelings concerning this affair, whatever your innocence, it is nothing to me.

The order of the Governor to me, were, that you should be exterminated, and not allowed to continue in the State, and had your leader not been given up and the treaty complied with before this, you and your families would have been destroyed, and your houses in ashes.

But if I have to come again, because the treaty which you have made here shall be broken, you need not expect any mercy, but extermination—for I am determined the Governor's order shall be executed. As for your leaders, do not once think—do not imagine for a moment— do not let it enter your mind, that they will be delivered, or that you will see their faces again, for their fate is fixed, their die is cast, their doom is sealed.

I would advise you to scatter abroad and never again organize with Bishops, Presidents, etc., lest you excite the jealousies of the people, and subject yourselves to the same calamities that have now come upon you. You have always been the aggressors—you have brought upon yourselves these difficulties by being disaffected, and not being subject to rule—and my advice is that you become as other citizens, lest by a recurrence of these events you bring upon yourselves irretrievable ruin.

The evening of October 31, an ad hoc military court found Joseph and Hyrum Smith and two associates worthy of death on charges of treason. Lucas ordered Brig. General Alexander Doniphan to execute them at dawn. Doniphan refused to carry out the order, declaring it cold-blooded murder and threatening to bring legal action against anyone who tried to do it. Sufficiently discomfited by the warning, the remaining officers agreed to suspend the execution. Joseph and about eighty associates were transported instead to a jail forty miles distant, in a frontier settlement curiously named "Liberty."

While Joseph Smith and four others[193] spent nearly six months in jail

---

[193]Sidney Rigdon was incarcerated until February, when he was released on bail due to failing health. Following his release, he thereafter wavered in both health and in faithfulness. (See for instance Leland H. Gentry, *Brigham Young University Studies*, Vol. 14, No. 4,

awaiting trial—frequently forced to eat poisoned food—twelve thousand Latter-day Saints began preparing for the exodus from Missouri. There was little to do but wonder where to go next. Roaming bands of "militia" constantly harassed the Saints, burning fields, stealing or shooting livestock, looting homes. The Saints turned to Brigham Young, who now, following the death of David Patten at Crooked River, was the senior apostle still in full church fellowship.

On January 29, 1839, Young led a number of men in a meeting at Far West to consider "the subject of our removal from the state." At the core of their discussion was the "seeming impossibility of complying with the orders of the governor of Missouri, in consequence of the extreme poverty of many, which had come upon them by being driven from place to place, deprived of their constitutional rights and privileges, as citizens of . . . the United States." Some were for petitioning the "citizens of Upper Missouri" with a full description of their plight, in hopes that such an appeal would touch the hearts of the people, bringing forth their generous assistance in kicking them out of the state.

Brother Brigham entertained no such illusions. "On motion of President Brigham Young, it was resolved that we this day enter into a covenant to stand by and assist each other to the utmost of our abilities in removing from this state, and that we will never desert the poor who are worthy, till they shall be out of the reach of the exterminating order of General [John] Clark, acting for and in the name of the state."[194]

Accordingly, the following covenant was drawn up and signed by more than two hundred men and women:

We, whose names are hereunder written, do for ourselves individually hereby covenant to stand by and assist one another, to the utmost of our abilities, in removing from this state in compliance with the authority of the state; and we do hereby acknowledge ourselves firmly bound to the extent of all our available property, to be disposed of by

---

p. 448.) At April Conference of 1844 he would admit with great effort that "want of health and other circumstances have kept me in silence for nearly the last five years. I am now come forth from a bed of sickness, and have enough of strength left to appear here for the first time in my true character. I have not come before a conference for the last five years in my true character. I shall consider this important privilege sacred in my family history during life." (*History of the Church*, Vol. 6, Ch. 12, p. 288)

[194]*History of the Church*, Vol. 3, Ch. 17, p. 250.

a committee who shall be appointed for the purpose of providing means for the removing from this state of the poor and destitute who shall be considered worthy, till there shall not be one left who desires remove from the state with this proviso, that no individual shall be deprived of the right of the disposal of his own property for the above purpose, or of having the control of it, or so much of it as shall be necessary for the removing of his own family, and to be entitled to the over-plus, after the work is effected; and furthermore, said committee shall give receipts for all property, and an account of the expenditure of the same.[195]

They would be forced to employ the same covenant again less than six years later.

Over the next several weeks, twelve thousand refugees packed up the little that remained to them and walked 450 miles across frozen wilderness to the east. In a courtroom nearly two years later, one man living along the course of their flight out of Missouri would testify how he had "beheld the blood-stained traces of innocent women and children, in the dreary winter, who had traveled hundreds of miles barefoot, through frost and snow, to seek a refuge from their savage pursuers."[196] In another in 1843: "[the mobbers were] frequently taking men, women, and children prisoners, whipping them and lacerating their bodies with hickory withes, and tying them to trees, and depriving them of food until they were compelled to gnaw the bark from the trees to which they were bound."[197] In November, the Latter-day Saints began crossing the Mississippi River into Illinois at Quincy, where they were granted asylum by the people of that state.

In a letter forwarded to Quincy in late March from his dungeon cell, Joseph Smith reflected on the Saints' recent experience.

If the inhabitants of the state of Missouri had let the Saints alone, and had been as desirable of peace as they were, there would have been nothing but peace and quietude in the state unto this day. . . . The cries

---

[195]*History of the Church,* Vol. 3, Ch. 17, p. 251.

[196]O. H. Browning, Monmouth. Illinois, June 9, 1841, in "Testimonies Given before the Municipal Court of Nauvoo," *Mormon Redress Petitions*, p. 619–620.

[197]Records of the Municipal Court at Nauvoo, June 30, 1843, cited in *Times and Seasons*, Vol. 4, p. 244.

of orphans and widows would not have ascended up to God against them. Nor would innocent blood have stained the soil of Missouri. But oh! the unrelenting hand! The inhumanity and murderous disposition of this people! It shocks all nature; it beggars and defies all description; it is a tale of woe; a lamentable tale; yea a sorrowful tale; too much to tell; too much for contemplation; too much for human beings; it cannot be found among the heathens; it cannot be found among the nations where kings and tyrants are enthroned; it cannot be found among the savages of the wilderness; yea, and I think it cannot be found among the wild and ferocious beasts of the forest—that a man should be mangled for sport! women be robbed of all that they have—their last morsel for subsistence, and then be violated to gratify the hellish desires of the mob, and finally left to perish with their helpless offspring clinging around their necks.[198]

Sidney Rigdon would describe it thus:

Suffice it to say, that our settlements were broken up, our towns plundered, our farms laid waste, our crops ruined, our flocks and herds either killed or driven away, our houses rifled, our goods, money, clothing, provisions, and all we had carried away; men were shot down like wild beasts, or had their brains dashed out: women were insulted and ravished until they died in the hands of their destroyers. Children were killed, while pleading for their lives. Men moving into the county with their families were shot down; their wagons, teams and loading, taken by the plunderers as booty, and their wives, with their little ones, ordered out of the state forthwith, or suffer death, as had their husbands; leaving them no means of conveyance but their feet, and no means of subsistence but begging. Soldiers of the revolution were slain in the most brutal manner while pleading for their lives in the name of American citizens. Many were thrown into prison to endure the insults of a mock trial that would have disgraced an inquisition.[199]

---

[198]Letter dated March 25, 1839, as cited in James R. Clark, *Messages of the First Presidency,* Vol. 1, p. 88.

[199]Letter addressed to "the Honorable, the Senate and House of Representatives of Pennsylvania, in legislative capacity assembled," January 1844, in *Times and Seasons*, Vol. 5, p. 418.

The incarceration was so tormentuous to Joseph and his companions that the Prophet almost reached his breaking point:

O God, where art thou? And where is the pavilion that covereth thy hiding place? How long shall thy hand be stayed, and thine eye, yea thy pure eye, behold from the eternal heavens the wrongs of thy people and of thy servants, and thine ear be penetrated with their cries? Yea, O Lord, how long shall they suffer these wrongs and unlawful oppressions, before thine heart shall be softened toward them, and thy bowels be moved with compassion toward them? O Lord God Almighty, maker of heaven, earth, and seas, and of all things that in them are . . . stretch forth thy hand; let thine eye pierce; let thy pavilion be taken up; let thy hiding place no longer be covered; let thine ear be inclined; let thine heart be softened, and thy bowels moved with compassion toward us. Let thine anger be kindled against our enemies; and, in the fury of thine heart, with thy sword avenge us of our wrongs. Remember thy suffering saints, O our God; and thy servants will rejoice in thy name forever.

The letter, written between March 20 and March 25, 1839, comprises much of sections 121–122 and 123 in the book *Doctrine and Covenants*. The Lord's reply to Joseph Smith, first published in *Times and Seasons* sixteen months later, would be instructive in its application and uncanny in its fulfillment:

Fools shall have thee in derision, hell shall rage against thee . . . thy people shall never be turned against thee by the testimony of traitors, although their influence shall cast thee into trouble, and into prisons. . . . If thou art called to pass through tribulation, if thou art in prison among false brethren . . . if thine enemies fall upon thee, if they tare thee from the society of thy parents, and if with a drawn sword, thine enemies tare thee from the bosom of thy wife and thy offsprings, while thy eldest son, although but six years of age, shall cling to thy garments, and shall say my father, my father why, can't you stay with us . . . Oh my father what are the men going to do with you? and then he shall be thrust from thee by the sword, and thou be dragged to prison and thy enemies prowl around thee like wolves for the blood of the lamb; and if thou shouldst be cast in to the hands of murderers, and the sentence of death be passed upon thee . . . know thou my son, that all these things shall give thee experience, and shall be for thy good. The son of man has descended below them all and are thou greater than he? . . . thy days are known, and thy years shalt not be numbered less; fear not what man can do, for God shall be with thee forever and ever.

The Lord inclined his ear: twenty-one days later, on April 15,[200] a sheriff and four guards transporting Joseph and four companions to a "change of venue" trial to the north in Boone County told the Prophet the Missouri governor was "now ashamed of the whole transaction, and would be glad to set [them] at liberty if he dared to do it." So inspired, that evening the sheriff and three of the guards sat down to have a "good drink of grog, and go to bed." To Joseph, the constable said openly, "You may do as you have a mind to."

While the others drank, the remaining guard loosed the Mormon leaders' bands and helped them saddle up a pair of horses. Then, in Joseph's words, "We took our change of venue for the state of Illinois."

---

[200]Some accounts give the date of April 6 for the escape, but most chronologies show this is premature.

CHAPTER 10

Road to Carthage

Joseph and his companions pulled into Quincy on April 22, where one contemporary claimed he later "saw the sheriff at Quincy making Joseph Smith, Jr., a friendly visit and receiv[ing] pay for the horses."[201]

In October, Joseph Smith, Sidney Rigdon, and Judge Elias Higbee, acting as church historian, traveled to Washington, D.C., to present to those in power affidavits signed by nearly ten thousand people regarding their losses in Missouri. To each official they met with they made their request for federal assistance—military or monetary—in aiding the Latter-day Saints to reoccupy their rightful properties in western Missouri.[202] Shuffled from one official to another, they languished in the nation's capital for more than four months. In February, they finally sat before U.S. President Martin Van Buren, whose "pusillanimous" reply is near proverbial in Mormon Sunday schools: "Gentlemen, your cause is just, but I can do nothing for you. If I take up for you, I shall lose the vote of Missouri."[203]

Thereafter, the Prophet left Washington to preach for a short time in New Jersey and Philadelphia, after which he returned to Quincy, leaving Judge Higbee to seek other avenues of redress. Eventually, the Saints' petition was referred to the Senate Judiciary committee, which counseled the Saints (through Higbee) to appeal for a redress of their wrongs to the U.S. district court in Missouri or, if they saw proper, to "apply to the justice and magnanimity of the State of Missouri—an appeal which the

---

[201]*Autobiography of Ebenezer Robinson*, p. 243.

[202]Land purchased from the government by the Latter-day Saints in Missouri likely exceeded 250,800 acres. (See B. H. Roberts, *Comprehensive History of the Church*, Vol. 3, Ch. 74, pp. 92–93, note 3.)

[203]*Documentary History of The Church of Jesus Christ of Latter-day Saints*, Vol. 4, Ch. 4, p. 80. It is interesting to note that the church had officially supported Van Buren's successful candidacy for U.S. president in 1835 (see Max H. Parkin, *Brigham Young University Studies*, Vol. 9, No. 4, p. 490).

committee feel justified in believing will never be made in vain by the injured or oppressed."[204]

In fact, it was never made at all.

Rebuffed, yet still needing a home for the twelve thousand Latter-day Saints now homeless in the environs of Quincy, church leaders began seeking property they could purchase on contract, because they had no money. They found it some fifty miles north where a "paper town" named Commerce had not yet taken hold. On May 1, they purchased from two brothers 660 acres of swampy ground bordering the Mississippi River. They named it Nauvoo and began draining the swamps.

Thus to Nauvoo, which Joseph said was a Hebrew derivative meaning "a beautiful location, a place of rest," came the great majority of all Latter-day Saint converts for the next seven years, swelling the population by 1846 to between fifteen thousand and seventeen thousand, only slightly behind Chicago. Many of these converts were from the British Isles, and most of these the product of the "apostolic mission" launched in the very midst of the town-making. The British mission would entrench for more than half a century the extent to which "the gathering" was to be understood. And as in more and more of recent church endeavor, Brigham Young was at the head of it.

Like many in the swamp community, he, and each member of his family, was sick with a malarial fever. "When I left [my family], they had not provisions to last them ten days, and not one soul of them was able to go to the well for a pail of water. I had lain for weeks, myself, in the house, watching from day to day for some person to pass the door, whom I could get to bring us in a pail of water. In this condition I left my family, and went to preach the Gospel."[205]

A clarification: Brigham did not go voluntarily; neither did he choose the date nor the destination. But he went willingly, and there is a clear distinction in Latter-day Saint theology. One is called to duty by those in authority over him or her. One can refuse, make excuses, or flat out say no. The underlying theology is that the Lord directs his church through revelation to leaders, one at a time, each for his or her purview

---

[204]"Report of the Senate Judiciary Committee on the Case of the Saints vs. Missouri, Twenty-sixth Congress, First Session, March 4th, 1840," as cited in *History of the Church,* Vol. 4, Introduction, p. 27.

[205]*Journal of Discourses*, Vol. 2, p. 19, Brigham Young, July 24, 1854.

and that the Lord's wisdom exceeds ours. Anyone who has served in capacities of church leadership can attest that this is the case. And sometimes you just can't get anyone else to take the job.

Whether general historical comment (old or new) likes him or not, Brigham Young never did anything halfway.

From his record: "We stayed in Liverpool one year and sixteen days, and during that time we baptized between eight and nine thousand persons, printed five thousand Books of Mormon, three thousand hymn books, over sixty thousand tracts that we gave people."[206]

Membership in the British Isles would soon surpass that in the United States.

In Nauvoo houses went up, streets were graded, stores began to prosper. A university was planned and a temple begun. A liberal city charter was granted in December 1840, presaging a future like the Saints had never known: Their own city! A newspaper![207] Visiting dignitaries! And full approval for a city militia, the Nauvoo Legion. By the governor, Joseph Smith was appointed its first commander.

Rising from a bluff overlooking the river, the Nauvoo temple would consume much of the energy of the people over the next six years, and certainly their resources. Built at a final cost of one million 1846 dollars, it was funded primarily from tithes and offerings of church members. At the beginning of temple construction, they were asked to contribute one-tenth of all funds then in their possession; toward the conclusion of the construction, one-tenth of any increase. Although many were employed full-time on the temple, most men in the area donated at least one day of labor out of very ten, either on the temple, in the quarries, or in the Wisconsin pineries, from which Wisconsin white pine logs were extracted and floated in rafts downriver. Women sewed clothing for the workers and provided meals, an effort launched by a handful of sisters in March 1842 but soon formalized by Joseph Smith as the "Female Relief Society of Nauvoo." Some donated their life savings. Many gave months of phys-

---

[206]*Journal of Discourses*, Vol. 14, pp. 80–81, Brigham Young, April 9, 1871.

[207]The *Wasp* (1842–1843); the *Nauvoo Neighbor* (1843–1845); *Times and Seasons* (1839–1846).

ical labor with little or no remuneration, working twelve- to fifteen-hour days in every kind of weather.

With all else that would happen in Nauvoo, however, it can appropriately be said that the temple occupied the central position in the contemplation and effort of the American Latter-day Saints in the first half of the 1840s. An initial menu of temple rites and possibilities had been taught in Kirtland five years before, but the doctrines and practices were expanded in Nauvoo. Among them were those regarding the eternal nature of the family relationship, the eternal progression of humans, and contingencies for postmortal salvation, like baptism for the dead—always a leading candidate for the most misunderstood doctrine of Mormonism.

Let me clarify something of Latter-day Saint temples, of which there are far more than a hundred today in nations around the world. Unlike our chapels, or meetinghouses, of which there are more than several thousand, temples are not open to the public except during open houses which precede their dedication. Once dedicated, only Latter-day Saints who attain a certain and prescribed level of faithfulness—payment of a full tithe, observance of the healthy code, strict observance of the law of chastity (for the unmarried) and fidelity (for the married), support of church leaders, and a commitment to Christian conduct—qualify for entrance.

The theology behind temples—sanctuaries for the offering and receiving of the highest and holiest of Latter-day Saint ordinances—developed gradually through a number of years, but primarily during the Kirtland and Nauvoo eras. In January 1841, Joseph scribed a revelation in which the Lord told him that "there is not a place found on earth that he ['The Most High'] may come to and restore again that which was lost unto you, or which he hath taken away, even the fulness of the priesthood."[208]

Such fullness of the priesthood would come soon, and it would include the "sealing" of marriages and families for all eternity and vicarious baptism—an essential ordinance of salvation—for those who die without it (and without proper, *authorized* baptism at that). Although Joseph Smith would give the first ordinances of this fuller priesthood to nine

---

[208]*Doctrine and Covenants* 124:28.

individuals on May 4, 1842, in the loft of his red brick store,[209] he was well aware that certain saving ordinances "belongeth to my house, and cannot be acceptable to me, only [except] in the days of your poverty, wherein ye are not able to build a house [temple] unto me."[210]

That house, in Nauvoo, was well under way.

But beyond public admission (to non-Latter-day Saints) that ordinances of the now-rising temple would serve to effectuate the binding of families into eternal units, and that even the dead would be offered the saving ordinances of the gospel, little was offered to explicate the specific procedures therein. Nor is much offered today.

A surprising number of individuals—usually apostates from the faith—have over time made great efforts to "expose" the wording, activity, and "true meaning" of temple ceremonies, even taking hidden portable recording devices into the ordinance "sessions." Such individuals have clearly understood very little. Temples of The Church of Jesus Christ of Latter-day Saints are considered by us the House of God, among the most sacred places on earth, and their ceremonies are the most sacred rites of faithfulness ever taken by Latter-day Saints. In conjunction with the making of these covenants, instruction offered in the temple teaches patrons of the plan for our salvation: the premortal existence, the Fall of Adam and Eve, the mortal probation, a Savior, and eternal progress. Much of it is review, straight out of the Scriptures, but some of it is symbolic— parabolic for those willing to "open their ears to hear."

Among the excuses offered by the ceremony "revealers" are that "other religions don't have these secret ceremonies." That's an irrelevant point at best—and an ignorant one in addendum. *Most* religions outside of Protestantism have proprietary ceremonies, none of which contemplate the exploratory "right to know" of outsiders to the faith. Those committed by covenantal integrity to the sacred rites of their own Hopi, Hindu, Muslim, or Mormon faith would no more pry into the sacred ceremonies of another than reveal their own. The very thought is absurd.

We go, we learn, we make covenants to be faithful and to consecrate our lives to Christian principles, and we hope we measure up. End of discussion.

---

[209]*History of the Church*, 5:1–2.

[210]*Doctrine and Covenants* 124:30.

Baptisms for the dead were first performed in the Mississippi River in August 1840. About fourteen months later, Joseph Smith instructed the Saints to discontinue the practice until an appropriate facility was completed in the temple. On November 21, 1841, a temporary wooden baptismal font was completed, secured, and used in the basement of the far-from-finished temple. No such facility had been built, or even contemplated, for the Kirtland temple.

As the temple rose, the Latter-day Saints sunk roots, and converts flowed into the city.

Then, on May 22, the Quincy (Illinois) *Whig* reported that ex–Missouri governor Lilburn Boggs had been "assassinated," although he had been only wounded on the sixth and was still alive on the date of publication (and for years afterward). The primary suspect was Orrin Porter Rockwell, one of Joseph Smith's bodyguards and one of the original members of the church.[211] Thus, in an affidavit signed eight weeks after the shooting, Boggs claimed "Joe Smith" was behind the murder attempt and convinced the current Missouri governor to seek his extradition from Illinois as an accessory. Illinois Governor Carlin agreed to the order, and Joseph was arrested on August 8. Nothing much came of the matter before Carlin's administration ended in December and Thomas Ford's began.

When Joseph petitioned the new governor to have the order rescinded, Ford, who had once opposed the Nauvoo city charter, consulted his supreme court. The court deemed the Missouri extradition attempt (including Carlin's participation) illegal, but suggested the Prophet appear before the district court in Springfield to have the charges formally cleared. The Prophet did so, and was summarily acquitted. Although O. P. Rockwell would eventually be cleared of any involvement in the assassination attempt, he would spend nearly nine months in miserable Missouri jails (some of the time for his "protection") before Alexander Doniphan could secure his release. And then he would become the embodiment of the Danite legend for the rest of his life.

If any among the Saints were entertaining visions of the Latter-day Saints taking their rightful and respected place in the mainstream of American society sometime soon, it wasn't Joseph Smith. In fact, his vision dictated exactly to the contrary. On Saturday, August 6, 1842, he

---

[211]And the man who would, more than anyone else, become the personification—in the minds of outsiders—of the Danite Avenging Angel.

wrote, "I prophesied that the Saints would continue to suffer much affliction and would be driven to the Rocky Mountains; many would apostatize, others would be put to death by our persecutors or lose their lives in consequence of exposure to disease, and some of you will live to go and assist in making settlements and build cities and see the Saints become a mighty people in the midst of the Rocky Mountains."[212]

And to a small public gathering on April 2, 1843, he said, "I prophesy, in the name of the Lord God, that the commencement of the difficulties which will cause much bloodshed previous to the coming of the Son of Man will be in South Carolina. It may probably arise through the slave question. This voice declared to me while I was praying earnestly on the subject, December 25th, 1832."[213]

What the voice dictated that Christmas Day eleven years before, recorded privately by Joseph's secretary, included the following: "For behold, the Southern States shall be divided against the Northern States, and the Southern States will call on other nations, even the nation of Great Britain, as it is called, and they shall also call upon other nations, in order to defend themselves against other nations; and then war shall be poured out upon all nations. And it shall come to pass, after many days, slaves shall rise up against their masters, who shall be marshaled and disciplined for war."[214]

Thus, a long tenure in "the states" was never a real component of Joseph's longing. But a few comfortable years would have been entirely welcome. Joseph hoped they would come in Nauvoo.

Unlike in Kirtland and Independence, the Latter-day Saints were building a Mormon city from the ground up here, and they were progressing a lot farther than they had in Far West. Church membership in the area was approaching sixteen thousand by 1843, and the "gathering" was in full swing.[215] Chartered steamships brought streams of British and Scandinavian converts up the Mississippi from New Orleans. Others came overland. The account of one journey is typical:

---

[212]*History of the Church*, Vol. 5, p. 85.

[213]Ibid., Vol. 5, Ch. 17, p. 324.

[214]Ibid., Vol. 1, Ch. 22, p. 302

[215]Some comparisons may be of interest: in 1840, Nauvoo had 7,000 residents, Chicago 4,500, and St. Louis 16,000. Source: *Historical Atlas of Mormonism*, p. 50.

We left Salem the 14th of October going to Boston where we stopped a few days with mother's sister, Elizabeth Stuart, and with a large company from neighboring towns, took passage by railroad for Albany, only stopping one night at Gloucester, thence we traveled by the Erie Canal to Buffalo. There was no railroad at this time across the state of New York. From Buffalo, we went by steamboat to Cleveland, Ohio; thence, by canal across the state of Ohio to Wheeling, near the head waters of the Ohio River, thence by steamboat down the Ohio to Cincinnati where we changed boats and continued down the Ohio and up the Mississippi to Nauvoo where we arrived on the 3 of November.[216]

To accommodate the ever-increasing boat traffic, averaging ten ships per week, [217] Joseph Smith for some time contemplated the rather aggressive ideas of dredging out the harbor and constructing a canal that would skirt the Des Moines rapids.

But other contemplations prevailed.

On the morning of the 12th of July, 1843, Joseph and Hyrum Smith came into the office in the upper story of the brick store, on the bank of the Mississippi River. They were talking on the subject of plural marriage. Hyrum said to Joseph, "If you will write the revelation on celestial marriage, I will take and read it to Emma [Joseph's wife], and I believe I can convince her of its truth, and you will hearafter have peace." Joseph smiled and remarked, "You do not know Emma as well as I do." Hyrum repeated his opinion and further remarked, "The doctrine is so plain, I can convince any reasonable man or woman of its truth, purity or heavenly origin," or words to their effect. Joseph then said, "Well, I will write the revelation and we will see." He then requested me to get paper and prepare to write. Hyrum very urgently requested Joseph to write the revelation by means of the Urim and Thummim, but Joseph, in reply, said he did not need to, for he knew the revelation perfectly from beginning to end.

[216]Benjamin Ashby autobiography, copy of holograph, Brigham Young University Studies, p. 7.

[217]Dennis Rowley, *Brigham Young University Studies*, Vol. 18, No. 2, p. 257.

Joseph and Hyrum then sat down and Joseph commenced to dictate the revelation on celestial marriage, and I [William Clayton] wrote it, sentence by sentence, as he dictated.[218]

Joseph was about to make public a matter that had burdened him for more than a dozen years. The latest scholarship suggests that he had likely first investigated the subject of the plurality of wives when scribing an inspired translation of the Bible in 1831,[219] or perhaps even during the Book of Mormon translation process two years earlier.

In that reading, of course, it becomes apparent that many Old Testament prophets, including the great patriarchs Abraham, Isaac, Jacob, had more than one wife at a time. Joseph undoubtedly went to the Lord in prayer regarding this practice. What the Lord told him we can only suppose from the dictation mentioned above, which, in the intervening twelve years, he had memorized. A number of people close to the Prophet were aware of "the principle" concerning plural marriage long before it was generally known, but they would also hear him state very clearly that, as in Old Testament times, "no man shall have but one wife at a time, unless the Lord directs otherwise."[220]

In Joseph's day, and for six decades afterward, he would direct otherwise.

Many outside of Nauvoo, and outside the church, would soon hear talk of "the principle" as well, but the revelation, now known as *Doctrine and Covenants* Section 132, would not be published until 1852, in Utah.

Among those standing in its trajectory in the early years was Joseph's wife, Emma, who shared her spouse with another woman, Fanny Alger, as early as 1831, and with others later. When Emma was finally shown the written revelation in 1843, she threw it into the lit fireplace without

---

[218]William Clayton, *Historical Record*, Vol. 6., pp. 225–226; cited in Otten & Caldwell, *Sacred Truths of the Doctrine & Covenants*, Vol. 2, pp. 354–355.

[219]This Inspired Version, or *Joseph Smith Translation*, is accepted by The Church of Jesus Christ of Latter-day Saints as an authentic and accurate book of scripture, although we continue to use the King James Version as the "standard" for church classes and curricula. According to the *Encyclopedia of Mormonism*, the JST "differs from the KJV in at least 3,410 verses and consists of additions, deletions, rearrangements, and other alterations." (*Encyclopedia of Mormonism*, Vol. 2, S. V. "Joseph Smith Translation of the Bible (JST)."

[220]October 5, 1843; *Documentary History of the Church*, 6:46.

delay. Knowing Emma as he did, Joseph had secured another copy of the document in another place.[221]

But the record reveals that neither Joseph nor Brigham Young, who would succeed him as church president four years later, ever spoke of the principle in the tittering tones of the titillated.[222]

Of Joseph, it is written: "He knew the voice of God—he knew the commandment of the Almighty to him was to go forward—to set the example, and establish Celestial plural marriage. He knew that he had not only his own prejudices and pre-possessions to combat and to overcome, but those of the whole Christian world . . . ; but God . . . had given the commandment."[223]

Brigham Young commented, "Some of these my brethren know what my feelings were at the time Joseph revealed the doctrine; I was not desirous of shrinking from any duty, nor failing in the least to do as I was commanded, but it was the first time in my life that I had desired the grave, and I could hardly get over it for a long time. And when I saw a funeral, I felt to envy the corpse its situation, and to regret that I was not in the coffin."[224]

National responses to Mormon polygamy would a few years hence find a substantial voice in the new Republican party's 1856 platform, declaring: "That the Constitution confers upon congress sovereign power over the territories of the United States . . . and that in the exercise of this power it is both right and the imperative duty of congress to prohibit in the territories those twin relics of barbarism—polygamy and slavery."[225]

---

[221]See *LDS Biographical Encyclopedia,* Vol. 1, p. 222, S. V. "Newell K. Whitney"; this copy would become the manuscript for the published revelation in 1852.

[222]A number of sources document Joseph's long reluctance to enter into this principle. One of Joseph's plural wives, Eliza R. Snow, summarizes the others, saying that an angel "stood by him with a drawn sword [and] told him that, unless he moved forward and established plural marriage his Priesthood would be taken from him." (*Biography and Family Record of Lorenzo Snow, One of the the Twelve Apostles of The Church of Jesus Christ of Latter-day Saints,* 1884, pp. 69–70. Another, Mary Elizabeth Lightner, said this angel appeared to Joseph on three separate occasions. (See *Brigham Young University Studies,* Vol. 38, No.1 p. 55, note 69.)

[223]*Biography and Family Record of Lorenzo Snow,* pp. 69–70 (Salt Lake City, 1884).

[224]*Journal of Discourses,* Vol. 3, p. 266, Brigham Young, July 14, 1855.

[225]Republican platform. Philadelphia. June 17th, 1856; *Cooper's American Politics,* bk, ii, Platforms, p. 39.

The reactions to polygamy would include plenty of humor. Mark Twain wrote, "The man that marries one of them [Mormon women in Utah Territory] has done an act of Christian charity which entitles him to the kindly applause of mankind, not their harsh censure—and the man that marries sixty of them has done a deed of open-handed generosity so sublime that the nations should stand uncovered in his presence and worship in silence."[226]

Meanwhile the Mormon response would grow increasingly defensive: "Whose business is it? Hands off here! Our belief is our own. We have a right to our opinions. If you don't believe them, that is nothing to us, we do. We have a right to our belief in that or any other doctrine . . . , whether our beliefs suits you or not, and we have the right to freely express that belief, and if you don't like it, you may go hang."[227]

Exploration into the specific reasoning behind an era of very limited polygamy by the Latter-day Saints (and many have pursued it) turns up few hard facts and even fewer clear explanations. The record shows that Joseph Smith was commanded by God, even against his initial will, to begin the practice. Six decades later, another prophet was commanded to end it.

And that's really all we know or claim.

But the gradually expanding knowledge of this peculiar Latter-day Saint practice was merely one component in the rapidly expanding dislike for the people practicing it. John Taylor would later write,

> In the year 1844, a very great excitement prevailed . . . in relation to the "Mormons," and a spirit of vindictive hatred and persecution was exhibited among the people, which was manifested in the most bitter and acrimonious language, as well as by acts of hostility and violence, frequently threatening the destruction of the citizens of Nauvoo and vicinity, and utter annihilation of the "Mormons" and "Mormonism," and in some instances breaking out in the most violent acts of ruffianly barbarity. Persons were kidnaped, whipped, persecuted, and falsely accused of various crimes; their cattle and houses injured, destroyed, or stolen; vexatious prosecutions were instituted to harass, and annoy.

---

[226]Mark Twain, *Roughing It,* p. 101.

[227]B. H. Roberts, *Defense of the Faith and the Saints,* Vol. 2, pp. 331–332.

In some remote neighborhoods they were expelled from their homes without redress, and in others violence was threatened to their persons and property, while in others every kind of insult and indignity were heaped upon them, to induce them to abandon their homes, the country, or the state.[228]

In late January 1844, following unsuccessful attempts to elicit government support for redress for the Missouri depredations, Joseph Smith met with his counselors and the twelve apostles to consider what course they should pursue regarding that fall's presidential election. The two leading candidates both had virulently anti-Mormon Missouri counties named for them.[229] The incumbent, Martin Van Buren, had already told the Saints he could do nothing for them lest he lose votes in Missouri. The other, Henry Clay, author of the Missouri Compromise, had suggested in that same 1839 meeting that the Latter-day Saints "had better go to Oregon."[230]

"It was then moved by Willard Richards and voted unanimously— 'That we will have an independent electoral ticket, and that Joseph Smith be a candidate for the next Presidency; and that we use all honorable means in our power to secure his election.' "[231] Against Joseph's wishes, Sidney Rigdon, who due to deteriorating mental and physical health appeared to be losing his hold on orthodoxy, was selected by the committee as his running mate.

Joseph Smith was never a real proponent of, nor believer in, his election. "I would not have suffered my name to have been used by my friends on anywise," he said, ". . . if I and my friends could have had the privilege of enjoying our religious and civil rights as American citizens, even those rights which the Constitution guarantees unto all citizens alike. But this as people we have been denied from the beginning. Persecution had rolled upon our heads from time to time . . . like peals of

---

[228]*History of the Church,* Vol. 7, Ch. 6, p. 57.

[229]James K. Polk would eventually gain the Democratic nomination over Van Buren and win the presidential election.

[230]*History of the Church,* Vol. 5, Ch. 20, p. 393.

[231]James R. Clark, *Messages of the First Presidency,* Vol. 1, p. 190.

thunder, because of our religion; and no portion of the Government as yet has stepped forward for our relief."[232]

Even so, Joseph had other things on his mind.

Mobocrats from Missouri kept up a relentless assault on the Saints, both through physical threat and harassment and through pretended legal means. Extradition orders on Joseph were extended at least twice by Missouri courts on the grounds that he was a fugitive from justice due to his "escape" from that state in April 1839. (These were in concourse with the accusations over the Boggs assassination attempt.)

In late February 1844, the twelve were directed to begin preparing for a journey to the West, where they were to scout out locations that might be amenable to another removal of the Saints in the near future. Before their intended departure, Joseph accompanied each of them to the as-yet-uncompleted temple and "sealed upon [their] heads all the keys of the kingdom of God." Said he, "I have sealed upon you every key, power, principle that the God of heaven has revealed to me . . . [my] brethren, upon your shoulders this kingdom rests; now you have got to round up your shoulders and bear off the kingdom."[233] "Now if they kill me, you have got all the keys and all the ordinances and you can confer them upon others, and the hosts of Satan will not be able to tear down the kingdom, as fast as you will be able to build it up."[234]

But in lieu of the western expedition, he soon sent them east to preach and make some noise about his candidacy, believing the protection of his people in their rights and religion his preeminent duty, whether that were at the hands of his own administration or the hands of another. In fact, few believed Joseph Smith would ever be elected, but with a concerted effort they might at least, through telling their story, swing votes away from any candidate "who might use the weapon they put into his hands to destroy them"[235]—that is, Martin Van Buren.

On March 11, Joseph organized a special council, later called the "Council of Fifty" in reflection of the number of members in it (there were initially fifty-three, including three non–Latter-day Saints). The

---

[232]*Times and Seasons*, February 15, 1844.

[233]*Collected Discourses*, Vol. 1, Wilford Woodruff, June 2, 1889.

[234]*Times and Seasons*, Vol. 5, p. 651.

[235]Ibid.

Council of Fifty would be engaged in two primary efforts, one being the searching out and selection of—in counsel with legitimate federal and territorial officials—a remote and available spot of land for resettling the Saints, and the other being a promulgation of Joseph's candidacy. In a more comprehensive way, however, the council was viewed, in the words of historian Kenneth W. Godfrey, "as the seed of a new political order that would rule, under Christ, following the prophesied cataclysmic events of the last days."[236]

Far too much has been made of this concept by writers, old and new, antagonistic to the church, and in fact the council would soon (and to the current day) be intertwined in the minds of those outside the faith as an extension or component of the retributive and anarchical Danite legend. The problem lay equally in the perception of its scope (world government) its tenor (by a theocracy), and its timing (constitutional America, 1844).

No way, no how, not here!

Unfortunately, all three perspectives were (and are) somewhat skewed from reality, and many are based on disreputable testimony offered in hothouse Hancock County courtrooms of the next few years. The 1840s Latter-day Saints (and those for some few decades afterward) really expected the apocalyptic confusion and the Second Coming to be very near, as did many of their other-Christian contemporaries, a perception that one writer has referred to as "imminent redemption."[237] Thus, a theocratic government functioning as precursor to the personal earth reign of Christ himself, in which a separation of church and state would be irrelevant, didn't even make sense. Ultimately, the Council of Fifty would mostly just help organize the exodus from Nauvoo two years later and, in early Utah, help establish economic and political stability and structure. (The Saints themselves would apply for territorial—that is, U.S. government—franchise a mere twenty-four months after arriving in the Salt Lake basin. But the Council of Fifty legend was born.)

With the temple in Nauvoo rising prominently, Joseph, if no other, knew the refuge they sought would be found in the remote American West. With the apostles and other members of the Fifty on their stump-

---

[236]*Encyclopedia of Mormonism*, Vol. 1, S.V. "Council of Fifty, Kenneth W. Godfrey.

[237]Val Norman Edwards, "Rhetorical Analysis of LDS Church Policy Statements," master's thesis, University of Utah, 1987, p. 87.

ing missions, he sent "a memorial and ordinance" to Congress seeking authorization to raise one hundred thousand armed volunteers to serve as mobile guardians of U.S. interests in the West, including "that noble extent of country lying between the Mississippi and the Pacific Ocean."[238] Apostles Orson Hyde and Orson Pratt "presented the matter to senators and representatives at Washington, and a number favored the . . . removal of the Mormons to the west, but generally urged that Joseph Smith go without seeking special authorization from the government."[239]

By the spring, Hancock County and vicinity was a veritable cauldron of spit and vinegar. The principal pot-stirrers were recent excommunicants like John C. Bennett (former Nauvoo mayor and assistant church president), William Law (former counselor in the church presidency), and the Higbee brothers, whose father had accompanied Joseph Smith on his ineffectual visit to the nation's capital six years earlier and who had died in full fellowship less than a year before. "Besides the above characters," wrote Taylor, "there were three other parties: the first of these may be called religionists, the second politicians, and the third counterfeiters, blacklegs, horse thieves, and cutthroats."

Among the religionists, particular issues like polygamy and baptism for the dead were the ostensible thorns piercing the flesh, when in fact the simple surging growth of the Mormon body was the greater threat. Likewise on the political horizon. The Mormon "bloc" vote had been sought and actively courted for more than five years in Illinois. Its courters, however, had frequently changed sides along the way. As the general mood began to turn against the Latter-day Saints—with their peculiar theocracy, their constantly drilling Nauvoo legion, and their multiethnic ever-changing populace—few remained willing to seek the Mormon vote. One candidate for governor went so far as to suggest another extermination order, this time from Illinois.[240]

By April 1844, Joseph's first counselor (Rigdon) had departed the city, never to fully rejoin the Saints, and his second (William Law) was about to be excommunicated. Facing increasing threats both from within

---

[238]*History of the Church,* Vol. 6, Introduction, p. 34.

[239]Ibid.

[240]See *History of the Mormon Battalion,* Introduction, pp. 12, 13, and *History of the Church,* Vol. 7, Ch. 6, p. 58.

and without, the Nauvoo Legion paraded visibly and practiced incessantly. Political maneuvering—now wagered largely *against* the Mormon vote, continued requests for Joseph's head by relentless Missourians not satisfied with their earlier conquests (six years earlier), and outright dissension bent on revenge—all conjoined to make of Nauvoo a bomb ready to explode. But the detonator would be newsprint.

On May 10, 1844, William Law and a handful of others, including the faithful Judge Higbee's unfaithful two sons, published a broadside in Nauvoo and environs touting a new weekly newspaper "worthy of the patronage of a discerning and enlightened public."[241] This publication, claimed the prospectus, would set things right in Nauvoo. It would tell the truth. It would also endeavor to promote "the unconditional repeal of the Nauvoo city charter" by the state of Illinois; "to restrain and correct the abuses of . . . power, to ward off the iron rod which is held over the devoted heads of the citizens of Nauvoo"; "to advocate unmitigated disobedience to political revelations, and to censure and decry gross moral imperfections wherever found, either in the plebeian, patrician or SELF-CONSTITUTED MONARCH" . . . and to oppose with uncompromising hostility any UNION OF CHURCH AND STATE, or any preliminary step tending to the same . . . in a word, to give a full, candid and succinct statement of FACTS AS THEY REALLY EXIST IN THE CITY OF NAUVOO!"[242]

In other words, to raise hell.

It worked.

When the first issue of the paper, the *Expositor*, was released on Friday, June 7, the community exploded. What one critic referred to as "dull or laughable" copy replete with "lame grammar and turgid rhetoric" was nothing compared to assistant editor Francis Higbee's assertion in print that Joseph Smith was "the biggest villain that goes unhung"[243] and the general call for violence against the Saints. To which the other Nau-

---

[241]From the "Prospectus of the Nauvoo Expositor," as cited in *History of the Church*, Vol. 6., Ch. 21, p. 443.

[242]Ibid; exclamations in the original.

[243]See Oaks, Dallin H. "The Suppression of the Nauvoo *Expositor*." *Utah Law Review* 9 (Winter 1965): p. 868. Interestingly, although this phrase ignited the defensive passions of the Latter-day Saints, the ordinance calling for the press's destruction would use nearly identical language in referring to the *Expositor*'s principals as "the most corrupt scoundrels and villains that disgrace the earth unhung."

voo paper, the *Neighbor*, responded, "The Church as a body and individually has suffered till forbearance has ceased to be a virtue."[244]

With clamor in the streets and fistfights in the barbershop, the city council convened three times over the next three days to consider the matter. In Joseph's account, "Upon investigating the matter, we found that our City Charter [modeled on that of the state capital, Springfield] gave us power to remove all nuisances; and, furthermore, upon consulting Blackstone upon what might be considered a nuisance, that distinguished lawyer . . . states . . . that a libelous and filthy press may be considered a nuisance, and abated as such. . . . [w]e conceived that we were acting strictly in accordance with law. It is possible there may have been some better way, but I must confess that I could not see it."[245]

After about fourteen hours of deliberations, the council (with Joseph Smith as mayor following John C. Bennett's firing) authorized the removal and destruction of the offending press, on the grounds that its product was a public nuisance and would certainly invite civil disturbance.

At approximately 7:30 P.M. on Monday, June 10, City Marshal John P. Greene and a hundred-person "posse" (Joseph was not with them) marched to the *Expositor* premises and, encountering Francis Higbee, stated his authority and his orders and demanded the key to the door. That denied, they forced the door, dragged the press into the streets, and bashed it to pieces.[246] According to bystander testimony offered later, the posse exhibited no sense of exultation nor of agitation. The only apparent chaos "was Higbee and his company throwing blackguard language to the posse," which language "was not answered to at all by the ranks."[247] They then returned to Joseph's residence, where he gave a brief speech to "three-times-three cheers" and sent them all to bed.

The following day Nauvoo started coming apart.

---

[244]*History of the Church*, Vol. 6, Ch. 22, p. 460.

[245]Ibid., Vol. 7, Ch. 8, p. 90. On this reading of *Chitty's Blackstone*, Church historian B. H. Roberts later wrote: "[Joseph] seemed not to have observed that the cited legal authority went no further than to scurrilous prints, not to printing presses." (*Comprehensive History of the Church*, Vol. 2, Ch. 54, p. 231, note 22)

[246]The Latter-day Saints' own press had been destroyed by a mob on July 20, 1833, in Independence, Missouri, as the first "Book of Commandments" (later *Doctrine and Covenants*) was being printed. Instead of taking legal action against the mob, the Latter-day Saints simply agreed three days later to abandon Jackson County.

[247]*History of the Church*, Vol. 6, Ch. 22, p. 457.

By Wednesday morning, Joseph Smith and seventeen companions, including his brother Hyrum and O. P. Rockwell, were under arrest due to a writ signed by Francis Higbee. The charge was inciting a riot. Although the writ directed the men to appear before any justice of the peace in Hancock County, including those in Nauvoo, the constable carrying it ordered them to appear before Justice Thomas Morrison in Carthage, eighteen miles to the east and a hotbed of anti-Mormon activity.

Joseph had faced Morrison before, in June 1841 when he was endeavoring to enforce one of the specious Missouri extradition writs "on behalf of the people." Thus the Prophet petitioned the Nauvoo City Court for habeas corpus which was granted. In the proceeding that evening, a number of witnesses claimed to have heard Francis Higbee threaten Joseph's life and to state quite publicly that if the citizens of Nauvoo "laid their hands on the press, from that hour they might date their downfall; that ten suns should not roll over their heads till the city was destroyed."[248]

The Nauvoo court then decided "that Joseph Smith had acted under proper authority in destroying the establishment of the Nauvoo *Expositor* . . . that his orders were executed in an orderly and judicious manner, without noise or tumult; that this was a malicious prosecution on the part of Francis M. Higbee; and that said Higbee pay the costs of suit, and that Joseph Smith be honorably discharged from the accusations and of the writ, and go hence without delay."[249]

That he did.

The same day, the openly and stridently anti-Mormon newspaper the Warsaw *Signal*, through the pen of its editor Thomas Sharp, launched a call for the extermination of the Latter-day Saints: "War and extermination is inevitable! CITIZENS ARISE, ONE and ALL!!! Can you stand by, and suffer such INFERNAL DEVILS! to ROB men of their property rights, without avenging them? We have no time to comment: every man will wage his own. LET IT BE MADE WITH POWDER and BALL!!!"[250]

By the next evening, June 13, several hundred mobbers were gath-

---

[248]Testimony of Joseph Dalton, "Hearing on the *Expositor* Affairs Before the Municipal Court of Nauvoo, Habeas Corpus Proceedings, Special session, June 12th, 1844," in *History of the Church*, Vol. 6, Ch. 22, p. 458.

[249]Ibid.

[250]Warsaw (Illinois) *Signal*, June 12, 1844.

ering in Carthage, the Hancock County seat, where a "mass meeting" resolved upon the following:

> to command the efforts and the services of every good citizen to put an immediate stop to the career of the mad prophet and his demoniac coadjutors. We must not only defend ourselves from danger, but we must resolutely carry the war into the enemy's camp. We will take full vengeance, terrible vengeance, should the lives of any of our citizens be lost in the effort; that we hold ourselves at all times in readiness to co-operate with our fellow-citizens in this state, Missouri and Iowa, to exterminate, utterly exterminate the wicked and abominable Mormon leaders, the authors of our troubles. A war of extermination should be waged to the entire destruction, if necessary . . . of his adherents."[251]

And as if clarification were needed: "To seek redress in the ordinary mode would be utterly ineffectual."

Faithful Latter-day Saints living anywhere in the vicinity outside Nauvoo were ordered to leave forthwith "on pain of instant vengeance." On Saturday, the fifteenth, Levi Williams, a Baptist preacher with a commission as colonel in state militia, rode into nearby Lima and demanded that all "Mormons" deliver their weapons, while crates of weapons began arriving in Carthage. By Sunday, city officers in Carthage were fearing for their lives, and Joseph sent a letter to Governor Ford requesting his appearance in person. The next morning an estimated fifteen hundred Missourians had crossed the Mississippi River into Warsaw. The Quincy (Illinois) Greys, a contingent of the state militia, were to accompany them to Carthage, with five cannons, where they would join the Carthage group and march on Nauvoo.

On Monday morning, June 17, Joseph Smith was arrested again on the same charges proffered earlier: inciting a riot. The charges were dismissed that afternoon, but Joseph instructed Nauvoo Legion Major-General Jonathan Dunham to begin preparing for war. Sometime that day, the Prophet's brother Hyrum wrote a letter to Brigham Young, still stumping through the eastern states, instructing him to call home the apostles: "Communicate to the others of the Twelve with as much speed

---

[251]"Resolutions, meeting of the citizens of Hancock county, convened at Carthage on the 13th day of June, 1844," cited in *History of the Church*, Vol. 6, Ch. 22, p. 463.

as possible," he wrote, "with perfect stillness and calmness. A word to the wise is sufficient; and a little powder, lead and a good rifle can be packed in your luggage very easy without creating any suspicion."[252] Joseph, however, instructed him not to send the letter.

On Tuesday morning, June 18, three thousand men of the Nauvoo Legion assembled in full dress and fully armed, and at 1:45 P.M. Lieutenant General Joseph Smith declared martial law in Nauvoo. He then gave a rousing speech from the steps of the Mansion House, Joseph's residence, which also served as a hotel. An excerpt follows:

> We are American citizens. We live upon a soil for the liberties of which our fathers periled their lives and spilt their blood upon the battlefield. Those rights so dearly purchased, shall not be disgracefully trodden under foot by lawless marauders without at least a noble effort on our part to sustain our liberties. I call upon all men, from Maine to the Rocky Mountains, and from Mexico to British America, whose hearts thrill with horror to behold the rights of freemen trampled under foot, to come to the deliverance of this people from the hand of oppression, cruelty, anarchy and misrule to which they have long been made subject.
>
> I call God and angels to witness that I have unsheathed my sword with a firm and unalterable determination that this people shall have their legal rights, and be protected from mob violence, or my blood shall be spilt upon the ground like water, and my body consigned to the silent tomb. While I live, I will never tamely submit to the dominion of cursed mobocracy. I would welcome death rather than submit to this oppression; and it would be sweet, oh, sweet, to rest in the grave rather than submit to this oppression, agitation, annoyance, confusion, and alarm upon alarm, any longer.[253]

Saints from all the outlying settlements were moving to Nauvoo as quickly as they could. As they traversed field and forest, camps of militiamen would send "balls whizzing past their heads." Many were without footwear, but all had been instructed to carry all the grain they were able.

---

[252]*History of the Church,* Vol. 6, Ch. 22, p. 487.

[253]Ibid., Ch. 24, p. 499.

On June 20, Joseph Smith sent a letter to President John Tyler seeking protection from the mobs and militias. An affidavit signed that day said that "cannons and ammunition" and upward of two thousand men were on their way from Missouri in steamships.

Shipments of feed grain and several hundred head of cattle from Missouri were moving toward the militia encampments around Carthage, but Nauvoo was largely cut off from external supplies, including food.

On June 20, Joseph finally decided it was time to call the twelve home from their various assignments in the East.[254] As the mail in and out of Nauvoo had been cut off, he sent a personal courier. He also asked Hyrum to take his family and make a break for Cincinnati, but Hyrum only replied, "Joseph, I can't leave you."

On Friday morning, June 21, Illinois Governor Thomas Ford arrived in Carthage. From there he sent two emissaries into Nauvoo to deliver a summons to Joseph Smith to send "one or more . . . discreet persons" to him in Carthage, where they could lay out the Nauvoo version of things. The individual(s) selected could expect full protection on the way back to Carthage—by the *two* officers sent.

When John M. Bernhisel and apostle John Taylor were appointed to accept the governor's invitation, they carried with them a packet of signed affidavits declaring the Nauvoo version, prominently that Joseph's blood would be split should he show his face outside the Nauvoo city limits. In Carthage, they made their presentation, but the governor's "headquarters" was so infested with mob rabble that the chief executive could hardly read between the oaths, curses, and catcalls, of which "he seemed to take no notice."

Of the visit, John Taylor noted: "After waiting the Governor's pleasure for some time, we had an audience—but such an audience! He was surrounded by some of the vilest and most unprincipled men in creation [including] Wilson and . . . William Law, Frank (Francis) and Chauncey Higbee . . . in all fifteen or twenty persons, most of whom were recreant to virtue, honor, integrity and everything that is considered honorable among men. I can well remember the feeling of disgust that I had in seeing the Governor surrounded by such an infamous group, and on being

---

[254]Ten of the Twelve were then on mission assignments; the remaining two, John Taylor and Willard Richards, were in Nauvoo.

introduced to men of so questionable a character . . . had I been on private business, I should have turned to depart."

Following the governor's reading of the affidavits, the Mormon apostle attempted to converse with him regarding each point of legal process now in question. "We represented to him the course we had taken in relation to this matter," wrote Taylor, "our willingness to go before another magistrate other than the Municipal Court, the illegal refusal by the constable of our request, our dismissal by the Municipal Court, a legally constituted tribunal, our subsequent trial before Esq. Wells at the instance of Judge Thomas (the circuit judge), and our dismissal by him; that we had fulfilled the law in every particular; that it was our enemies who were breaking the law, and, having murderous designs, were only making use of this as a pretext to get us into their power."

To this, the governor replied "that the people viewed it differently, and that, notwithstanding our opinions, he would recommend that the people should be satisfied."[255]

The next day, Joseph sent another letter to the governor, asking him to come to Nauvoo and see things for himself. But before that communication could be delivered, Taylor and Bernhisel returned with an ominous and conclusive letter from Governor Ford, a missive so *dis*missive of the Mormons' case that Joseph later wrote of Ford "he is [either] under the influence of the mob spirit . . . and is conniving at our destruction, or else he is so ignorant and stupid that he does not understand the corrupt and diabolical [men] that are around him."

Ford's letter (in part) said: "In the particular case now under consideration, I require any and all of you who are or shall be accused to submit yourselves to be arrested by the same constable, by virtue of the same warrant and be tried before the same magistrate [Morrison in Carthage] whose authority has heretofore been resisted. Nothing short of this can vindicate the dignity of violated law and allay the just excitement of the people. You are wrong in the first instance, and I can call out no portion of the militia for your defense until you submit to the law. I would say that your city was built, as it were, upon a keg of powder which a very little spark may explode."[256]

---

[255]*History of the Church*, Vol. 6, Ch. 28, pp. 543–544.

[256]Ibid., Ch. 27, p. 536.

Ford ordered Joseph and the others named in the original warrant to come immediately to Carthage in the accompaniment of no one but the two officers previously sent. In one breath, Ford promised them protection, and in the next, he warned that the tendency of the thus-employed militia "may assume a revolutionary character, and the men may disregard the authority of their officers."

In his letter of response, Joseph said, "We are left to the mercy of the merciless. Sir, we dare not come, for our lives would be in danger, and we are guilty of no crime."

So instead, Joseph met in council with several companions that evening. An initial decision was made to sneak out the back and head for Washington, D.C., where Joseph would seek audience with President Tyler. But then "Joseph's countenance brightened up and he said, 'The way is open. It is clear to my mind what to do. All they want is Hyrum and myself; then tell everybody to go about their business, and not to collect in groups, but to scatter about. There is no doubt they will come here and search for us. Let them search; they will not harm you in person or property, and not even a hair of your head. We will cross the river tonight, and go away to the West.'"

The Prophet Joseph Smith's final dictation to his secretary, Willard Richards, records the following: "I told Stephen Markham that if I and Hyrum were ever taken again we should be massacred, or I was not a prophet of God."[257]

At about 9 P.M., tears streaming down their faces, Joseph and Hyrum bid farewell to their families (having asked William Phelps to see them to safety in Cincinnati) and accompanied Willard Richards through the dark streets to the river, where they hoped to board a skiff. Failing in that, they awoke Porter Rockwell in his cabin at about midnight and were soon employing his skills in rowing the skiff across the Mississippi. The boat they "borrowed" from Aaron Johnson leaked so much they were all put to bailing with boots and hats. (Willard Richards, a physician weighing in at nearly 300 pounds, was certainly part of the problem.)

From the Iowa side the next morning, Rockwell was sent back with instructions to return that night with fresh horses "and be ready to start for the Great Basin in the Rocky Mountains." But by early afternoon,

[257]Tullidge, *Life of Joseph the Prophet*, p. 491.

Rockwell had returned with Reynolds Cahoon, bringing no horses but a letter from Joseph's wife Emma, pleading for him to return, give himself up to the authorities, and trust in the Lord.

Cahoon reported that Ford's troops were prepared to march on Nauvoo and "guard the city until they were found, if it took three years to do it." He urged Joseph to return, lest everyone's homes and property be destroyed.

Joseph replied, "If my life is of no value to my friends it is of none to myself."

Joseph then asked Cahoon to have a boat ready at half-past five to carry them back across the river.

Bank of the River Mississippi, Sunday, June 23rd, 1844, 2 P.M.

His Excellency Governor Ford:

SIR.—I wrote you a long communication at 12 last night, expressive of my views of your Excellency's communication of yesterday. I thought your letter rather severe, but one of my friends has just come to me with an explanation . . . which . . . gives us greater assurance of protection, and that your Excellency has succeeded in bringing in subjection the spirits which surround your Excellency to some extent.

I now offer to come to you at Carthage on the morrow, as early as shall be convenient for your posse to escort us into headquarters, provided we can have a fair trial, not be abused nor have my witnesses abused, and have all things done in due form of law, without partiality, and you may depend on my honor without the show of a great armed force to produce excitement in the minds of the timid.

Joseph Smith, Hyrum Smith

Joseph sent the letter with two messengers who did not arrive in Carthage until 9 P.M. After initially signaling that Joseph should have an armed escort into the town, the governor gave in to his rabble and retracted the offer, saying such was an honor not afforded other ordinary citizens. He then commanded the messengers to leave the city, although it was well past nightfall. Their horses exhausted, they arrived in Nauvoo at approximately four in the morning.

At 6:30 A.M., Joseph Smith, the seventeen others named in the original writ (from which they had once been acquitted), and a dozen assistants and legal counselors, trusting in the earlier assurance of the governor that they would be protected in their journey, started up Mulholland Street on their journey to Carthage. As they topped the bluff that overlooks Nauvoo, Joseph looked back over his fair city and its still uncompleted temple. Said he, "This is the loveliest place and the best people under the heavens; little do they know the trials that await them."

At a farmhouse about four miles west of Carthage, the procession met a company of militia. Joseph was ordered off his horse and presented a document from the governor commanding all members of the Nauvoo Legion to surrender their state-issued weapons upon demand. Feeling certain the hostilities upon his people would abate with his surrender, Joseph countersigned the order and then spoke to those around him: "I am going like a lamb to the slaughter, but I am calm as a summer's morning. I have a conscience void of offense toward God and toward all men. If they take my life I shall die an innocent man . . . and it shall be said of me 'He was murdered in cold blood!' "

Knowing the enormity of his charge, the militia captain requested that Joseph return to Nauvoo with him to oversee the surrender of arms, to which Joseph consented. They arrived back in Nauvoo at a little past two, and Joseph directed the surrender. Although entirely cognizant of the real possibility of another "Missouri massacre," the legionnaires complied. Not a single person outside of Nauvoo was asked to give up his state-issued weapon.

Before departing the final time for Carthage, Joseph met with his family, expressing his conviction that he would soon be dead. The accused and their protectors arrived back in Carthage just before midnight, yet the streets were aflame with passion. Hundreds of people, most members of the Carthage militia (the "Carthage Greys"), filled the town square, where riotous shouts of "Where's the damned Prophet?" and "Let us shoot the damned Mormons" split the night incessantly.

The Carthage Greys in the back of the crowd repeatedly threw their guns in an arc over their heads, allowing them to come down and spear the earth with their bayonets

when they would run back and pick them up, at the same time whooping, yelling, hooting and cursing like a pack of savages.

On hearing the above expressions, the Governor put his head out of the window and very fawningly said, "I know your great anxiety to see Mr. Smith, which is natural enough, but it is quite too late tonight for you to have the opportunity; but I assure you, gentlemen, you shall have that privilege tomorrow morning, as I will cause him to pass before the troops upon the square, and I now wish you, with this assurance, quietly and peaceably to return to your quarters." When this declaration was made, there was a faint 'Hurrah for Tom Ford,' and they instantly obeyed his wish.[258]

Though it was frequently reported to the governor that a number of men, in the militia and out of it, were swearing to kill the Prophet themselves, he "suffered [them] . . . to run at liberty and mature their murderous plans."

At 8 A.M. Tuesday morning, June 25, Joseph and Hyrum, incarcerated, were arrested for treason (for having activated the Nauvoo Legion). At approximately 9:45 A.M. Ford ordered Joseph, Hyrum, Willard Richards, and John Taylor to accompany him on a stroll through the troops, where the governor repeatedly introduced the brothers, locking arms, as the "Generals Smith" to the boisterous crowd. As a number of the Greys offered to greet the "Mormons" in their own way, Ford told them they would have "full satisfaction" in due course.

Just before noon, it was announced that the "militia" from Warsaw, comprised of about two thousand Missourians, was nearing Carthage. In midafternoon, Ford informed Joseph that he was dispatching a company of soldiers to Nauvoo to help keep the peace. He told Joseph that should the need arise he would even utilize the (unarmed) members of the Legion to protect the inhabitants of Nauvoo. Although Joseph was promised he could accompany the governor on that journey to Nauvoo, to assuage the citizens, by 5 P.M. he was taken before Robert Smith, a justice of the peace who was concurrently serving as the commanding officer for the Carthage Greys, and charged—again—with riot for destroying the *Expositor* press. When reminded that both the governor and the prosecutors of this charge had repeatedly insisted that the group appear only before the officer of the court who had issued the writ—Thomas Morrison—

---

[258]*History of the Church*, Vol. 6, Ch. 29, p. 560.

the justice agreed to an adjournment granted bail could be posted. Thinking the amount ordered beyond their reach, he was surprised when the surety was raised. At about 7:30 P.M., the men were released.

Seeking another way to keep Joseph and Hyrum, if no others, incarcerated, Robert Smith appealed to Governor Ford. Ford replied: "You have the Carthage Greys at your command." That he did, and with some of them he soon served another writ on Joseph and Hyrum.

When confronted by John Taylor as to the procession of illegalities to which the Mormons had long been and were presently being exposed, the governor said he could not interfere with the judicial process but would be happy to see Taylor and Richards escorted to safety by a military guard, if they thought that necessary. Taylor "expressed my dissatisfaction at the course taken, and told him that if we were to be subject to mob rule, and to be dragged contrary to law into prison, at the instance of every infernal scoundrel whose oath could be bought for a dram of whiskey, his protection availed very little, and we had miscalculated his promises."

Soon the remaining "prisoners" were escorted to jail. Stephen Markham walked on one side of Joseph and Hyrum, wielding a massive hickory walking stick he often referred to as "the rascal beater," and the Welsh *Maid of Iowa* steamboat captain Dan Jones walked on the opposite side, carrying, likewise, a stout walking stick. The jailer placed them in the single prisoner cell, but later transferred them to the one-bed, two-mattress "debtor's apartment," where the six men (the two Smiths, Markham, Taylor, Jones, and Richards) settled down to discussion, evening prayer, and a fitful night of half-rest.

The next morning, Stephen Markham and Dan Jones spent several hours whittling the apartment's door into repair so that it could be hung and latched properly, affording the prisoners, to their way of seeing it, a greater degree of safety. Joseph and Hyrum spent most of the time preaching to the guards. Willard Richards took notes in his official history, and John Taylor sang. Throughout the day, the prisoners heard comment that "if the law could not reach them, powder and ball would."

At about 2:30 P.M. a request was made for the prisoners to attend an examination, "but as Mr. Stigall, the jailor, could find no law authorizing a justice of the peace to demand prisoners committed to his charge, he refused to give them up until discharged from his custody by due course of the law."

An hour and a half later, the justice returned with a command of the

Carthage Greys and overpowered the jailer and took their prisoners, saying they weren't really incarcerated, but there for their "safety." Sensing mayhem, Joseph stepped boldly into the crowd, locked arms with one of the rowdies, and walked to the courtroom. Standing for the prosecution were Chauncey Higbee and Thomas Morrison. Requests by the defense attorneys to subpoena witnesses were at first denied, but then the meeting was adjourned till the next day at noon.

Meanwhile, Governor Ford received a dispatch from his captain in Nauvoo saying that there had as yet been no reason to keep vigil in the quiet city, but perhaps they would be of better use in Carthage, where things were quickly and obviously getting difficult. Further, he wrote, "while the police were at Carthage they were treated as soldiers, but since they came to Nauvoo they have been treated as gentlemen."

At about 8 P.M., Governor Ford and his captains decided they would ride for Nauvoo in the morning with all soldiers minus fifty, "in order to gratify the troops." The fifty would be left to guard the prisoners.

In the early hours of the night, several of the prisoners expressed their conviction that they would get through this and return to Nauvoo free men. Joseph upheld no such illusions for himself, saying he had had a number of premonitions of his impending death.

When all the others were apparently asleep, Joseph whispered to his Welsh riverboat captain, Dan Jones, "Are you afraid to die?" Jones replied, "Has that time come, think you? Engaged in such a cause [as we are] I do not think that death would have many terrors."

Joseph replied, "You will yet see Wales, and fulfill the mission appointed you before you die."

As Joseph would fulfill his own mission.

In the morning, Jones asked the guard on duty how the night had gone. The officer replied, "We have had too much trouble to bring Old Joe here to let him ever escape alive, and unless you want to die with him you had better leave before sundown. You'll see that I can prophesy better than Old Joe, for neither he nor his brother, nor anyone who will remain with them will see the sun set today."

Jones returned and told Joseph what he had just heard, and Joseph asked him to take that same message to the governor, which he did. On his way across the square, he heard the same threat a number of times.

"You are unnecessarily alarmed for the safety of your friends," the governor replied upon hearing Jones's report. "The people are not that cruel."

Jones insisted on what he had heard, demanding a stronger guard.

Governor Ford's face turned pale, and Jones remarked, "If you do not do this, I have but one more desire, and that is if you leave their lives in the hands of those men to be sacrificed—"

"What is that, sir?" he asked in a hurried tone.

"It is," said Jones, "that the Almighty will preserve my life to a proper time and place, that I may testify that you have been timely warned of their danger."[259]

Jones then returned to the jail, but was denied entrance. It would save his life.

At 8:20 A.M., Joseph wrote a letter to Emma, in which he asked her to instruct the commander of the Nauvoo Legion to welcome the governor and afford him all courtesies. Then he closed: "I am very much resigned to my lot, knowing I am justified, and have done the best that could be done. Give my love to the children and all my friends . . . May God bless you all. Amen."

In preparation for his departure, Ford placed the Carthage Greys, including a number who had two days before been arrested for insubordination, in charge of the prisoners. Hundreds he discharged, telling them to go home, although military protocol demanded troops were to be discharged by their immediate commanding officers in close proximity to their homes, so as to preclude acts of lawless violence in the lands of the subjected. Another three hundred remained camped, and armed, 8 miles away on the Warsaw road under the command of the preacher, Colonel Levi Williams.

Sometime during the morning, Cyrus Wheelock was allowed to visit the prisoners, and to do so without a search of his overcoat (it was raining). Inside, he extracted from the coat's deep pockets a "pepperbox" six-shooter and handed it to Joseph. Joseph handed to Hyrum a single-shot pistol he had received in a similar exchange early in the day.

At about 10 A.M., Ford pulled out for Nauvoo. Sometimes after noon, Willard Richards began feeling ill. Stephen Markham sought leave from the guard so as to procure some medicine but, having attained it and attempting to return, was surrounded by a group of militia and forced to leave the city at the point of bayonet. That saved his life.

---

[259]Ibid., Ch. 33, p. 603.

In midafternoon, as the Greys began to grow more and more boisterous outside the jail, Joseph asked John Taylor, an Englishman converted in Canada, to sing several verses of "A Poor Wayfaring Man of
Grief," and then to sing it again. Hyrum read from the Book of Josephus.

At 4 P.M., the shift of eight guards was changed. At 5, the good jailer
Stigall came on shift and suggested to Joseph that they might be safer in
the actual jail cell. Joseph agreed, saying they would go in after dinner.
Joseph then turned to Willard Richards, not named in the writ and accompanying Joseph only out of a sense of duty as his personal secretary,
and asked, "If we go into the cell, will you go in with us?" Richards
answered, "Brother Joseph you did not ask me to cross the river with you;
you did not ask me to come to Carthage; you did not ask me to come to
jail with you; and do you think I would forsake you now? But I will tell
you what I will do; if you are condemned to be hung for treason, I will
be hung in your stead, and you shall go free."

Sometime after 5 P.M., there was a scuffle from downstairs, the
sound of gunfire, and a cry of surrender. Looking out the window, Richards could see a hundred men, perhaps two, crowding into the jail door,
their faces painted black with mud and gunpowder, their firearms drawn.
In a rush they came up the stairs, firing. Hyrum raised his pistol toward
the door, and Taylor, Richards, and Joseph attempted to bar the door,
which burst open in a rush. Taylor and Richards attempted to fight off
the mob with the rascal beaters, but their efforts were futile.

Hyrum was shot first, a lead ball smashing in through the left side
of his nose. He fell exclaiming, "I am a dead man!" As he fell, another
ball came through the window of the jail, entering his left side and passing
through his body with such force that it broke to pieces the watch in his
vest pocket. Another from the door deflected off his chest and then
pierced his throat. Finally, a fourth ball smashed into his left leg.

Lead was coming through the floor, the windows, and from a dozen
guns in the doorway. Joseph, his eyes mostly on his dear brother Hyrum,
fired his six-gun blindly into the stairwell. John Taylor parried with his
stick a couple more times and then ran for the window opposite, but a
ball caught him in the thigh and he fell across the windowsill, where a
ball fired from outside hit him with such force it threw him back into
the room. Two more balls smashed into his wrist and his knee as he
struggled to crawl for cover to a mattress lying on the floor. Then a fifth

ball smashed into his left thigh with such force that it threw scraps of flesh and spattered blood across the wall.

Assuming his exit would stop the internal killing, Joseph ran for the window and attempted to jump from it. Two balls from the doorway hit him in the back, and two more fired from outside hit him in the chest. But his momentum carried him through the window and out, where he smashed to the ground 12 feet below. There, according to affidavits, one man grabbed him and set him up against the well, and several more balls were dispatched into his lifeless body.

As a cry went up outside, the mobbers retreated down the stairwell, leaving big Willard Richards alone and unscathed but for a graze on the tip of his left earlobe. Fearing the mob's return at any moment, he dragged the bleeding Taylor into the corner and stuffed him under the mattress. Then he awaited his fate.

It was 5:17 P.M.[260]

Governor Ford and his troops were in Nauvoo, making a great show for the people of just how in charge they were. To an assembly of unarmed civilians Ford issued the following warning: "A great crime has been done by destroying the *Expositor* press and placing the city under martial law, and a severe atonement must be made, so prepare your minds for the emergency. Depend upon it, a little more misbehavior from the citizens, and the torch, which is already lighted, will be applied, and the city may be reduced to ashes, and extermination would inevitably follow; and it gives me great pain to think that there is danger of so many innocent women and children being exterminated. If anything of a serious character should befall the lives or property of the persons who are prosecuting your leaders, you will be held responsible."[261]

In fact, both those who prosecuted the Mormon leaders and those who killed them would all go scot-free.

---

[260]The ball fired from outside that struck John Taylor in the chest and threw him back into the room hit his vest-pocket watch, probably saving his life. Its hands were stilled at 5:16: 26.

[261]*History of the Church*, Vol. 6, Ch. 35, p. 623.

CHAPTER 11

Aftermath

On the morning of Friday, June 28, 1844, "the sun rose on as strange a scene as the broad Hancock prairies had ever witnessed. At the three corners of a triangle eighteen miles asunder stood a smitten city [Nauvoo], and two almost deserted villages [Warsaw and Carthage], with here and there a group of questioning men, anxious to hear the news of the night. Toward the two villages the more courageous ones were returning to find their several abodes unsacked and untouched. The wet and heavy roads leading to the county seat from the south and east were being traversed by the refugees of the night, now returning and wondering that they had homes to return to. All knew that a great crime had been committed, by whom they knew not; and they knew not how, upon whom, where, or in what manner retribution might fall."[262]

From one of those backroads just past sunrise emerged Arza Adams, one of the signers of the "poor covenant" five years before, suffering from the effects of the flu and his long night ride from Carthage. Although rumor had preceded him, he carried to Emma and others gathered at the Mansion House word that Joseph and Hyrum were in fact dead. The note was written and signed by the doctor, Willard Richards.

Carthage Jail.
8 o'clock, 5 min., P.M., June 27.

Joseph and Hyrum are dead. Taylor wounded, not badly. I am well. Our guard was forced as we believe, by a band of Missourians from 100 to 200. The job was done in an instant, and the party fled towards Nauvoo instantly. This is as I believe it. The citizens here are afraid of the "Mormons" attacking them; I promise them no.
W. Richards.[263]

---

[262]*History of Hancock County,* Gregg, p. 323.

[263]B. H. Roberts, *Comprehensive History of the Church,* Vol. 2, Ch. 58, p. 289–290.

Having delivered his warning speech, Ford and his troops had spent just a bit of time looting in the Nauvoo Temple[264] and then departed Nauvoo about 6:30 the previous evening, arriving in Carthage just in time to have all public documents and courthouse records retrieved and to spread the word for the few remaining Carthage residents to flee for their lives.

Sometime after midnight, he took his troops and departed himself, traveling in haste to Augusta, 18 miles to the south. It was near that hour before Richards could get any help to move the wounded Taylor to safety at a local lodge. At about 8 A.M., he loaded the two corpses,[265] covered with tree branches to protect them from the summer sun, into a pair of wagons and departed for Nauvoo under escort of eight soldiers. At about 3 P.M., the procession reached the eastern terminus of Mulholland Street, where several thousand mourners were awaiting their arrival.

The bodies of Hyrum and Joseph Smith were taken for preparation for burial, while Dr. Richards, Stephen Markham (who had been run out of town before the murders), and the brothers' legal counselors addressed the crowd in front of the Mansion House. Richards admonished the people to keep the peace, stating that he had pledged his honor toward their good conduct.

The next day, Saturday, the two brothers lay in state at the Mansion House from 8 A.M. until 5 P.M., and an estimated ten thousand people filed past their coffins. Most were in a state of near shock.

"With all that had been said by the Prophet Joseph to his brethren and the Saints," wrote apostle Francis Lyman years later, "there was not one soul, save it might be the Prophet himself, that was prepared for the sacrifice of his life. No one ever thought that he would be slain. They were not prepared for it. They had not thought it would be just that way. . . . Many people have turned away from the truth because things did not come exactly to suit them."[266]

Emma Smith, for example.

No one would ever deny that Emma had walked a hard road with

---

[264]Affidavit of Wm. G. Sterrett, published in Church Historians' Compilation. *Millennial Star*, Vol. xxiv, pp. 421–422.

[265]John Taylor remained under the care of his wife and doctor in Carthage until July 2, when he was well enough to return to Nauvoo.

[266]Francis M. Lyman of the Quorum of the Twelve, General Conference, April 5, 1892.

Joseph. But the murder of her beloved husband would ask her to take one more step than she was willing to take. On the heels of her growing discomfort with the principle of polygamy, her unabashed dislike of senior apostle Brigham Young, and the general confusion as to who now presided over the Latter-day Saints, Emma began her break from the church.

She would try to take Joseph with her.

On the evening of June 29, following the public viewing, the doors to the Mansion House were closed and bolted. The bodies were removed and hidden in a distant bedroom, and the coffins were filled with a measure of sand and gravel and nailed shut. Then a procession led to the family cemetery some 80 yards away, and about that same distance from the gently lapping waves of the Mississippi River. There the coffins were buried with full ceremony. Around midnight, winds whipping their hair and rain spraying their faces, ten men took the bodies from their hiding place in the Mansion House and carried them quickly to a prepared sepulture in the lower reaches of a nearby building then under construction. By morning, all traces of their nighttime traverse had been obliterated.

In the next few months following what Latter-day Saints would forever after term "the Martyrdom," Emma Smith and Brigham Young would tug open a breach that would find no repair. Others would jump into it, taking at least a dozen tiny "Mormon" splinter groups out into Texas, Wisconsin, Michigan, and elsewhere in the next few years. Finding herself associating less and less with the larger body of Saints and their concerns, sometime in the late fall or early winter of 1845, Emma had the two bodies disinterred and reburied, again clandestinely, somewhere nearby, and possibly even closer to the river. Not even Hyrum's widow, Mary Fielding Smith, was invited to the event. Few people, among them Emma and those who dug, knew where the brothers' remains ended up, and they weren't talking.

Thus it stood for eighty-four years.

In the interim, in the early 1850s, a small group of Brigham-rejectors gathering just over the border in Wisconsin decided that only a literal descendant of Joseph Smith should lead the Latter-day Saints. But it took them seven more years to convince Joseph III, the oldest surviving son, that such was the case. When the "Reorganized Church of Jesus Christ of Latter-day Saints (RLDS)" was officially incorporated in 1860, many of Joseph's family, including Emma, joined up. The RLDS Church eventually headquartered itself in Independence, Missouri; the other church, as we shall soon see, in Utah.

Now back to the bodies.

In January 1928, with the Mississippi River chewing away at its flanks, a grandson of Joseph Smith, now presiding over "the Missouri church," initiated an effort to have the bodies found; modern and structurally sound coffins constructed; and a fitting monument to the martyrs erected. In the six-day process of popping exploratory holes all over the homestead hillside, the diggers first found Emma (who died in 1879) and then, on January 16, Joseph and Hyrum about 10 feet away. On a windy, 12 degree afternoon four days later, three new coffins were laid side by side in a concrete monument and duly memorialized by the few invited participants.[267]

Some in "the Utah church" were not entirely pleased with the exhumation, thinking it a desecration of a sacred site. The digging and removal may have, in fact, further damaged the skulls. Recent computer imaging and reconstruction of the death masks made in 1928 suggests the men's graves as now marked may be reversed.[268] But faithful Latter-day Saints, who honor Hyrum nearly as much as his younger brother, find what is in the grave to mean very little compared to what is in the record.

Joseph Smith recorded or referred to having at least seventy-seven visions/conversations with at least fifty-nine separate heavenly beings,[269] including Peter, James, John, John the Baptist, Adam, Seth, Enoch, Noah, Elijah, Abraham, Isaac, Jacob, Moroni, Mormon, and Nephi (the last three are Book of Mormon characters), as well as numerous other resurrected or translated American and Middle Eastern saints. He saw the Father and the Son (separate and distinct beings) together on five occasions and the Savior individually on four.[270] The Book of Mormon:

---

[267]Including only one from "the Utah church." For a full account see Bernauer, Barbara Hands, "Still Side by Side—The Final Burial of Joseph and Hyrum Smith," in *John Whitmer Historical Association Journal,* Vol. 11, 1991, 17–33.

[268]See Shannon Michael Tracy, "In Search of Joseph," KenningHouse, 1995; and *Deseret News,* January 28, 1996, B1.

[269]See "Personages Who Appeared to the Prophet Joseph Smith or Who Were Seen by Him in Vision," *Church History Regional Studies,* Brigham Young University Department of Church History and Doctrine, New York, H. Donl Peterson, p. 65.

[270]For a recounting see Alexander L. Baugh, "Parting the Veil: The Visions of Joseph Smith," *Brigham Young University Studies,* Vol. 38, No. 1, pp. 23–69.

Another Testament of Jesus Christ has since been printed more than ninety million times in ninety-seven languages, and *Doctrine and Covenants* (containing many of his revelations—some visions, some not) has been printed in thirty-eight.

Of Joseph Smith, the badly wounded John Taylor (who in another thirty-six years, still limping, would become the church's third president after it had added more than one hundred thousand members) would write: "He lived great, and he died great in the eyes of God and his people; and like most of the Lord's anointed in ancient time, has sealed his mission and his works with his own blood; and so has his brother Hyrum. In life they were not divided, and in death they were not separated!"[271]

Joseph's own summation of his brief life, given some twenty-one months before, would be more modest, but nonetheless frank: "As for the perils which I am called to pass through, they seem but a small thing to me, as the envy and wrath of man have been my common lot all the days of my life; and for what cause it seems mysterious, unless I was ordained from before the foundation of the world for some good end, or bad, as you may choose to call it. Judge ye for yourselves. God knoweth all these things, whether it be good or bad. But nevertheless, deep water is what I am wont to swim in."[272]

Outside of Nauvoo, from Carthage and beyond, the world thought Mormonism had come to its end. But they didn't know Brigham Young. Nor just how clear Joseph's vision had been.

---

[271]*Doctrine and Covenants* 135:3.

[272]*History of the Church*, Vol. 5, Ch. 8, p. 143; September 2, 1842.

CHAPTER 12

Prelude to a Finale

On the eve of the martyrdom, most of the apostles were still in the eastern states preaching and promoting Joseph Smith's candidacy for president of the United States. Although each of the apostles, in their disparate locales, would record having feelings of inexplicable sorrow and discomfort the evening of June 27, it would be nearly two weeks before any of them would hear rumors of the murders in Nauvoo, and mid-July before most had them confirmed.

A letter from his wife, Mary Ann, finally reached Brigham Young in Vermont. It speaks of much more than just a murder:

> My Dear Companion. I set down to communicate a few lines to you at this time. My heart is full. I know not what to write to comfort you at this time. We have had great afflictions in this place since you left home. . . . You have now been gone allmost six weeks. I have not had a line from you since you left home. I have not time to write much now. We are in great affliction at this time. Our Dear Br. Joseph Smith and Hiram has fell victiams to a verocious mob. The great God of the creation only knows whithe[r] the rest shall be preserved in safety or not. We are in tolable good health at presant. I have been Blessed to keep my feelings quite calm through all the storm. I hope you will be careful on your way hom and not expose yourself to those that will endanger your Life. Yours in hast[e].
>
> If we meet no more in this world may we meet where parting is no more. Farewell.[273]

Sidney Rigdon, out of Joseph's favor both as first counselor in the church presidency and as his vice-presidential running mate (and in deteriorating health), was in Pittsburgh politicking when he heard the news.

---

[273]As rendered in Dean C. Jessee, *Brigham Young University Studies*, Vol. 18, No. 3, p. 327.

There he received a letter from Young and others of the Twelve, who had gathered in Boston, asking him to meet them as soon as possible in Nauvoo to discuss privately what their next step was to be.

Sidney hastened to Nauvoo, arriving August 3, well ahead of the members of the Twelve. The next morning, a Sunday, he preached a disjointed and wandering sermon in which he claimed to be "the identical man that the ancient prophets had sung about, wrote and rejoiced over" as he who would lead the church following Joseph's death, and that were it not for two or three things that only he knew about, "this people would be utterly destroyed, and not a soul left to tell the tale."[274] He then called for a meeting of all the Saints for the following Thursday, a meeting in which he would lay out for them the plan of the church's future under his "guardianship."

To most in attendance, the called-for meeting seemed clearly premature and ill-advised. Finally, Brigham Young and all but four remaining members of the Twelve arrived in Nauvoo at 8 P.M. Tuesday. Brigham called a meeting for the next afternoon at 4 to be attended by the Nauvoo high council, the high priests, and the eight members of the Twelve then in Nauvoo. Again, Rigdon told them he was ordained to be the guardian of the church, to build it up unto Joseph.

Offered his turn, Brigham Young said, "I do not care who leads the church, even though it were Ann Lee[275]; but one thing I must know, and that is what God says about it. You [by voting] cannot fill the office of a prophet, seer and revelator: God must do this."[276]

And there, in a nutshell, Brigham Young reiterated a foundational doctrine of Mormonism, one made evident from the first vision of Joseph Smith and clarified a number of times in both Latter-day Saint and (to LDS eyes) biblical scripture. But a doctrine no one in this assembly had had to think about since their initial conversion to Joseph Smith and his restoration: God calls his prophets. Electioneering is pointless.

With that niblet for them to chew on a while, Brigham adjourned the meeting, and instructed the leaders to have all the available Latter-

---

[274]Elder Parley P. Pratt of the Twelve subsequently said, "I am the identical man the prophets never sang nor wrote a word about."

[275]Ann Lee brought a small group of Shakers, or Shaking Quakers, to the U.S. in 1774.

[276]*History of the Church*, Vol. 7, Ch. 19, p. 233.

day Saints present the following morning. At 10 A.M. on August 8, the temple behind him carving a silhouette in the morning sun, Sidney stood up in a wagon and "harangued" an approximated five thousand Saints for about an hour and a half, again playing the guardian card. According to one historian, many in the crowd began to see that Rigdon's unconcealed "ambition had diluted his sincerity."[277] But what really changed the course of events is what many in the crowd saw that afternoon.

Following a noontime break, Brigham would address the crowd for about two hours. But his last 119 minutes were largely superfluous. Wrote one attendee: *"Mother had the baby on her knee, who was playing with a tin cup. He dropped it, attracting our attention to the floor. Mother scooped over to pick it up, when we were startled by hearing the voice of Joseph. Looking up quickly we saw the form of the Prophet Joseph standing before us. Brother Brigham looked and talked so much like Joseph that for a minute we thought it was Joseph."*[278]

Accounts enumerate a physical change, including height (Brigham Young was approximately four inches shorter than Joseph Smith), body shape (unlike Joseph, Brigham was often described as "stout"), mannerisms, and voice. One account even noted a whistling through the teeth that Joseph often had due to the broken tooth he suffered in the Ohio tar-and-feathering.

Although this "transfiguration"—interpreted (then and now) as a manifestation of the transfer of the mantle of Prophet to Brigham Young—was not seen by everyone in the crowd and not detailed by most until some years later, more than one hundred written accounts—fifty-seven of them eyewitness[279]—testify to the event. And though such a manifestation was and is nonessential from a doctrinal point of view, it served its purpose in exactly the same way that the passing of the mantle from Elijah to Elisha[280] did in ancient Palestine. The people had a sign.

The specific text of Brigham's address, which he would later describe in his journal that evening as an effort simply "to comfort the harts of

[277]Leonard J. Arrington, *Brigham Young: American Moses*, 1985, pp. 114–115.

[278]Eight-year-old Mary Field, as cited in Jorgensen, p. 143.

[279]Lynne Watkins Jorgensen, "The Mantle of the Prophet Joseph Smith Passes to Brother Brigham: A Collective Spiritual Witness," *Brigham Young University Studies* 36, No. 4 (1996–7).

[280]2 Kings 2:1–15.

the Saints," would deal not with miracles and manifestations but with practicalities and principles. In essence, he taught the people, saying that an immediate reorganization of the First Presidency was probably not the course to follow. The Quorum of the Twelve was intact, he explained, and an 1835 revelation to Joseph Smith[281] made clear that, in the absence of the presidency, this quorum was to preside. As always in Brigham's mind, he asked the people to wait and see what the Lord had in *his* mind. With their sustaining vote, the Twelve would lead for now.[282] As for Rigdon, Young said, "We are of one mind with him and he with us. We want such men as Brother Rigdon."[283]

All but an estimated twenty people (out of five thousand) sustained the Twelve as the presiding authorities of the church. The twenty wanted Rigdon. Rigdon wanted none of it. He would be excommunicated one month later and leave the Saints forever, although he would hold to his testimony of the early years to the end of his life.

The Twelve, Brigham at their head, would preside over the church for the next three and a half years. And they would waste no time in getting up to full speed. Exactly seven days following the two leadership speeches (and a unanimous sustaining on August 12 of the Twelve's right to lead), by August 15, Brigham Young and the Twelve released a general epistle to the Saints "in Nauvoo and all the world." Of immediate focus were to be completion of the temple and a renewed emphasis on the tithing of every member or candidate for admission to the church so as to weed out those practicing "mock membership." In addition, Young began to outline a refined geographic/ecclesiastical organization for the church. "The time has come when all things must be set in order."

On Sunday, August 18, Brigham preached a discourse in which he discussed "a disposition in the sheep to scatter, now the shepherd is taken away." Rigdon was leaving; dozens would follow him, including members of the Twelve.

---

[281]In 1844 this would have been *Doctrine and Covenants* 3:11; the verses are now found in *Doctrine and Covenants* 107:22–24.

[282]Even sixteen years later, Brigham was still playing the aw-shucks role: "The brethren testify that brother Brigham Young is brother Joseph's legal successor. You never heard me say so. I say that I am a good hand to keep the dogs and wolves out of the flock." (*Journal of Discourses,* Vol. 8, p. 69, Brigham Young, June 3, 1860).

[283]*History of the Church,* Vol. 7, Ch. 19, p. 240.

Yet Brigham's focus was on the temple, and what the people would get out of completing it; specifically, their "endowment." As he would later explain, "Your endowment is, to receive all those ordinances in the House of the Lord, which are necessary for you, after you have departed this life, to enable you to walk back to the presence of the Father, passing the angels who stand as sentinels, being enabled to give them the key words, the signs and tokens, pertaining to the Holy Priesthood, and gain your eternal exaltation in spite of earth and hell."[284]

Thus the temple was key. It was central to the faith. And in Brigham's mind, and under his growing leadership, it would take precedence over all other concerns, some of them not petty.

The air of trepidation in Nauvoo had lessened little if at all since the death of the Prophet. Throughout that summer, the citizens in surrounding Hancock County, Illinois, had continued to petition Governor Ford for an extermination or deracination of the Mormons, now almost all gathered in Nauvoo for their own safety, yet deprived of safe access to their own farms and crops.[285] Many were going hungry.

To aid them, tithing funds were to be used. Beyond that, the temple: "We want to build the Temple in this place," said Brigham, "if we have to build it as the Jews built the walls of the Temple in Jerusalem, with a sword in one hand and the trowel in the other. I would rather pay out every cent I have to build up this place and get an endowment, if I were driven the next minute without anything to take with me."

Which is about how it went.

Through the fall of 1844, the Latter-day Saints worked the temple with one hand on the trowel and the other on the gun. In late September, they received word that the Baptist preacher Levi Williams and the Warsaw *Signal* editor Thomas Sharp were getting up a "wolf hunt" to drag some of the church leaders back to Carthage to kill them like Joseph and Hyrum. Invited to the hunt were residents of three states. On September 24, a contingent of the Quincy Greys made camp on the eastern fringes of the city, and the Saints began importing weapons up the river from

---

[284]*Journal of Discourses*, Vol. 2, p. 31, Brigham Young, April 6, 1853.

[285]In a directive to his regional commander regarding the merit of such evictory petitions, even the duplicitous Ford evinced a growing distaste for the animosity. "I am afraid," he wrote, "that the people of Hancock are fast depriving themselves of the sympathy of their fellow citizens, and of the world."

St. Louis. An underground arsenal was begun near the temple. After a prayer dedicating the construction site, Brigham Young lifted the first spadeful of earth.

On September 26, the Nauvoo Legion, still unarmed, was advised by the governor to have troops ready for inspection in the morning. The following day, Ford rode into town with about 470 soldiers, "all that would volunteer in nine counties to help maintain the supremacy of the laws." Their intent was peaceful; in fact, they wanted a Mormon posse to help track down and capture Williams and Sharp, who were eluding warrants for their arrest. In this, the Latter-day Saints respectfully declined, and Ford accepted. This assemblage of the authorized force did, however, serve to disband an unauthorized one. According to the *History of Hancock County*, its perpetrators "abandoned their design, and all the leaders of it fled to Missouri."[286]

It was there, on September 30, that Governor Ford's troops finally convinced Williams and Sharp to surrender. Part of the agreement was that they would be tried in a Carthage court. Thus, on October 21, a grand jury impaneled in Carthage began their investigation into the murders, and by the 26th, nine individuals had been indicted on two counts of murder. But the trial was then postponed until the following May. The first twelve jurors selected for the trial were soon dismissed, however, as charges of impartiality were levied: several of the selectors were Latter-day Saints. For the second attempt at selection a week later, not an active Latter-day Saint was in sight. According to Ford's *History*, "as more than a thousand men had assembled under arms at the court to keep away the Mormons and their friends, the jury was made up of these military followers of the court, who all swore that they had never formed or expressed any opinion as to the guilt or innocence of the accused."[287]

On May 30, each of the defendants was found not guilty in regard to Joseph's murder. Hyrum's trial was postponed until the following June. In January 1845, the Nauvoo city charter was repealed by the state legislature,[288] and the residents of Nauvoo began to lose heart and faith in

---

[286]*History of Hancock County*, pp. 326–328.

[287]*History of Illinois*, p. 367.

[288]"Of this act on the part of the state legislature, the state's attorney, Josiah Lamborn, in a letter to Brigham Young, dated at Springfield, Ill., Jan. 1845, said: "I have always considered that your enemies have been prompted by political and religious prejudices, and by a

the system. Come June, with no witnesses for the prosecution presenting themselves, those accused of Hyrum's murder walked away, fully acquitted. Sharp would become the superintendent of schools in Hancock County and later a county judge. Levi Williams would continue to preach and would die in relative anonymity thirteen years later.

In early September, Missouri started all over again.

On the 10th, houses outside of Nauvoo reoccupied by Latter-day Saints began to burn in Morley Settlement. Noting the return of hostilities, the editor of the Quincy *Whig* wrote: "These outrages should be put a stop to at once; if the Mormons have been guilty of crime, why punish them; but do not visit their sins upon defenseless women and children. It is feared that this rising against the Mormons is not confined to the Morley Settlement, but that there is an understanding among the [anti-Mormons] in the northern part of this (Adams) and Hancock counties to make a general sweep, burning and destroying the property of the Mormons wherever it can be found. If this is the case, there will be employment for the executive of the state, and that soon."[289]

Hancock County Sheriff Jacob B. Backenstos pled with the Latter-day Saints to do nothing in retaliation, as it could turn into all-out civil war. He proposed to a Hancock County crowd that "The Mormon community had acted with more than ordinary forbearance, remaining perfectly quiet, and offering no resistance when their dwellings, their buildings, stacks of grain, etc., were set on fire in their presence. They had forborne until forbearance was no longer a virtue."[290]

In his journal entry of September 11—the day twenty-nine houses

---

desire for plunder and blood, more than the common good. By the repeal of your charter . . . our legislature has given a kind of sanction to the barbarous manner in which you have been treated. Your two representatives exerted themselves to the extent of their ability in your behalf, but the tide of popular passion and frenzy was too strong to be resisted. It is truly a melancholy spectacle to witness the lawmakers of a sovereign state condescending to pander to the vices, ignorance and malevolence of a class of people who are at all times ready for riot, murder and rebellion." (B. H. Roberts, *Comprehensive History of the Church*, Vol. 2, Ch. 67, p. 468–469)

[289]B. H. Roberts, *Comprehensive History of the Church*, Vol. 2, Ch. 67, p. 475.

[290]Ibid., p. 477. According to Gregg in his *History of Hancock County*, "The manner was to go to a house and warn the inmates out, that they were going to burn it. Usually there would be no show of resistance: but all hands, burners and all, would proceed to take out the goods and place them out of danger. When the goods were all securely removed, the torch would be applied and the house consumed. Then on to another."

burned to the ground in Morley Settlement—John Taylor clarifies what may have been in the minds of Latter-day Saints standing tall in the face of such civil and personal outrage: "We [are] going west in the spring."

That decision—and Taylor's journal mentions it as one reached by the Twelve together—would be publicly announced on September 24 in response to a query from a citizens' committee in Quincy "as to when the Mormons could be expected to leave the country."

The Apostles' circular stated, in part: "We would say to the committee above mentioned, and to the Governor, and all the authorities and people of Illinois, and the surrounding States and Territories; that we propose to leave this county next spring, for some point so remote that there will not need to be a difficulty with the people and ourselves."

Certain dispensations were requested:

> that the Latter-day Saints, particularly their leaders, be left alone in regard to frivolous lawsuits that continued to vex them (including a continual flow of *Expositor* grievances);

> that the residents of surrounding counties assist them in the sale of their properties "so as to get means enough that we can help the widow, the fatherless and destitute to remove with us"[291];

> that the Latter-day Saints be not abused in their efforts to buy grain, draft animals, foodstuffs and expeditionary gear;

> that such removal be not forced "so early in the spring, that grass might not grow nor water run."

On October 1 and 2, fifty-eight delegates from nine counties (Hancock County was excluded) met in Carthage to discuss the fate of the Mormons in their midst. Their resolution: "It is the settled and deliberate conviction of this convention that it is now too late to attempt the settlement of the difficulties in Hancock county upon any other basis than that of the removal of the Mormons from the state; and we therefore accept and respectfully recommend to the people of the surrounding

---

[291]Brigham Young estimated that the Latter-day Saints had several hundred farms and more than two thousand houses to sell in the area. Overnight resale was not a pretty prospect.

counties to accept the proposition made by the Mormons to remove from the state next spring, and to wait with patience the time appointed for removal."[292]

Yet patience was in great want.

Even Sylvester Bartlett, previously charitable editor of the Quincy *Whig,* wrote that "it is [the Mormons'] duty to obey the public will, and leave the state as speedily as possible."

In their response to the Twelve's circular, the Quincy committee tendered the following "soulless" response:[293] "After what has been written and said by yourselves, it will be confidently expected by us and the whole community, that you will remove from the state, with your whole church, in the manner you have agreed in your statement to us.

"Should you not do so we are satisfied, however much we may deprecate violence and bloodshed, that violent measures will be resorted to, to compel your removal; which will result in most disastrous consequences to yourselves . . . and that the end will be your expulsion from the state."

Their city disenfranchised, their legion annulled, their hopes for justice and closure denied, their neighbors hating them—and Joseph's prophecy fresh in their minds—Brigham Young announced plans at the October 1845 General Conference, held in the partially completed temple, to evacuate Illinois by the following spring. And as with the Missouri exodus in 1838, he put the members under covenant to assist the poor among them.

By early November, Saints throughout the United States were being counseled to join with the Nauvoo Saints in their exodus the following spring. In the words of apostle Orson Pratt, presiding over the mission that covered most of the eastern United States as far south as Kentucky, "We do not want one saint to be left in the United States after that time. Let every branch [congregation] in the east, west, north and south be determined to flee out of 'Babylon,' either by land or sea, as soon as then."[294] Many began moving toward Nauvoo before Christmas.

---

[292]Resolution, Citizens' meeting, Oct. 2, 1845, Carthage, Illinois, as cited in B. H. Roberts, *Comprehensive History of the Church,* Vol. 2, Ch. 68, p. 506.

[293]*Nauvoo Neighbor,* October 29, 1845.

[294]B. H. Roberts, *Comprehensive History of the Church,* Vol. 3, Ch. 71, p. 25.

By late November, the attic level of the temple was complete enough that it was dedicated for temple ordinance work, and labor began in earnest and in haste.

The beginning of temple work seemed to elevate mob action to renewed heights. Brigham Young, spending twenty-hour days at the temple, came and went in disguise or under curtain of night. The police force was strengthened, and almost every man and boy who was unemployed or awake at any given hour was set to guarding. Preparations for a long journey consumed the minds of the people, but so did the receipt of their temple blessings. By February 3, more than fifty-six hundred people had received their temple work.

Young, fearing another violent "rupture" at any moment, one that they would surely lose and lose miserably, decided the time had come to go.

Their seven-year sojourn in "the City of Joseph" had come to an end.

CHAPTER 13

The American Exodus

"For Brigham Young and his associates, the 1846 exodus from Nauvoo, far from being a disaster imposed by enemies, was foretold and foreordained—a key to understanding LDS history and a necessary prelude for greater things to come. From a later perspective, too, scholars of the Mormon experience have come to see the exodus and colonization of the Great Basin as the single most important influence in molding the Latter-day Saints into a distinctive people."[295]

In his "transfiguration address" the summer before, Brigham had told the people: "Heretofore you have had a Prophet as the mouth of the Lord to speak to you, but he has sealed his testimony with his blood, and now, for the first time, are you called to walk by faith, not by sight."[296]

It would be a long walk. Neither had the grass sufficiently grown (or even begun to sprout) nor had the life-preserving streams scattered across the Great Plains begun to flow freely on February 4, 1846, when the first wagons pulled out of Nauvoo, easing their own way down Parley Street toward the Mississippi River docks. The exit road would soon be known as the "street of tears."

Though a variety of locations for their ultimate destination—including Texas or the "Oregon country," specifically Vancouver Island[297]—had been studied and discussed following the martyrdom, records show that by the date of the Exodus, Brigham Young knew quite well where they were heading. That the Saints' destiny lay in the Rocky Mountains, said Young, had been "fulfilled . . . long before we left Nauvoo."[298]

---

[295]*Encyclopedia of Mormonism*, Vol. 4, Western Migration and Planning.

[296]*History of the Church*, Vol. 7, Ch. 19, p. 232.

[297]In early 1846, British-born apostle John Taylor was in England trying to gain the interest of the throne in letting the (British) Latter-day Saints have Vancouver Island as a place of settlement and refuge.

[298]March 16, 1856, *Journal of Discourses*, III:257, 258. In a meeting of the Council of Fifty on Tuesday, September 9, 1845, Brigham Young presiding, it was "resolved that a company

Joseph Smith's short but eventful life would end here, in the Carthage, Illinois jail, where vigilantes with their faces smeared black with axle grease and gunpowder shot him and his brother Hyrum to death on June 27, 1844.

This granite monument was constructed in 1905 near the Sharon, Vermont birthplace of Joseph Smith. It is 38.5 feet high, one foot for each year of Joseph's life.

The Smith family farmstead in Palmyr township, New York, near the forested grove where young Joseph received his First Vision and launched the story of the Latter-day Saints.

Adam-ondi-ahman, or "the place where Adam dwelt." In Latter-day Saint theology, this tranquil landscape some fifty miles north of today's Kansas City, Missouri, is where it all began: the biblical Garden of Eden.

In this tiny frontier cabin, the Peter Whitmer, Sr. homestead in Fayette, New York, Joseph Smith officially organized The Church of Jesus Christ of Latter-day Saints on April 6, 1830 with six original members. It would reach one million members in 1947, it will reach 11 million by 2001.

A 1997 sesquicentennial reenactment of the great 1847 exodus to the Salt Lake Valley would see more than 10,000 individuals—LDS and non-LDS—take part at some point along the 1000-mile trail from Winter Quarters, Nebraska. An estimated 400 people went all the way, about 60 of them walking every step, in memory of the Handcart Pioneers of 1856-1860. Here, the principal wagon train approached the Utah/Wyoming border just south of Evanston, Wyoming.

Joseph Smith, founder and first Prophet of The Church of Jesus Christ of Latter-day Saints (1805-1844). Detail of larger painting, 1959, by Alvin Gittins.

Following Joseph Smith's murder in 1844, Brigham Young led the Latter-day Saints across half the North American continent to a safe haven in the Rocky Mountains, earning him the nickname "the American Moses." He presided over The Church of Jesus Christ of Latter-day Saints for 30 years, dying of natural causes on August 29, 1877. Photo taken circa 1875.

Salt Lake City today: the city's tallest building (foreground) is the 28-story Church Office Building, anchoring one end of the six-building world headquarters plaza. Adjacent and to the west lies ten-acre Temple Square, whose multi-spired namesake oversees one of the most fastidiously kept inner city garden paradises in the world.

Perhaps the most iconic images in Mormondom are the Tabernacle (left) and Salt Lake temple (background, spires) on Temple Square in the heart of Salt Lake City, Utah. The tabernacle, completed in 1875, is home to the world famous Tabernacle Choir and its weekly broadcasts; the 250,000-square-foot temple, one of more than a hundred now built around the world (although it remains by far the largest), took 40 years to complete.

Between 1847 and 1869, the year the Transcontinental Railroad was completed (in Utah), an approximated 68,000 people walked or wagoned their way across the American continent to the Salt lake Valley. Here a wagon train completes the final leg of the journey through Echo Canyon, Utah Territory, in 1866.

For the first 80 years of the Church's history, converts from around the world were encouraged to emigrate to "Zion," the Salt Lake Valley of the Rocky Mountain Great Basin. Here a group of European converts pose for a photo on the dock at Plymouth, England before embarking for America in 1863.

Many sites along the Mormon Trail are considered sacred ground to millions of Latter-day Saints, but easily the best known is Martin's Cove, in central Wyoming, where more than 160 pioneers died seeking shelter from early snows in 1856.

That same day, a chartered ship named the *Brooklyn* sailed out of New York Harbor with 238 Latter-day Saints and "two or three" non-Mormons on board under the leadership of Samuel Brannan. Their voyage around Tierra del Fuego, north to Hawaii, and east to San Francisco Bay would take five months and twenty-seven days. Ten passengers would die en route; two new ones would be born.

Brigham Young and other church leaders remained in Nauvoo until mid-February, endeavoring to organize the eviction. Young and several others had upward of a year's supply of dried meat and flour and other goods on their family wagons, but once in Iowa, they would quickly begin depleting their stores in feeding others not so well prepared.

Church emissaries traveled throughout the region, including to St. Louis, soliciting financial aid for the Saints. They raised a hundred dollars.[299]

At the river, wagons were ferried across on barges, and then directed seven miles south to a staging ground that became known as the "Sugar Creek Camp." According to church historian Joseph Fielding Smith, "It was an extreme winter. They were without sufficient food, clothing, and provender for their teams. Their covered wagons would not successfully shed the snow and rain, and many wagons were without covers.

On the first night of the encampment, nine infants were born."[300] Wrote Eliza R. Snow:

"from that time, as we journeyed onward, mothers gave birth to offspring under almost every variety of circumstances imaginable, except those to which they had been accustomed; some in tents, others in wagons—in rainstorms and in snowstorms. I heard of one birth which

---

of 1500 men be selected to go to Great Salt Lake valley and . . . gather information relative to emigration and report the same to the council." (*History of the Church*, Vol. 7, Ch. 32, p. 439)

[299]See Bennett, *Dialogue*, Vol. 19, No. 4, p. 105.

[300]Joseph Fielding Smith Jr., *Doctrines of Salvation*, Vol. 3, p. 337. Some commentators place the Sugar Creek birth of nine babies during the second occupation of the camp, after the Battle of Nauvoo in September. (See "Nine Children Were Born": A Historical Problem from the Sugar Creek Episode, Carol Lynn Pearson, in *Brigham Young University Studies*, No. 4, Fall 1981.)

occurred under the rude shelter of a hut, the sides of which were formed of blankets fastened to poles stuck in the ground, with a bark roof through which the rain was dripping. Kind sisters stood holding dishes to catch the water as it fell, thus protecting the newcomer and its mother from a showerbath as the little innocent first entered on the stage of human life; and through faith in the Great Ruler of events, no harm resulted to either.

Let it be remembered that the mothers of these wilderness-born babies were not savages, accustomed to roam the forest and brave the storm and tempest . . . [m]ost of them were born and educated in the eastern states . . . and, for the sake of their religion, had gathered with the saints, and under trying circumstances had assisted, by their faith, patience and energies, in making Nauvoo what its name indicates, 'the Beautiful.' There they had lovely homes, decorated with flowers and enriched with choice fruit trees, just beginning to yield plentifully.

To these homes, without lease or sale, they had just bade a final adieu, and . . . had started out, desert-ward, for—where? To this question the only response at that time was, God knows.[301]

It would only get worse.

On February 28, wagons and walkers still rolling in from Nauvoo, the wide expanse of the Mississippi River (nearly a mile at Nauvoo) froze solid enough to allow the wagons to come across on their own power. The cold would combine with poor preparation on the part of many—or access to few resources on the part of many others—to make life in the camp generally miserable and desperate. In many cases, food supplies for both people and draft animals were exhausted in a few days.

Brigham Young wrote:

Sugar Creek Refugee Camp, Iowa Territory

Saturday, 28 [February, 1846], Six A.M., thermometer 20° above zero. Wind variable, changing toward the north.

---

[301]Quoted by Tullidge, *Women of Mormondom*, ch. xxxii.

I met in council with the Twelve in my tent. We read and approved the following to the governor of Iowa [James Clark]:

To His Excellency,
Governor of the Territory of Iowa,

Honored Sir: The time is at hand, in which several thousand free citizens of this great Republic, are to be driven from their peaceful homes and firesides, their property and farms, and their dearest constitutional rights—to wander in the barren plains, and sterile mountains of western wilds, and linger out their lives in wretched exile far beyond the pale of professed civilization; or else be exterminated upon their own lands by the people, and authorities of the state of Illinois. As life is sweet we have chosen banishment rather than death. But Sir, the terms of our banishment are so rigid that we have not sufficient time allotted us to make the necessary preparations to encounter the hardships and difficulties of those dreary and uninhabited regions. We have not time allowed us to dispose of our property, dwellings, and farms; consequently, many of us will have to leave them unsold, without the means of procuring the necessary provisions, clothing, teams, etc. to sustain us but a short distance beyond the settlements: hence our persecutors have placed us in very unpleasant circumstances.

To stay is death by 'fire and sword', to go into banishment unprepared is death by starvation, But yet under these heart-rending circumstances, several hundreds of us have started upon our dreary journey, and are now encamped in Lee county, Iowa, suffering much from the intensity of the cold. Some of us are already without food, and others barely sufficient to last a few weeks: hundreds of others must shortly follow us in the same unhappy condition.

Therefore, we, the Presiding Authorities of the Church of Jesus Christ of Latter-day Saints, as a committee in behalf of several thousand suffering exiles, humbly ask your Excellency to shield and protect us in our constitutional rights, while we are passing through the territory over which you have jurisdiction. And should any of the exiles be under the necessity of stopping in this territory for a time, either in the settled or unsettled parts, for the purpose of raising crops, by renting farms or upon the public lands, or to make the necessary preparations for their exile in any lawful way, we humbly petition your Excellency to use an influence and power in our behalf: and thus preserve thousands of American citizens, together with their wives and children from intense sufferings, starvation and death.

And your petitioners will ever pray.[302]

No reply to this communication was ever received.

At high noon on March 1, five hundred wagons moved out for the West. Fighting the bitter cold and the snow, and alternating between foot-deep mud and frozen mishmash, the westering wanderers traveled 4 to 5 miles per day. Most nights, Englishman William Pitt's Nauvoo Brass Band "often beguiled the exiles into forgetfulness of their trials and discomforts."[303] But Pitt and his players served in other ways, too. Having early on been invited to play a concert in an eastern Iowa town, Pitt's brass band frequently sought out such opportunities in communities along the trail route. They were frequently welcomed. It seemed amazing to many in these crowds, wrote one chronicler, that these wandering exiles "could thus forget all their sorrows and their wrongs and minister to the pleasure of those who, at best, had but small sympathy with them."[304]

On the banks of Locust Creek, another Brit, William Clayton[305], wrote down the words for the quintessential and beloved Mormon anthem, "Come, Come Ye Saints" (using the English folk tune "All is well" for melody):

> Come, come, ye Saints, no toil nor labor fear;
> But with joy wend your way.
> Though hard to you this journey may appear,
> Grace shall be as your day.
> 'Tis better far for us to strive
> Our useless cares from us to drive;
> Do this, and joy your hearts will swell—
> All is well! All is well!

---

[302]History of Brigham Young, Ms., entry 28 February, 1846, p. 65.

[303]B. H. Roberts, *Comprehensive History of the Church*, Vol. 3, Ch. 72, p. 47.

[304]B. H. Roberts, *Comprehensive History of the Church*, Vol. 3, Ch. 72, p. 48.

[305]It has been estimated that more than four thousand English converts were among those fleeing Nauvoo.

Why should we mourn or think our lot is hard?
'Tis not so; all is right.
Why should we think to earn a great reward
If we now shun the fight?
Gird up your loins; fresh courage take.
Our God will never us forsake;
And soon we'll have this tale to tell—
All is well! All is well!

We'll find the place which God for us prepared,
Far away in the West,
Where none shall come to hurt or make afraid;
There the Saints will be blessed.
We'll make the air with music ring,
Shout praises to our God and King;
Above the rest these words we'll tell—
All is well! All is well!

And should we die before our journey's through,
Happy day! All is well!
We then are free from toil and sorrow, too,
With the just we shall dwell!
But if our lives are spared again
To see the Saints their rest obtain,
Oh, how we'll make this chorus swell—
All is well! All is well!

On April 25, the advance company made camp at a place they named Garden Grove, seventy-nine days and 150 miles from Nauvoo. Here, spring finally in the air, a council meeting was held in which it was determined that a large company of the Saints would remain and build up a temporary trail camp, its primary purpose being to supply and sustain those coming behind (and many of those in the present company). Accordingly, 359 men reported to Brigham Young for duty in the camp. Various appointments set them to felling trees to build fences and houses, digging wells, building bridges, and preparing the land for cultivation. Seed was sown, and the welcome mats came out.

"There was no place for idlers there," wrote B. H. Roberts, "indeed idleness persisted in was made cause for disfellowship from the camp."[306]

The only idlers may have been the dying.

We . . . had a young boy given into our care by his father, his mother being dead; his father wished him to go with us to the mountains and we were to look after him the same as our own. On Saturday, the 25th, we reached a grove which they named "Garden Grove." . . . This was a beautiful place, plenty of timber and water. Our boy, George Patten, still got worse and became as helpless as a babe—was out of his head, and to all appearance could not live.

[George] had by this time become unconscious. I got up and went to the bedside of the sick boy while my husband and Brother Brownell could have a little rest. They both thought the boy could not possibly live many hours. So I took my seat beside the poor sick boy and began to reason with myself. My reasoning was something like this. I thought to myself this poor dying boy was put into our charge to watch over the same as one of our own children; could we give up one of our own children to die without using all the faith within our reach to plead with the Lord to spare the dear one and not take it away from us; this boy had no mother living to plead with the Lord to spare the dear one and not take it to impress it upon me what to do for poor George—for he was a good boy, and we all loved him.

So when I got up from praying I was led by my feelings to put a teaspoonful of consecrated oil in his mouth; his tongue was drawn far back in his mouth and was very black, and his breathing rattling and heavy, and his eyes to all appearance set in his head. I did not see that he swallowed the oil, so I anointed his face and head with the oil, asking the Lord to bless the same; then, in a little while gave him another teaspoonful of oil, asking the Lord at the same time with a humble heart to spare the boy and accept of my feeble efforts in his behalf.

I felt broken-hearted before the Lord, and to my great joy, I noticed that George opened his eyes and looked upon me as though he was astonished.

---

[306]B. H. Roberts, *Comprehensive History of the Church*, Vol. 3, Ch. 72, p. 54.

I said, "George do you know me?"

He spoke in a whisper, "Yes."

Oh, how glad I felt by this time. Mr. Rich had woken up and inquired how the boy was, saying afterwards that he almost feared he was gone. I said to him come and see; the boy looked at him and smiled which astonished Mr. Rich so much that he turned to me and said, 'What has caused such a change?' I said to him prayer and faith, and hope in our Father in Heaven. My husband was truly affected, and told me the boy's life would be spared to yet be a blessing to me in some future time.

And from that time on the dear boy continued to mend slowly and got well and proved himself to be a blessing to me and my children many years afterwards when my husband was away from home on a mission, and me and my children were destitute and needed help. . . . And when George would help me he would always say "Mam," for that is what he calls me, he would say, "Mam, I owe my life to you, for your faith and prayers saved me from death."[307]

In late April, a matter that had been discussed several times to no firm conclusion finally came to a head on the Iowa prairies. A letter from Apostle George A. Smith to Brigham Young sums up and responds to the decision: "If you in your wisdom should think it best to sell the [Nauvoo temple] for to help the poor in the present emergency, we frankly concur notwithstanding we feel opposed to a Methodist Congregation listening to a Mob Priest in that holly [sic] place."[308]

Brigham even set the price: two hundred thousand dollars, a paltry one-fifth of its construction cost.

It never sold, but it would soon change hands nonetheless.

On May 18, some 27 miles farther west near what is today the small town of Thayer, a similar temporary town was established. Apostle Parley P. Pratt named this one Mount Pisgah, like the mount from which Moses was allowed to glimpse the Promised Land.[309] Again, fences, farms, and appointed stewards were left behind.

---

[307]Sarah Rich Autobiography, typescript, Brigham Young University Studies, p. 55.

[308]Brigham Young Papers, cited in *Dialogue,* Vol. 19, No. 4, pp. 102–103.

[309]See Num. 20:10–11; Deut. 1:37, 3:26.

From Pisgah, Brigham Young led an advance company onward, reaching "Indian Town" (today's Council Bluffs) on the Missouri River June 14. From there, it could have been possible to complete the journey to the valley of the Great Salt Lake, 1,050 miles away, by fall. However, at least two things changed Brigham's mind. The first was Iowa itself: 300 miles, every one of them brutal, had devoured nearly four and a half months. And the second was the U.S. Army. They caught up with the stragglers in Mount Pisgah.

On June 26, Captain James Allen of the U.S. Regular Army out of Fort Leavenworth rode into the refugee camp with a retinue of three and a request: five hundred able men to join U.S. forces in the recently declared war with Mexico (May 13, 1846). You can imagine the reception he got: the nation which had refused to aid them when they were residents now had the audacity to ask for five hundred of their best men to fight in the war against the landlord of the territory to which they were now fleeing for their own safety. Nevertheless, Wilford Woodruff, presiding elder of the camp, stated he could only refer the captain to Brigham Young, 130 miles west at the Missouri River. So Allen and his men continued west. Woodruff sent his own messenger, who arrived one day ahead of the captain. Brigham Young saw it an answer to prayer.

Back in January, he had sent an epistle to President James K. Polk offering to build "block houses and stockade forts" along the trail to the Rocky Mountains for the benefit of all future travelers. If the U.S. government would compensate them for their efforts, the Saints would build, then politely abandon, a string of secure shelters on their way out of the United States. The request was ignored.

Now with the Mexican problem—the Latter-day Saints were heading west anyway—Polk saw his answer. He confided in his diary of June 2, 1846, "Col. [Stephen W.] Kearny . . . authorized to receive into service as volunteers a few hundred of the Mormons who are now on their way to California, with a view to conciliate them, attach them to our country, and prevent them from taking part against us."

Although the prolonged absence of five hundred able-bodied men would severely challenge the exodus to the West, Brigham Young recognized that the promised military pay, clothing, and supplies—which battalion volunteers would be entitled to keep—could be of great benefit to isolated pioneers wresting a new life from the untried soil of a yet distant home.

But it may have been more fundamental than that. Fourteen and a half years later, from a pulpit in Salt Lake City, Brigham Young revealed what he hadn't dared reveal to the disheartened masses on that windswept Iowa plain. In a conference address given February 17, 1861, Young referred to Missouri Senator Thomas Hart Benton as "the mainspring and action of governments in driving us into these mountains." Brigham's claim was that Benton, who had abetted their expulsion from Missouri eight years before, had made a deal with President Polk to try the Mormons loyalty, and "unless they turned out five hundred men to fight the battles of the United States in Mexico," the state militia in Missouri was authorized to "destroy every man, woman, and child" among them.[310]

The reality of the matter is not entirely clear from the historical record. At least one non-Latter-day Saint contemporary agreed with Brigham's summation, however.[311]

In any case, Young, Willard Richards, and Heber Kimball took up the reins and headed back toward Mount Pisgah, passing more than eight hundred westering wagons along the way and encouraging volunteers among all. "Shirt-sleeved Heber, standing before a deal table and under the flag, gave them, in his rough-and-ready manner, what he thought was a pep talk. He said he did not think the men would have to fight, assured them their wives would be taken care of, that they would never want, and then, in a curious appeal to their faith and manhood, added, 'If any of you die, why die away and the work will go on . . . we will go on and put in a crop.' In spite of, or perhaps because of, this talk their work of recruitment was a success."[312]

To Allen, Brigham promised, "You shall have your men, and if we have not enough men we will furnish you women."[313] Allen got a little of everything. When the newest contingent of the army of the West marched out of Miller's Hollow, Iowa Territory, on July 20 under the command of Captain Allen, it was comprised of 513 men, 34 women, and 51 children, some of them employed as launderers. For many who

---

[310]Journal of Discourses, Vol. 8, p.   t335–p. 336.

[311]see "Views of Colonel Thomas L. Kane on a Government for Deseret" in Wilford Woodruff's Journal, 26th Nov., 1849)

[312]Stanley B. Kimball, *Heber C. Kimball: Mormon Patriarch and Pioneer*, p. 139.

[313]The context of this comment about women would suggest that Brigham was speaking facetiously.

had already forfeited nearly everything they owned, families were part of the deal.

So for the next year, the Mormon Trail would follow two routes (okay three, but we'll get to that later). For now, we'll stick with the army.

By the time the Mormon Battalion reached Fort Leavenworth, 150 miles down river, Captain Allen was finding the unusual demographic makeup of his entourage the least of his worries. He reached the fort waning from sickness and died within days. From Leavenworth, Lieutenant Andrew Jackson Smith pushed the battalion onward to Santa Fe. Presumably annoyed with the nature of his force, Smith employed frequent forced marches and other inequities with a dictatorial demeanor. One chronicler of the events stated that any other body of people not already accustomed to being herded from one place to the next "would have mutinied rather that submit to the oppressions."

As the battalion entered Mexican territory, three "sick" detachments were ordered to Fort Pueblo, Colorado, first from western Kansas and later from Santa Fe. Against the contentions of many that families were not to be separated, these detachments included most of the women and children. Fortunately for the remaining volunteers, there was a new commander awaiting their arrival in Santa Fe: Lieutenant Colonel Philip St. George Cooke.

Thus, 340 men, four officers' wives (the wives were all commissioned as privates), and a few children continued on their grueling 2,000-mile, six-month desert march to California, reaching San Diego on January 29, 1847. Along the way, they mapped the country (an effort which played prominently in the Gadsden Purchase of 1853), opened a wagon road, and established a U.S. presence that would, two years later, be officially recognized with the annexing Treaty of Guadalupe Hidalgo. Of their exploits, Commander Cooke offered this example: "The garrison of four presidios of Sonora concentrated within the walls of Tucson gave us no pause. We drove them out, with their artillery, but our intercourse with the citizens was unmarked by a single act of injustice."

Four women and at least six children completed the march; one of them, Lydia Hunter, would die following childbirth in San Diego.

When the battalion completed its march to the Pacific Ocean, fifteen men turned around and escorted Army General Stephen W. Kearny back to Fort Leavenworth with a prisoner: California-based Army Colonel John C. Fremont, for "among other things . . . stirring up a conspiracy with the

Spaniards against the Mormon Battalion, holding forth some of his Missouri mobocratic spleen."[314] Fremont, son-in-law of Missouri Senator Benton, would never forget the ignominy, either. He would hold forth his spleen against the Latter-day Saints again in less than a decade—and to much greater effect.

Eighty-one of the battalion reenlisted and were reassigned to Fort Moore (Los Angeles). The rest, about 245 of them, were honorably discharged. Moving north, most found employment for some time in the area of San Francisco or at Sutter's Mill, where six of them were instrumental in the first discovery of gold on January 24, 1848. By the summer of 1848, having cut yet another wagon road over today's Carson Pass into Nevada and fed survivors of the Donner-Reed expedition, nearly all were in the Valley of the Great Salt Lake.

Which was, after all, their destination in the first place.

The Mormon Battalion's only "battle" was the "Battle of the Bulls," a wild cattle stampede that resulted in the death of fifteen bulls (shot), two mules (gored), and three wounded men. Perhaps its accomplishments were best catalogued by its commanding officer, Colonel Philip St. George Cooke, in his official summation of the journey for his commanders:

History may be searched in vain for an equal march of infantry. Half of it has been through a wilderness, where nothing but savages and wild beasts are found, or deserts where, for want of water, there is no living creature. There, with almost hopeless labor, we have dug deep wells, which the future traveler will enjoy. Without a guide who had traversed them we have ventured into trackless tablelands where water was not found for several marches. With crowbar and pick and axe in hand, we have worked our way over mountains, which seemed to defy aught save the wild goat, and hewed a pass through a chasm of living rock more narrow than our wagons. Thus, marching half naked and half fed, and living upon wild animals, we have discovered and made a road of great value to our country.[315]

---

[314]William Pace Autobiography, *Brigham Young University Studies*, pp. 16–17. "Among other things" includes the fact that Fremont had recently been named governor of California by U.S. Navy Commodore Robert Stockton, an appointment not recognized by incoming General Kearny, who replaced him with another man.

[315]Daniel W. Tyler, *History of the Mormon Battalion,* 254–255.

A country, ironically, from which they had been fleeing for their lives and freedom.[316]

Which, of course, brings us back to Iowa.

Following the mustering of the battalion—and the unexpected labor crossing Iowa—Brigham Young had to consider the wisdom of moving onward to the Salt Lake Valley that summer. Establishing a layover of sorts, a winter quarters, would give the pioneer company time to prepare wagons, gather foodstuff, and make a solid plan. And to gather in a bit of money.

On August 6, in Fort Leavenworth, the battalioneers were paid approximately twenty-one thousand dollars in advance for a year's allotment of uniforms and clothing. Nearly six thousand of it was immediately dispatched to Brigham Young by way of apostle Parley Pratt. Sometime later, another four thousand was received.[317]

But Saints were still flowing out of Nauvoo, three hundred miles away. Hundreds of people remained in the city (including some of Brigham's wives and children), owing either to sheer poverty or assignment. Many worked to complete the temple, and attended to ongoing ordinance work, both for the living and for the dead. On April 30, 1846, with a gilded angel holding a trumpet gracing the tower, the edifice was privately dedicated by Brigham Young's brother, Elder Joseph Young, and then publicly dedicated by Elder Orson Hyde of the Twelve on May 1. The dedicatory process was repeated in sessions covering a three-day period. Those wishing to attend were asked to pay a one-dollar admission fee, the funds being gathered to help those still in Nauvoo move their families and join the main body of the church strung out across Iowa.

Thus, through May and June, an additional nine thousand people, including the families of Elder Hyde and Elder Wilford Woodruff, left Nauvoo in successive waves and set themselves to the task of crossing Iowa.

On June 29, the pioneers encamped at the Missouri completed building a ferryboat on the east bank of the river. The next day, President Young, most of the Twelve, and about three hundred wagons crossed the river seeking a site for the location of the camp, even though some viewed

---

[316]And even more ironically, according to Brigham Young University professor Larry C. Porter, a country in which approximately fifteen percent of the battalion soldiers did not even hold citizenship.

[317]See B. H. Roberts, *Comprehensive History of the Church*, Vol. 3, Ch. 74, pp. 96–97.

the Omaha Indians on the Nebraska side of the river as "not so friendly."[318]

On June 30 or July 1 (accounts vary), Captain Allen and his dragoons rode into the camp with their request. While Brigham saw the silver lining in the request, he also saw the difficulty. His current plans called for an advance company of the pioneers to continue into Nebraska Territory, probably as far as Grand Island, 150 miles away on the Platte, to establish winter quarters. Another group presided over by Bishop George Miller had been instructed to push twenty or thirty wagons as far west as Fort Laramie. But both the land upon which they were currently situated and that to the west were within the boundaries of the Louisiana Purchase, most of it Indian reservation, and could therefore be occupied by whites only by permission of the government. Therefore, proposed Brigham, what did the good captain think of this logic: "[does not] an officer enlisting men in an Indian country [have] a right to say to their families, 'You can stay till your husbands return' "?[319]

Captain Allen thought, in fact, that he did.

With that assurance, Young said he would use whatever influence he had to raise the battalion, although he warned that he "would rather have undertaken to raise 2,000 a year ago in 24 hours than 100 in one week now."[320]

It was soon agreed that, unless later decided otherwise by President Polk, whom he was contacting immediately, Captain Allen would see that the pioneers were given safe quarter in the Indian lands, and throughout their western journey, should they serve their country in this way.

Headquarters, Mormon Battalion
U.S. Volunteers,

July 16th, 1846

The Mormon people, now en route to California, are hereby authorized to pass through the Indian country on that route, and they may

---

[318]Joseph Fielding Smith Jr., *Doctrines of Salvation*, Vol. 3, p. 339.

[319]History of Brigham Young, Ms., 1846, bk. 2, pp. 4, 5

[320]Ibid., p. 44.

make stopping places at such points in the Indian country as may be necessary to facilitate the emigration of their whole people to California, and for such time as may be reasonably required for this purpose.

At such stopping points they may entrench themselves with such stockade works or other fortification as may be necessary for their protection and defense against the Indians. This during the pleasure of the president of the United States.

[Signed] J. Allen,
Lt. Col. U.S.A. Commanding Mormon Battalion of U.S. Volunteers.[321]

Fortunately, President Polk's "pleasure," although history would show him no great friend of the Latter-day Saints, lasted long enough.

Soon, several chiefs of the Pottawattamie tribe on the Iowa side of the Missouri were persuaded to sign a permission for the pioneer encampments to occupy "for a time" their lands. As Iowa was on the threshold of statehood, however, the duration of Mormon encampment and their "real intention"[322] in pausing on their trek was of some concern to Washington. The Latter-day Saints, however, soon found with the Nebraska-side Omahas a friendlier offer: the smallpox-decimated and Sioux-threatened Omahas offered "written permission to remain on their lands two years or as long as might suit their convenience, and to use all the wood and timber they might require."[323] The Latter-day Saints, in return, could offer protective services and food (they were herding upward of thirty thousand head of cattle); "also to assist [the Indians] in building some houses, enclosing fields, teaching their young men husbandry, doing some blacksmithing for them, and trading with them."[324]

Plans for moving onward to Grand Island were abandoned, and

---

[321]Ibid., pp. 98–99.

[322]Letter from the War Department on Saints Occupancy of Indian Lands, Sept. 2, 1846, in B. H. Roberts, *Comprehensive History of the Church*, Vol. 3, Ch. 76, p. 139.

[323]B. H. Roberts, *Comprehensive History of the Church*, Vol. 3, Ch. 76, pp. 140–141.

[324]B. H. Roberts, *Comprehensive History of the Church*, Vol. 3, Ch. 76, p. 140–141.

Bishop Miller and his wagons were called back.[325] In early September, it was finally determined to select winter quarters at a "high plateau overlooking the river" from the Nebraska side some twelve miles north of the ferry crossing.[326] About the same time the battalion reached the Arkansas River on September 11 in what is today western Kansas, several thousand Saints were beginning to scratch the earth and topple trees for cabins in what would become their home for the next eight months. The Latter-day Saints no longer entertained any ideas of finding a permanent residence within the boundaries of then-occupied U.S. territory. The sunset side of the Rockies was the only vision in their minds.

Literally, in Brigham's case. "President Young had a vision of Joseph Smith," church historian George A. Smith would later write, "who showed him the mountain that we now call Ensign Peak, immediately north of Salt Lake City, and there was an ensign [flag] fell upon that peak, and Joseph said, 'Build under the point where the colors fall and you will prosper and have peace.' "[327]

On September 10, the festering over, Nauvoo came under bona fide siege. "Some 1800 armed men, supplied with scientific engineers, and good artillery, attacked the remaining few, who were chiefly lame, blind, widows, fatherless children, and those too poor to get away."[328]

Estimates of the number of Latter-day Saints remaining in the city vary from one hundred to one thousand (and there were many able men among them, both by assignment and by choice). It must be understood that converts immigrating from the eastern states and Europe continued to flow into and through Nauvoo during this period; thus, numbers are fluid at best. In any case, most had spent their life savings just getting to Nauvoo.

"[This] is truly a lonesome and dismal place," wrote one such faithful transient to Brigham Young. "I want to know what I shall do. Is it best for me to remain among the gentiles? . . . My body is almost worn out a struggling to get a shelter for my head. . . . If you think it wisdom for me to come

---

[325]Miller's group wintered approximately one hundred and fifty miles northwest of Winter Quarters at L'Eau qui Coule, or Running Water River.

[326]The remnants of Winter Quarters occupies a site in present-day Florence, Nebraska.

[327]*Journal of Discourses*, Vol. 13, p. 85.

[328]Ibid., Vol. 2, p. 23.

out [to Winter Quarters] this fall, how shall I gather . . . ? Council me as though I was your child or Sister and whatever you say that I will do."[329]

And another wrote: "If you was to see me and my family at this moment, you would say we had either been whitewashed or had risen out of our graves—we have not the least idea where our next meal is to come from. . . . Some subsist by selling their clothes for food. There have been many saints who were preparing as fast as they could to go to the West who have gone to the grave, many literally dying for want—two or three dying in a house."[330]

The Saints weathered cannon artillery bombardment and sniping for the duration of the week. At some point during the fray, Hyrum Smith's widow, Mary Fielding Smith, fled the city with four children and crossed the river, where they lived tentless in the trees along the banks for most of the week.[331] Seven-year-old Joseph would soon drive a team of oxen across Iowa, and another team clear to the Rocky Mountains a year and a half later. At the age of sixty-two he would become the sixth president of the church.

On September 16, church leaders in Nauvoo surrendered the keys of the temple to a government agent, and by the next day most were crossing the river with whatever they could carry, in many cases no more than a hobo's satchel of food and clothing. Called the "poor camp," from three hundred to six hundred people would await rescue from Winter Quarters throughout much of October. Some, like Mary Fielding Smith, would leave in spurts; others, in cottonwood boxes. On October 9, the famished refuges would be the beneficiaries of flocks of exhausted quail that would land in the camps and render themselves easy prey for "sudden succulence."[332]

Having received word of the final siege in Nauvoo, in late September Brigham Young would call upon the faithful in Winter Quarters to go rescue their brethren: "Let the fire of the covenant which you made in the House of the Lord burn in your hearts like flame unquenchable, till

---

[329]Elizabeth Gilbert to Brigham Young, 13 August 1846, Brigham Young Papers.

[330]Thomas Bullock Papers, cited in Bennett, *Dialogue*, Vol. 19, No. 4, p. 103.

[331]Joseph's widow, Emma, would remain in Nauvoo and separate herself from the Utah church. Mary Fielding Smith, though widowed and wandering impoverished, would distribute both money and flour to the even poorer as she crossed Iowa later that month.

[332]With all thanks to Wallace Stegner for his more creative and inimitably original "sudden beef."

you, by yourselves or delegates . . . rise up with his team and go straight-away and bring a load of the poor from Nauvoo . . . [for] this is a day of action and not of argument."[333] By mid- and late October, two rescue parties had returned to eastern Iowa to gather the final refugees and help them to the banks of the Missouri three hundred miles away.

The battalion was just south of Albuquerque, well into Mexican ter-ritory, and cutting back to half rations.

Thus "while the flower of Israel's camp was sustaining the wings of the American eagle by their influence and arms in a foreign country, their brothers, sisters, fathers, mothers and children were driven by mob vio-lence from a free and independent State, of the same national republic, and were compelled to flee from the fire, the sword, the musket and the cannon's mouth as from the demon of death."[334]

The demon would yet find them.

---

[333]*Journal History,* Sept. 28, 1846.

[334]General epistle from the Council of the Twelve Apostles, to the Church of Jesus Christ of Latter-day Saints abroad, dispersed throughout the Earth, December 23, 1847, in *Bi-ography and Family Record of Lorenzo Snow,* Ch. 22, pp. 159–160.

CHAPTER 14

The Camp of Israel

What formed and cohered in Winter Quarters was a people apart: separate, unique, and alone. No longer did they face the antipathy of Carthage or Quincy, nor even the near-at-hand recurring curiosity of beat reporters in St. Louis or Chicago. To most previous and casual observers, they were simply gone.

Though the term "Camp of Israel" had been used by some among the Saints during various travels dating as far back as the summer of 1839, at Winter Quarters it would become the common, accepted and even preferred appellation. This was modern Israel, with its Prophet, its Exodus from bondage, and its sojourn toward the Promised Land well under way. Winter Quarters would be the staging ground for the biggest and most historic human migration in American history.

At the time of the formal organization of the camp into companies back in March, Brigham Young had been unanimously sustained as its leader—his rightful and able assumption of Joseph's mantle was becoming ever clearer. Already amongst his own people, and within a mere two years among those outside the faith, he was being referred to as "the American Moses." And he was just getting started.

It was Brigham that Colonel Thomas L. Kane sought when he approached from the east.

They were collected a little distance above the Pottawattamie agency. [The] landing, and the large flat or bottom on the east side of the river were crowded with covered carts and wagons; and each each one of the Council Bluff hills opposite was crowned with its own great camp gay with bright white canvas, and alive with busy stir of swarming occupants. In the clear blue morning air the smoke steamed up from more than a thousand cooking fires. Countless roads and bypaths checkered all manner of geometric figures on the hillsides. Herd boys were dozing upon the slopes; sheep and horses, cows and oxen, were feeding around them, and other herds in the luxuriant meadow of the then-swollen river. From a single point I counted four thousand head of cattle in view at one time. As I approached it seemed to me the children there were to prove still more numerous.

Hastening by these, I saluted a group of noisy boys, whose purely vernacular cries had for me an invincible home-savoring attraction. It was one of them, a bright-faced lad, who, hurrying on his jacket and trousers, fresh from bathing in the creek, first assured me I was at my right destination. He was a mere child; but he told me of his own accord where I had best go and seek my welcome, and took my horse's bridle to help me pass. . . .

There was something joyous for me in my rambles about this vast body of pilgrims. I could range the wild country wherever I listed, under safeguard of their moving host. Not only in the main camps was all stir and life, but in every direction, it seemed to me I could follow "Mormon roads" and find them beaten hard, and even dusty, by the tread and wear of the cattle and vehicles of emigrants laboring over them. By day, I would overtake and pass, one after another, what amounted to an army train of them; and at night, if I encamped at the places where the timber and running water were found together, I was almost sure to be within call of some camp or other, or at least within sight of its watchfires. Wherever I was compelled to tarry, I was certain to find shelter and hospitality, scant, indeed, but never stinted, and always honest and kind. After a recent unavoidable association with the border inhabitants of western Missouri and Iowa, the vile scum which our own society, to apply the words of [another], "like the great ocean washes its frontier shores," I can scarcely describe the gratification I felt in associating again with persons who were almost all of eastern American origin—persons of refined and cleanly habits and decent language, and every day seemed to bring with it its own special incident, fruitful in the illustration of habits and character.[335]

Non-Mormon Kane's association with the Latter-day Saints was relatively young, but not untested. A twenty-four-year-old lawyer and soldier from Pennsylvania and the son of a prominent judge, he had first heard

---

[335]From Kane's Lecture before the Historical Society of Pennsylvania. *The Mormons*, March 26, 1850, pp. 25–27.

of the plight of the Latter-day Saints only months before in Philadelphia, where Jessee Little was making public pleas for assistance to aid his embattled people then being driven from their own homes in Nauvoo. Kane immediately drafted some letters of introduction for Little to carry to Washington, D.C., and soon joined him there, where, in due time, the idea for a Mormon Battalion came forth from the halls of power. Kane was in the Missouri River camp by the time Captain Allen arrived with his request.

In a letter written to President Polk on August 9, Young thanked the chief executive for his generosity in forming the battalion. He also praised his choice of Kane as an unofficial ambassador between them: "[His] presence in our midst, and the ardor with which he has espoused the cause of a persecuted and suffering people . . . have kindled up a spark in our hearts which had been well nigh extinguished."[336]

Though official church records do not record Kane as ever having formally converted to the faith (rumors contend to the contrary), he would move in and out of church history for the next forty years, always in the role of an effective champion.

In Winter Quarters, a town—however impermanent—began to rise. Kane would later write that it was as if the "people and improvements [had been] transplanted there unbroken" from another place. Although the practice of establishing winter quarters was nothing new to transient inhabitants of the western frontier, the practice of doing so according to a detailed plat map was. Brigham Young helped survey and lay out the town, following a "City of Zion" design envisioned some years before by Joseph Smith. "The city was laid off into 41 blocks; and there were 820 lots," according to the History of Brigham Young.[337] Winter Quarters soon had residential street names, stockyards, foundries, and a gristmill. Most men in the community were employed building wagons, repairing equipment, securing food supplies from around the region, or in making willow baskets and washboards to be sold to the other Iowa and Missouri settlers in the spring. To queries of why there was so much infrastructure in a settlement not meant to last more than a year or two, Brigham Young

---

[336]James R. Clark, *Messages of the First Presidency*, Vol. 1, p. 300.

[337]History of Brigham Young Ms., bk. 3, p. 61.

explained that "if the saints did not reap any [financial] benefits from it, the Indians whose lands they then occupied, probably would."[338]

By late December 1846, the west-side town was host to nearly six hundred and fifty homes (log and sod) and about thirty-five hundred people, with another twenty-five hundred or so living on the eastern side of the river. But not all of them lived in rigid, nor warm, shelters. Hundreds of dugouts were hewn into the riverbanks and covered with willow branches and dried grass for roofs. Eventually, more than a thousand shelters went up. An additional estimated ten thousand people spent the winter on the open prairies of Iowa.

Yet everyone in sight knew that, come spring, the town builders would move on. The Rocky Mountains were their fixed and immutable goal. Workshops of various kinds were erected, and carpenters, mechanics, and blacksmiths established and plied their trades—all with their eye on the western horizon. Perhaps this time the grass would be allowed to grow and the streams run free before an evacuation was required.

In December, the Saints gave shelter and cattle to a couple of bands of Omaha Indians who had been "roughly treated" by the Sioux. But even by late fall, the Latter-day Saints were well into their own rough treatment at the hands of twin killers, malaria and scurvy. The malarial fever, emanating from the mosquito-clouded marshes of the Missouri River bottoms, soon earned them the nickname of the "Misery Bottoms." The plague seemed to hit the downwind, Iowa-side campers the worst. The "black canker" (scurvy) was less discriminating, taking victims on either side with equal dispatch. The mosquito-borne fever was quick and, for the most part, given their circumstances, unavoidable. But shipments of potatoes from Missouri and the discovery of an abandoned crop of horseradish some miles to the north brought some alleviation to those suffering from scurvy. In all, upward of six hundred people died in the camps by the end of that winter.[339]

---

[338]B. H. Roberts, *Comprehensive History of the Church*, Vol. 3, Ch. 77, pp. 150–151.

[339]"The accrued death rate [at Winter Quarters] comes to 82.1 per thousand. In laymen's terms, that is catastrophic. The most deprived third world regions in this century rarely reach 50 per thousand death rate. Utah in the 1850 census, three years after the Mormons' arrival there, registered a death rate of 21 per thousand." Additionally, an infant mortality rate of 35.5 percent is most likely from available data. (*Women in Winter Quarters*, Maureen Ursenbach Beecher, Sunstone, July 1983)

Diarist Helen Mar Kimball Whitney, who lost a baby there, wrote that "the outlook was indeed a gloomy one, and needed all the faith and hope that could be mustered to sustain us under the circumstances, for death was sweeping away its victims, and want and suffering seemed staring us in the face. . . . That was among the saddest chapters in my history."[340]

A brief look at the demographics of the Winter Quarters camps is instructive. In a census taken that first winter, Shadrach Roundy, named bishop of one of twenty-two Winter Quarters "wards,"[341] said the 101 congregants over whom he had ecclesiastical responsibility included three widows and members of twenty-nine families, comprised of nineteen men in good health, three in distress, three in the battalion, and six absent. Specifically, "twelve of his twenty-nine families, or nearly half, were headed by women."[342]

While adding its own weight of trial and suffering to the backs of men, women, and children full up to the brim with such, Winter Quarters served to transfer the emotional and memorial gaze of Latter-day Saints away from the past—including Jackson County, Nauvoo, and Joseph Smith—and toward the future: the Rocky Mountains, true refuge, and the presidency of Brigham Young. Young would tell the Winter Quarters Saints that he "did not think there had ever been a body of people . . . placed under the same unpleasant circumstances that this people have been, where there was so little grumbling."[343]

Most conversation, in fact, was not concerned with the present at all. According to historian B. H. Roberts, leaving "was the chief topic of

---

[340]Helen Mar Kimball Whitney, "Scenes and Incidents at Winter Quarters," *Women's Exponent* 14 (September 1885):58, as cited by Beecher in *Women in Winter Quarters*, Sunstone 8:4/11 (July 1983).

[341]A ward is the standard congregation in LDS geography and administration. Comprised of between three hundred and six hundred members, it is larger than a "branch" and smaller than a "stake," the latter comprised of five to ten wards. As of year-end 1998, there were 25,550 wards and branches worldwide, growing at a rate of approximately one thousand per year.

[342]*Women in Winter Quarters*, Maureen Ursenbach Beecher, Sunstone, July 1983, citing Shadrach Roundy, Record Book 1845–48, holograph, LDS Church Archives.

[343]*History of the Church*, Vol. 7, Ch. 40, p. 608.

conversation and of discussion wherever two or three were gathered together."[344]

Through the dark days of that midwestern winter, Brigham Young and his leaders consulted maps and published accounts of the Great Basin region. Although John C. Fremont's maps of the region (published in 1845) were an aid to their deliberations, "the great Intermountain West," wrote Roberts, "had not, as yet, inspired a great amount of interest [by the explorers]." Fremont's own account, probably the most extensive, said the intermountain Great Basin was "a region surrounded by lofty mountains; contents almost unknown."

Perfect.

On January 14, 1847, Brigham Young announced to the Saints in Winter Quarters (and subsequently elsewhere) a revelation that would direct the Latter-day Saints for the next ten months and firmly establish him as the new Joseph.

Camp of Israel
Winter Quarters, Iowa Territory

The Word and Will of the Lord concerning the Camp of Israel in their journeyings to the West:

Let all the people of the Church of Jesus Christ of Latter-day Saints, and those who journey with them, be organized into companies, with a covenant and promise to keep all the commandments and statutes of the Lord our God. And this shall be our covenant: That we will walk in all the ordinances of the Lord.

Let each company provide themselves with all the teams, wagons, provisions, clothing, and other necessaries for the journey, that they can. When the companies are organized let them go to with their might, to prepare for those who are to tarry. Let each company, with their captains and presidents, decide how many can go next spring; then choose out a sufficient number of able-bodied and expert men, to take teams, seeds, and farming utensils, to go as pioneers to prepare for putting in spring crops. Let each company bear an equal proportion, according to the dividend of their property, in taking the poor, the

---

[344]B. H. Roberts, *Comprehensive History of the Church*, Vol. 3, Ch. 77, pp. 154–155.

widows, the fatherless, and the families of those who have gone into the army, that the cries of the widow and the fatherless come not up into the ears of the Lord against this people.

Let each company prepare houses, and fields for raising grain, for those who are to remain behind this season; and this is the will of the Lord concerning his people.

I am the Lord your God, even the God of your fathers, the God of Abraham and of Isaac and of Jacob. I am he who led the children of Israel out of the land of Egypt; and my arm is stretched out in the last days, to save my people Israel.

Amen.[345]

Almost immediately following the reading of this document to the pioneers, preparations for the departure were under way. Messengers were dispatched to the various encampments—Miller and his company on the Running Water River to the northwest, the Iowa-side camps, and those still on the prairies—and to all Saints abroad and asunder, naming the men Young wanted to accompany him in the Vanguard Company and those who were to take the lead in organizing other companies to follow. While most of Miller's group began to gather in Winter Quarters, where they were instructed to join in the planting and harvesting of spring crops, Miller himself and about thirty companions separated themselves from Brigham's leadership and headed to Texas.

On Monday, April 5, 1847, the streams were running freely, and crops were just beginning to show. Under instructions from President Young, Apostle Heber C. Kimball moved out with six of his company's wagons and moved about four miles to the west. On April 6, at the seventeenth Annual General Conference of the church, Brigham Young was sustained by the membership as the presiding elder of the church. The next day, he and another twenty-five wagons of the Vanguard Company pulled out.[346] Together, the aggregating Vanguard, or Pioneer, Com-

---

[345]See James R. Clark, Messages of the First Presidency, Vol. 1, p. 315; or *Doctrine and Covenants*, Section 136.

[346]Winter Quarters (the west side of the river) would be emptied of residents after the summer of 1848. By 1853, only the cemetery remained, and in 1856 settlers moving into the area named it Florence, which was eventually absorbed in the growth of Omaha, Nebraska, and became a part of that city. The Iowa side of the river will yet regain our attention.

pany—143 men, 3 women, and 2 children—traveled to a spot about 35 miles west of Winter Quarters on the Elkhorn River, where they engaged themselves in building a ferry to enable those following the subsequent luxury of not getting their feet wet. Mormon ferries and bridges would soon dot the course all the way to the Great Basin.

Of those in this Vanguard Pioneer Company, "as far as we can determine," wrote Joseph Fielding Smith, "21 were natives of New York, 14 were natives of Vermont, 11 of Ohio, 10 of Massachusetts, four of Pennsylvania, four of Connecticut, three of North Carolina, two of Illinois, two of Virginia, two of Maine, three of New Hampshire, two of Mississippi, two of New Jersey, three of Tennessee, and one each of Alabama, Indiana, South Carolina, Kentucky and Rhode Island. . . . Five were natives of Canada, four of England and one each of Ireland, Scotland, Denmark, Norway, and Germany."[347]

Knowing little about the rigors of the journey ahead of them, it was not initially planned to include women and children in the Vanguard Company. "But Harriet Page Wheeler Young, the wife of Lorenzo D. Young, brother of Brigham Young, being in feeble health, and her life imperilled by the malaria atmosphere of the Missouri bottoms, pleaded successfully for the privilege of accompanying her husband to the mountains. The other two women were Clara Decker Young, [plural] wife of President Brigham Young, and Ellen Sanders Kimball, wife of Heber C. Kimball. The success of the first of the trio—born of her necessities— made possible the permission for the other two."[348]

On April 15, Brigham Young "called the Pioneer camp together and addressed the brethren on the necessity of being faithful, humble and prayerful on the journey. Exhorted the camp to vigilance in guarding and informed the brethren that I had intimations that the Pawnee Indians were advised to rob us. Said we should go in such a manner as to claim the blessings of heaven."[349]

Finally, they would get some.

---

[347]Joseph Fielding Smith Jr., *Doctrines of Salvation*, Vol. 3, p. 350.

[348]B. H. Roberts, *Comprehensive History of the Church*, Vol. 3, Ch. 78, pp. 163–164.

[349]History of Brigham Young, Ms., bk. 3, p. 83.

CHAPTER 15

Road to Zion

"We traveled the first 500 miles without any grass," wrote Wilford Woodruff of their early spring exodus. "With the exception of the little grain we fed our animals, they lived entirely on the bark of cottonwood limbs and saplings which they gnawed from the cottonwood we would lay before them for their night's meal."[350]

The austere circumstances of the sojourn were, in fact, largely voluntary. By the summer of 1847, the route along the wide, shallow, and meandering Platte[351]—the Oregon Trail—was "a national highway." On the south side of the river, that is. The Mormons traveled the north.

"Church leaders were persuaded that the inconvenience of making a new trail over the Platte plains was preferable to contact with the western emigration pressing up the [south] bank of the stream, a large portion of which was from western Missouri, and among the companies were many of the old enemies of the saints, who less than a decade before had aided in their expulsion from that state."[352]

At one point in early May, having been informed by an eastern-bound group of fur trappers that the southside trail was indeed the easier track, the leaders met to consider crossing over. Wrote Woodruff:

We were convinced that it would be better for us as a company to cross the river and take the old traveled road to Laramie, as there was good grass all the way on that side, while the Indians were burning it all off on the north of the river where we were traveling.[353] But when

---

[350]Wilford Woodruff, *Collected Discourses*, Vol. 1, July 24, 1888.

[351]"The consensus regarding this river was that it was a mile wide, six inches deep, too thick to drink, too thin to plow, hard to cross because of quicksand, impossible to navigate, too yellow to wash in, and too pale to paint with." (Stanley B. Kimball, *Heber C. Kimball*, p. 154)

[352]B. H. Roberts, *Comprehensive History of the Church*, Vol. 3, ch. 78, pp. 166–167.

[353]"It was the custom of the Indians in the spring to set fire to the dry grass left over from the previous year in order to give the new growth a better and earlier start, and thus bring

we took into consideration the situation of the next company, and the thousands that would follow, and as we were the Pioneers and had not our wives and children with us—we thought it best to keep on the north side of the river and brave the difficulties of burning prairies to make a road that should stand as a permanent route for the saints independent of the then-emigrant road, and let the river separate the emigrating companies that they need not quarrel for wood, grass, or water; and when our next company came along the grass would be much better for them than it would be on the south side, as it would grow up by the time they would get along; and the vote was called and it was unanimous to go on the north side of the river; so the camp again moved on.[354]

Which, as it turns out, is exactly what happened.

Self-enforced penury aside, for the most part, the Pioneer Company of the Camp of Israel traveled without incident and little suffering, following the Platte River to Confluence Point (central Nebraska) and then the North Platte past Chimney Rock, Scotts Bluff, and into today's Wyoming, where the blue line of the Rockies began to rough up the western horizon.

Here, "in one instance we had to form a guard of a wedge shape for three days and nights to keep our company from being trampled to death by an enormous herd of buffalo that had gathered from the mountains and were migrating in a solid body to the plains below. The herd was judged to be sixty miles in length, and numbered not less than one million. They were traveling east, and we were traveling west. We were three days passing through the herd, and we all breathed freer when we were clear of them. No other class of men will ever witness the same scene again upon the face of the earth."[355]

---

the buffalo herds to these new pastures. The desire to have the grass of the plains start to grow as early as possible in the spring had led those interested in traveling along the route on the south side of the Platte to fire the grass in the fall, and thus provided earlier pasturage for immigrant and fur traders' trains. But the Indian 'spring-burning' on the north side of the Platte often left the Mormon Pioneers only blackened plains in which to camp." (Ibid, pp. 173–174)

[354]Wilford Woodruff's journal, entry for May 4, 1847.

[355]Wilford Woodruff, *Collected Discourses*, Vol. 1, July 24, 1888; I cannot read the verse without growing emotional.

As they approached Fort Laramie on June 2, exactly halfway to the Salt Lake valley, the grass was growing just fine.

And the Mississippians were waiting. Enter Great Basin Route No. Three.

Three days after the initial exodus from Nauvoo fourteen months before, knowing his fellow Saints were on their way west, a tough Tennessee-born missionary named John Brown had led a number of wagons loaded with about sixty converts—men, women, and children—out of Greenwood Springs, Mississippi, and on toward the Rocky Mountains. Thus, news of the battalion recruitment in central Iowa and the resultant stopover on the Missouri River never reached them.

This "Mississippi Company" (Alabamans and others among them) pushed their ox teams the 420 miles to St. Louis and trudged cross-state to Independence, where another sixteen people joined the company. Now numbering approximately eighty people, they then angled northwest amidst the mounting movement on the Oregon Trail (on the south side), intending to rendezvous with the larger body of Saints at the Platte River somewhere around Fort Kearny in what is today south-central Nebraska. The larger body was nowhere in sight. Their fellows, in Winter Quarters, were about 170 miles to the east.

Knowing they were on the intended route of the general exodus, and supposing they were running behind, the Mississippi Company decided to go west at a faster clip and catch up. They beat Brother Brigham to Fort Laramie by nearly a year.

There, within sight of mountains several thousand feet higher than anyone in the group had ever seen, the members of the Mississippi Company finally learned that no Mormons had yet been this way. Although it was still midsummer, Brown and his Mississippi captain, William Crosby, realized they knew less about Young's plans than they wished and much less about the high country to the west than they cared to guess at. When a French trapper named Jean Richards invited them to winter near his camp 260 miles to the south, they tarried but a moment. Four weeks later, on August 7, 1846, the Mississippi Company pulled into the tiny four-year-old trading post known as "Fort" Pueblo, on the Arkansas River in what is now southern Colorado.

His converts soon comfortable in log cabins, John Brown and six companions turned back to the east to gather their families still in that region for the exodus west. On September 12, they met the Mormon

Battalion preparing to ford the Arkansas River in the vicinity of today's Dodge City, Kansas.

Regular Army Lieutenant Andrew Jackson Smith could hardly believe his good luck. Hearing of a comfortable settlement of Latter-day Saints several days west up this very river, he ordered a group of ailing soldiers and most of the women and children detached from the crusade. Under escort of ten soldiers, he sent them 270 miles upriver to this instant city at the foot of the Rockies.

Within the next couple of months—first from Santa Fe, then from the area of today's Truth or Consequences—another three "sick detachments" would be escorted to Pueblo, boosting the Latter-day Saint population in that locale to near three hundred by November.

In his landmark *The Oregon Trail,* Francis Parkman described his own autumn entry to that well-timbered site in the Arkansas River bottoms, until then just a small trading post: "After half an hour's riding we saw the white wagons of the Mormons drawn up among the trees. Axes were sounding, trees were falling and log huts going up along the edge of the woods and upon the adjoining meadow. As we came up the Mormons left their work and seated themselves on the timber around us, when they began earnestly to discuss points of theology."

In exchange for supplies—the preaching was free—the Latter-day Saints helped the perhaps fifteen trader-trappers (most with wives and children) homebased in that vicinity to erect a number of cabins in a fashion so as to protectively circumscribe and buttress the inner mud-walled "fort." They built a row of cabins for themselves about a half mile away, on the south side of the Arkansas. According to John Brown's autobiography, the settlers then put in a turnip patch, pumpkins, beans, and melons.

There, planting, preaching, and patiently waiting, the combined companies passed an unusually mild winter. It was, in reality, a fortuitous commingling: the previous establishment, however recent, of the well-heeled Mississippi Company at Fort Pueblo likely saved the lives, or unquestionably eased the way, for the furloughed battalioneers. And as they were then a mere two days' ride from Bent's Fort—an authentic military installation on the Colorado plains—the battalion soldiers were enabled to secure military provisions and even occasional employment at the fort.

The still-marching battalioneers were just turning west about 500 miles to the south. Tripe for dinner was starting to sound good. And the

Saints in Winter Quarters were trying to keep their sod chimneys from collapsing in on them as the frost-laden "bricks" melted.

By the middle of the following April, however, natural movement of both goods and gossip along the growing western trail system assured the Pueblo Saints that Brigham was finally on his way. Toward the end of the month, a group of seventeen of them (six were women/girls) began the trek north to Fort Laramie. They had been encamped in the vicinity of the fort for two weeks when Brigham Young and the Pioneer Company arrived. With him was John Brown.

Following their encounter with the battalion eight months before, Brown and his companions had made good time back to Mississippi and Alabama, arriving in late October. But before they could load the wagons, word came from Winter Quarters that Brown should delay the southern exodus, but come himself, with "some able-bodied men." Thus, Brown and three other Mississippians (two additional men died on the trek north) were in that high plains reunion. It was the second time in less than a year that John Brown and the seventeen campers had been at Fort Laramie.

Being then apprised of the situation 260 miles to the south, Brigham sent four men to retrieve and accompany the remainder of the Pueblo company back up to Fort Laramie. They were already two days north of Pueblo.

At Fort Laramie, the pioneers were suddenly in regular contact with other westering immigrants, with supply trains, traders, mountain men, and news. Of the latter, immigrants by the thousands were in motion on the Oregon Trail. A small party of men moving rapidly from Saint Joseph, Missouri, reported they had passed perhaps two thousand wagons en route for the West. Some of them would reach the fort within days.

Moving out on June 4, Brigham's company, now joined by the Mississippi group on the south side of the Platte, began to experience the gradual but perceptible rise toward the Rockies. Flora and fauna began to change. Streams began to be more frequent. "Excellent feed, thrifty timber, plenty of game, beautiful scenery. . . . Instead of sand and continual barrenness without water," wrote Erastus Snow, "we have found hard roads through the hills, and at convenient distances beautiful creeks skirted with timber, and bottoms covered with grass."[356]

---

[356]Erastus Snow's journal, entry June 10, cited in *Improvement Era*, Vol. xv, p. 165.

On June 8, the pioneers met a small party of men hauling pelts toward the east, coming from Fort Bridger, 300 miles to the west. From them, the company learned that a healthy man on a strong horse could ride from Fort Bridger to the Great Salt Lake in two days, "and that the Utah country was beautiful."[357]

The trapper's captain, James Grieve, also told the pioneers of a small boat made from buffalo skins that his party had concealed some miles north, and he gave the Pioneer Company permission to appropriate it. Thus, Young dispatched a company of about forty men to move ahead quickly, secure the boat, and make preparations for ferrying the whole Pioneer Company across the river.

By the time the main camp reached "last crossing" of the North Platte River on June 12, the advance boys had certainly secured the boat and were in fact making a secure wage ferrying the Oregon immigrants across. To date: "1,295 lbs. of flour, at the rate of two and a half cents per pound; also meal, beans, soap and honey at corresponding prices, likewise two cows, total bill for ferrying $78.00."[358] "It looked as much of a miracle to me," wrote Wilford Woodruff, "to see our flour and meal bags replenished in the midst of the [Wyoming] Hills, as it did to have the children of Israel fed on manna in the wilderness."[359] Brigham Young thereafter referred to the boat as "the revenue cutter."

The Pioneer camp remained at the "last crossing" for five days, during which Brigham directed the beginning of construction of a more permanent ferry across the river. It would become known throughout the region (along with at least one other site) as "Mormon Ferry." And then, leaving ten men to man the ferry, they pulled out. As noted by historian Stanley B. Kimball, "the easy part . . . was over."[360]

They had followed the Platte for more than 600 miles. Now they were in the Sweetwater country, where some of the most desperate and compelling drama of the American pioneering era would occur eight years later. Climbing toward the spine of the continent, they were frequently forced to zigzag back and forth across the Sweetwater, using the revenue

---

[357]History of Brigham Young. Ms., 1847, p. 92.

[358]Ibid., p. 94.

[359]Woodruff's journal, entry for June 13.

[360]Stanley B. Kimball, *Heber C. Kimball*, p. 164.

cutter again and again to ferry supplies. On June 26, 275 trail miles from Fort Laramie, they topped South Pass, crossed the Continental Divide, and gazed, for the first time, on country that drained not to the east and the Atlantic, but to the west and the Pacific.

It looked about like what it looked like straight behind them: high, windswept sage country laced with rocky ridges and cold meandering streams. But to the west was freedom, solitude, a place to start once again.

Just beyond South Pass, at Pacific Springs, they met up with Moses "Black" Harris, a mountaineer with extensive knowledge of the country into which they were heading, including the Salt Lake basin. His summation of the colonization possibilities within the latter, wrote Apostle Orson Pratt, was "unfavorable."

Perfect.

Two days later they came upon Jim Bridger. Each man's reputation having preceded him to this confluence in the wilderness, the famed mountain man asked for a parley with Brigham Young, who happily agreed. Inquiring as to the Mormons' destination, the mountaineer attempted to dissuade them. "Bridger considered it imprudent to bring a large population into the Great Basin," wrote Brigham Young, "until it was ascertained that grain could be raised; he said he would give $1,000 for a bushel of corn raised in that basin."[361] Young replied: "Wait a little, and we will show you."[362]

In fact, Bridger's comment has oft been misconstrued. Wilford Woodruff records (others concur) that "[Bridger] spoke more highly of the Great Basin for a settlement than [Moses] Harris did; that it was his paradise, and if this people settled in it, he wanted to settle with them. There was but one thing that could operate against it becoming a great grain country, and that would be the frost. He did not know but the frost would kill the corn,"[363] and thus the $1,000 reward to whomever could show him his "paradise" was indeed arable country.

Brigham would indeed grow the bushel. As far as is known, he never got, not sought, his thousand dollars.

---

[361]History of Brigham Young, Ms., bk. 3, p. 95.

[362]Erastus Snow, *Utah Pioneers,* July 25, 1880, p. 43.

[363]Woodruff's journal, entry for June 28.

Arriving at the Green River two days later, they encountered Samuel Brannan, who had taken a ship full of eastern-states immigrants around the Horn and up to San Francisco Bay. He shared with the pioneers his good news from the coast, that the soldiers of the battalion were safe, employed, and enjoying a season of honor in the heavenly clime of the Pacific. Additionally, Brannan was getting rich there and would tolerate no suggestion that anything but the coast was the proper home for the Saints. He had just passed through the Great Basin (by way of Fort Hall), and it was no place for raising up a kingdom to the Most High.

Brigham never wavered. Joseph's prophecy had been that the Latter-day Saints would go on to become "a mighty people in the midst of the Rocky Mountains." Brigham had even seen in clear vision the summit under which he was to build a city for the Saints, and he would find that summit. He told Brannan he intended to plant his people "on the back-bone of the animal (continent)," where he could raise and eat his own potatoes in peace.

On Monday, July 5, a contingent of five men took the revenue cutter, now mounted on axles and outfitted like a wagon, and headed back toward Fort Laramie, where they hoped to encounter and direct the trailing pioneers. Accompanying them as far as the river ferry (which they had just completed), Brigham Young and his companions encountered an advance team of the Pueblo Saints, waiting to cross. From the opposite bank, they (Young and company) greeted them with a cheer. The remainder of the group was about seven days behind them.

The Pioneer Company broke camp on the morning of July 9, leaving the well-traveled Oregon Trail (which headed northwest) and angling south on a route "but dimly seen," according to Orson Pratt. This highly promoted "Hastings Cutoff" had hosted only four small previous wagon companies the year before. [364] The fourth, composed mainly of members of the James Reed and George Donner families, had gained tragic fame in the Sierra Nevadas of California.[365] But on their way to the Salt Lake

---

[364]It is reported that members of one of these parties "left letters advising others with families and wagons not to attempt it [the Hastings Cutoff]," but the letters were never delivered. (*History of California*, Bancroft, Vol. v, pp. 529–530) Lansford Hastings himself, whose guide was published the year before he actually tried the route with wagons, nearly destroyed the two companies he guided through it.

[365]The Donner party tragedy in the snows of the Sierra Nevada—a result in large measure of the inordinate amount of time it took them to pursue and conquer the Hastings Cutoff

Valley, the Donner party had broken a trail and carved a rough road that would soon favor the Latter-day Saints tremendously.

A day later, Brigham Young and several other members of the company became ill, and soon gravely so with "mountain fever," likely Colorado tick fever. Orson Pratt and a party of men and tools were instructed to move ahead, seeking the Donner-Reed route. Dropping rapidly in elevation down the course now followed by Interstate 80 through Echo Canyon, they entered the broad, fertile valley today occupied by the little town of Henefer. To the northwest stood 300-foot vertical rock walls, flanking the Weber River almost to the water's edge. Straight to the west, along a row of low bluffs, they found traces of Donner's wagon passage, rising gradually to the west. Out came the picks and shovels.

For the next several days, Pratt's advance party hacked and whacked its way up the willow-choked stream bottoms and sage-matted hillsides. Here the Donner party's efforts were clearly visible, and while substantial, they were insufficient to satisfy either Pratt or the needs of the thousands of Mormon wagons that would soon be rolling over this track. Pratt's company chopped, graded, in-filled, backfilled, buttressed, and bridged, even working behind themselves once their wagons had passed over a section.

On July 17, a typical day on the road crew, Pratt's company moved just over 8 miles, criss-crossing the stream thirteen times. The grade was ever upward, with no end to the ascent. What appeared to these pioneers to be mountains—and to Jim Bridger as mere foothills—occupied the landscape in every direction. Wrote Orson Pratt: "Leaving our horses at the foot [of one hill], we ascended to the summit . . . which appeared to be about 2,000 feet high. We had a prospect limited in most directions by still higher peaks; the country exhibited a broken succession of hills piled on hills, and mountains in every direction."[366]

In fact, what even Jim Bridger would have called mountains would soon come into view. Fortunately for the pioneers, they wouldn't have to scale any of them.

On Monday, July 19 (the Sabbath was spent in rest and worship),

---

into the Salt Lake Valley—would claim the lives of thirty-nine of the eighty-seven immigrants. Their remains would be seen by Brannan on his way east and buried by Salt Lake–bound members of the Mormon Battalion on theirs.

[366]Orson Pratt's journal entry for July 17, 1847.

Orson Pratt and John Brown of the Mississippi Company ascended a tall hill, possibly today's "Big Mountain," and caught the first narrow glimpse of the Valley of the Great Salt Lake, about 10 miles away and 4,000 feet below them. Descending now on a grade that would later require the wagons to have poles run through their rear wheels to prevent them from skidding downhill, the two men explored the route as it entered a steep walled canyon hosting a small stream.

Two days later, William Clayton would describe the route: "[There was] hardly room for a road. It is evident that the emigrants who passed this way last year must have spent a great deal of time culling a road through the thickly set timber and heavy brush wood. It is reported that they spent sixteen days in making a road through from Weber River which is thirty-five miles but as the men did not work a quarter of their time much less would have sufficed. However, it has taken us over three days after the road is made although a great many hours have been spent in improving it. In this thick brush wood and around here there are many very large rattlesnakes lurking, making it necessary to use caution while passing through."[367]

Pratt and Brown then returned to their camp, which had moved just over 6 miles in their absence. The main Pioneer Company had nearly caught up. A third group, moving slowly with the head of the apostles, brought up the rear some miles back.

Just after noon on Wednesday, July 21, Apostle Erastus Snow rode into Pratt's advance camp at the foot of Little Mountain carrying a letter from Willard Richards and George A. Smith (with Brigham's blessing). It instructed Snow and Pratt to proceed ahead of the work crew and determine the final course into the valley. With one horse between them, the two continued down the canyon through the afternoon. They soon reached a point at which they could glimpse through trees open country straight to the west. Signs of a great struggle on the hillside to the south revealed the site where the Donner party decided to pull their wagons with horse and chain over a steep hill rather than fight the stream bottom with its choking assemblage of plant life.

"Mr. Snow and myself ascended this hill," recorded Orson Pratt that evening, "from the top of which a broad open valley, about twenty miles wide and thirty long, lay stretched out before us, at the north end of

---

[367]William Clayton's journal, Thursday, July 22, 1847.

which the broad water of Great Salt Lake glistened in the sunbeams, containing high mountainous islands from twenty-five to thirty miles in extent. After issuing from the mountains among which we had been shut up for many days, and beholding in a moment such an extensive scenery open before us, we could not refrain from a shout of joy which almost involuntarily escaped from our lips the moment this grand and lovely scenery was within our view."[368]

Mr. Snow's own account: "From the view we had of the valley from the top of the mountain, we supposed it to be only an arm of prairie extending up from the Utah valley, but on ascending this butte we involuntarily, both at the same instant, uttered a shout of joy at finding it to be the very place of our destination, and beheld the broad bosom of the Salt Lake spreading itself before us."[369]

Pratt and Snow entered the valley and traveled through waist-high grass some distance to the southwest, before recalling that Brigham Young had instructed them to go north upon entering the valley. The place he sought would be to the north. Accordingly, they changed their course. In the late afternoon heat of July (Orson Pratt would record the temperature two days later as 96 degrees), Snow realized at some point that his jacket, which he had laid across his saddle, had fallen off. Thus, he told Pratt to go on ahead, he'd meet him back at the canyon mouth. Pratt did so, eventually wandering over what would become downtown Salt Lake City. He rejoined Snow late in the evening, and the two returned to their camp in the canyon at about 9 P.M.

Meanwhile, the rest of the Pioneer Company moved toward them.

"We have crossed this creek which Elder Pratt names Canyon Creek eleven times during the day," William Clayton would write, "and the road is one of the most crooked I ever saw, many sharp turns in it . . ."

Eventually they would arrive at "Donner Hill."

After traveling one and three-quarters miles, we found the road crossing the creek again to the north side and then ascending up a very steep, high hill. It is so very steep as to be almost impossible for heavy wagons to ascend and so narrow that the least accident might precipitate a wagon down a bank three or four hundred feet—in which case it would

---

[368]Orson Pratt's journal, entry for July 21.

[369]Erastus Snow's journal, entry for July 21, 1847.

certainly be dashed to pieces. Colonel Markham and another man went over the hill and returned up the canyon to see if a road cannot be cut through and avoid this hill. While passing up, a bear started near them but soon was out of sight amongst the very high grass. Brother Markham says a good road can soon be made down the canyon by digging a little and cutting through the bushes some ten or fifteen rods [between 55 and 80 yards]. A number of men went to work immediately to make the road which will be much better than to attempt crossing the hill and will be sooner done.[370]

That evening the England-born and-bred William Clayton would write: "When I commune with my own heart and ask myself whether I would choose to dwell here in this wild looking country amongst the Saints surrounded by friends, though poor . . . or dwell amongst the gentiles with all their wealth and good things of the earth, to be eternally mobbed, harassed, hunted, our best men murdered and every good man's life continually in danger, the soft whisper echoes loud and reverberates back in tones of stern determination: give me the quiet wilderness and my family to associate with, surrounded by the Saints and adieu to the gentile world. . . . If I [only] had my family with me, how happy could I be."

On July 23, Woodruff would top Big Mountain, Brigham Young still prostrate with mountain fever in the back of his wagon, and tell the chief apostle he thought he might want to take a look.

Brigham would write: "I directed Elder Woodruff, who kindly tendered me the use of his carriage, to turn the same half way round, so I could have a view of a portion of Salt Lake Valley. The Spirit of the Lord rested upon me and hovered over the valley, and I felt that there the Saints would find protection and safety. We descended and encamped at the foot of the Little Mountain."

The following day, Woodruff and Young would emerge from the canyon. Most of the Pioneer Company, the advance team of the Pueblo battalioneers, and a good number of the Mississippi Saints were already settling in. In the words of historian Leonard Arrington, "the Mississippians had already mowed the grass and planted a turnip

---

[370]William Clayton journal, Thursday, July 22.

patch." In fact, more than five acres had already been flooded by diverting the waters of what would soon be known as City Creek, and seeds were in the ground.

Gazing over the valley, Brigham spied 12 miles to the northwest an otherwise inconspicuous hill snuggled up to the outer flanks of much more topographically significant summits. It was the hill of his vision, the landmark, the sign. He would name it Ensign Peak.

"This is the right place," he said to Woodruff. "Drive on."[371]

By late fall, another 1,948 pioneers would flow into the Valley off the trail. According to one report:

> As the year 1847 closed there were approximately 10,000 church members in England; 2,000 in Scotland; and 4,160 scattered on a worldwide basis. The church population in the Great Salt Lake Valley was about 2,000, and between 5,000 and 13,000 were at Winter Quarters in Nebraska [in fact, most of these were on the Iowa side of the river, in an area known as Miller's Hollow], and between 2,000 and 4,000 in the various settlements in Iowa [i.e., Garden Grove and Mount Pisgah]. Less than 200 remained in Nauvoo, and between 200 and 300 in the city of St. Louis, Missouri. There were between 7,000 and 13,000 scattered throughout the eastern and the southern states, and 2,000 in the Society [Tahitian] Islands.[372]

That Saturday, July 24, 1847, Brigham Young had completed the first installment of one of the most monumental treks in American history. Over the next twenty-two years, when the Union Pacific Railroad would connect its east- and west-bound tracks at a point just north and west of Salt Lake City, effectively ending the pioneer era, Brigham would be followed by an estimated 68,000 Latter-day Saints,[373] and by the time of his death in 1877, by another 12,000. Their immigration to the Salt Lake valley—a recommended policy for the next five decades—would route an

---

[371]Or so the story goes. The specific quotation cannot be found in the historical record until twenty-two years later (in Woodruff's journal).

[372]Alma Sonne, Conference Report, April 1963, p. 26.

[373]Exact numbers are impossible to calculate. I use here the "correlated" figure incorporated in most of the official church material created for the Mormon Trail sesquicentennial celebration in 1997.

endless supply of converts from dozens of nations to the new seat of Zion.[374]

Some had been there at Palmyra; most had not. Many, but not all, had suffered through Jackson County and made the long walk to Nauvoo. Thousands of others had witnessed Nauvoo only on their way through it for points west. By the mid-1850s, Nauvoo wasn't even on the route. It was hardly on the map.

But all—to the present day—would come to claim the same heritage, a spiritual descendancy from men and women and children who walked some of it, saw any of it, and believed all of it. It would become their story, too.

Yet, it was clearly not the context of a common background that would bring them together, but the vision of a common future. Brigham, for one, hoped his long journey across the continent would bring full closure to one of the most pathetic eras in American history.

He would be half-right: the rest of the United States would indeed forget about it.

[374]The 1997–98 Church Almanac records data on more than three hundred ships sailing from eight nation-ports bringing Latter-day Saints to America between 1840 and 1869.

CHAPTER 16

Transition

I'm one of those Americans (the majority, I'm sure) who never heard the story of the Mormon Trail as a child, even though my grandparents lived within miles of Rebecca Winters's grave outside Scotts Bluff, Nebraska. I remember learning about Mississippi steamboats and the Missouri Compromise, the Gadsden Purchase, and gold at Sutter's Mill, but never that Mormons were in the middle of every one of those events.

I remember fervent discussions about the Little Bighorn, the Long Walk to Bosque Redondo, and the Sandcreek Massacre (a Colorado specialty), but nary a word about an outright gubernatorial extermination order on card-carrying American citizens. We read accounts of the flood of immigrants that came in through Ellis Island, but nothing of the twenty thousand residents (most American citizens) who were driven out the opposite side of the country. And I certainly couldn't have told you anything about their faith. In fact, I don't recall ever meeting an actual Mormon until I fell in love with one at sixteen (I converted to her faith two years later and married her five years after that.)

The Mormon Trail of most Latter-day Saints didn't weave across the frozen prairies of Iowa, nor through the bitter snows of Wyoming. As my New York–born convert friend, Bill Luce, is fond of saying, he "crossed the plains in a '62 Ford Falcon" on his way to a good engineering program at Utah State University. The journey from Out to In is certainly a process, however—sometimes long, sometimes brief. On the surface, my own journey from zero to Zion took seven days.

But just like with that "other" trail and that other experience, it is the journey that defines, makes, and molds men and women from a cornucopia of cultures into a people with a common heritage and common purpose. The next decades would do that for the Latter-day Saints, making of them—German, Greek, Dutch, Jew, and British—a cohesive and singular people as closely defined as any ethnic community on earth. The Trail experience would inform and influence and flavor part of that common identity; the struggle toward Utah statehood would flavor some more of it, and Utah's subsequent station as home for nearly the entirety of the Saints would impart a very strong flavor. For a while.

The sixth president of the church would be born at Far West, Missouri, and walk across the country as a boy. The seventh would do neither.

My point is this: just about everything that happened to The Church of Jesus Christ of Latter-day Saints in the United States[375] between Joseph Smith's First Vision and Brigham Young's entry into the Salt Lake valley twenty-seven years later influences Latter-day Saint identity worldwide. This is true even though, at the end of the second millennium, approximately 69 percent of all Latter-day Saints in the world are first-generation converts due to the Church's expanding growth. (Of church members outside the United States and Canada, the number is 90 percent.) Only a few things that happened over the next five decades color the formative identity and doctrine of the Latter-day Saints as strongly as do the Exodus and pre-Exodus years we have just looked at. There are essential components remaining, however, components of the "Utah story" with which we are all involved at some visceral if not doctrinal level.

Thirty-three days after Brigham Young entered the Salt Lake valley, a settlement well underway,[376] he mounted his horse and began a return journey to Winter Quarters with seven of the apostles and about one hundred other pioneers serving in various capacities, not the least of which would be as cheerleaders for those still in the east. Along the way, they picked up Apostle Ezra T. Benson, who had been sent out previously to greet nine additional wagon trains en route to the valley, and continued east with him. An additional seventy pioneers were just ahead of them on that return journey, many of them members of the Mormon Battalion returning, for the first time in more than a year, to their families still encamped on the Missouri.

Back in Miller's Hollow on December 5, the assembled apostles resumed a trail-long discussion on reestablishing the First Presidency of the

---

[375]Certainly, noteworthy things in church history happened outside the United States during this period, but for the most part, excepting rapid growth in and emigration from the British Isles, they didn't influence Mormonism in general.

[376]Initially called the "City of the Salt Lake," it was revised to "Great Salt Lake City" in 1851 and eventually just called Salt Lake City.

church. It was suggested that if Brigham Young, as president of the Twelve felt the Lord's approval for such a move, they would proceed. Subsequently, Orson Hyde, in whose home they were meeting, moved that Brigham be sustained as the new church president and pick two new counselors. All agreed.

Brigham Young and most of the apostles remained in the Winter Quarters area throughout that winter. On December 23, they issued an "epistle" to be carried to Latter-day Saints throughout the globe directing all—except those in California—to emigrate "to Zion."

"Should any ask, 'where is Zion?,' " they wrote, "tell them in America; and if any ask: 'what is Zion?' tell them the pure in heart."[377]

That same day, 300 miles to the east, Emma Smith remarried in Nauvoo, taking as her husband a non–Latter-day Saint named Lewis Bidamon with whom she would finish her days. It would have been Joseph Smith's forty-second birthday.

In a conference held from December 24 to 27 in the brand new log tabernacle in Miller's Hollow, members of the church in that region—the largest body of church members then assembled in any one area—sustained the ordination of Brigham Young as the new president of The Church of Jesus Christ of Latter-day Saints.

In February, the Twelve assembled once again in council. Orson Hyde recorded: "The voice of God came from on high, and spake to the Council. Every latent feeling was aroused, and every heart melted. What did it say unto us? 'Let my servant Brigham step forth and receive the full power of the presiding Priesthood in my Church and kingdom.' This was the voice of the Almighty unto us."[378]

Of the event, Hyde later recorded: "Men, women, and children came running together where we were, and asked us what was the matter. They said that their houses shook, and the ground trembled, and they did not know but that there was an earthquake. We told them that there was nothing the matter—not to be alarmed; the Lord was only whispering to us a little, and that he was probably not very far off."[379]

At the Eighteenth General Conference of the church held in the log

---

[377]General Epistle of the Quorum of the Twelve, December 23, 1847.

[378]*Journal of Discourses*, Vol. 8, p. 234, Orson Hyde, October 7, 1860.

[379]Ibid.

tabernacle on April 6, 1848—during which Miller's Hollow was officially renamed Kanesville in honor of Thomas L. Kane—the sustaining of Brigham Young as Prophet, Seer, and Revelator and second president of the Church of Jesus Christ of Latter-day Saints was officially rendered. The assembled Saints in the British Isles likewise sustained the action in August, as did those back in the City of the Salt Lake in October, "there being about five thousand people in the valley by that time."[380]

Thus, a new prophet led the Saints, the very one of whom Joseph had once said, "that man will yet preside over this Church."[381]

On February 2, 1848, the Saints' two hundredth day in the valley, at about the same time the "earthquake" was rattling Iowa, James K. Polk signed the U.S. Treaty of Guadalupe Hidalgo, making the Great Salt Lake part of U.S. territory. When they had entered the valley, as B. H. Roberts points out, church leaders were "smarting under the sense of injustice and wrong permitted if not inflicted under quasi-sanction of the United States." Yet, in general, they still considered the U.S. Constitution the finest document for political rule ever written. And within that same view, statehood was their best course toward political autonomy. Thus, they first petitioned for statehood in July 1849 and organized a provisional legislature for the "State of Deseret," a term taken from the Book of Mormon and signifying industry. The proposed boundaries were enormous, ranging from central Oregon to Mexico, and from San Diego to southern Colorado, including portions of nine present-day states, or approximately 490,000 square miles.[382]

New president Millard Fillmore went partway, granting them territorial status (Utah) and wisely appointing as governor the only man they would have chosen for themselves: Brigham Young. The heretofore "state" of Deseret was dissolved by the spring of 1851.

"With no friends anywhere upon the face of the earth, no credit . . . and hardly a dollar," wrote early apostle Reed Smoot, the Latter-day Saints occupied, settled, and sustained a vibrant new community in the heart of the wilderness. Within weeks of the initial arrival in the Salt Lake Valley, some were being dispatched to colonize the far reaches of the

---

[380]B. H. Roberts, *Comprehensive History of the Church*, Vol. 3, Ch. 84, pp. 317–318.

[381]See Orson F. Whitney, *The Life of Heber C. Kimball*, p. 28.

[382]*Historical Atlas of Mormonism*, p. 90.

territory, a move calculated by Brigham Young to ensure self-rule and freedom from oppression by establishing the first or at least the most prevalent presence in the vast territory, even in those areas they would not eventually control. Over the next decades Latter-day Saint colonizers would establish more than three hundred settlements in western North America. Today, many of these communities—many the first nonnative communities in the state—dot the western landscape throughout Utah, Nevada, New Mexico, Arizona, Colorado, California, Montana, Idaho, Texas, Wyoming, Canada, and Mexico.

It could be assumed that the Latter-day Saints' establishment in the remote and arid interior of the North American continent would discourage a mass in-migration of settlers. *Au contraire.* Through the fifties and sixties, tens of thousands of converts poured into the Valley of the Great Salt Lake. Many, especially those from the eastern states, were not thrilled from a visual standpoint, but "at least it was a land of liberty, uninfested by mobs and heartless priests and politicians . . . [and] they felt safer far in the society of wild Indians and savage wolves than in the midst of the Christian civilization they had left behind."[383]

A Perpetual Emigrating Fund established in 1849 used church assets and private contributions to sponsor emigrants to Salt Lake. Monies were extended as a loan rather than as a gift, and sponsored emigrants signed a note obligating themselves to repay the PEF once having arrived in Utah. This obligation could be met through cash, commodities, or labor. It has been estimated that previous to its dismantling in 1887, the PEF aided more than thirty thousand people in traveling to Utah, but the high price of the journey put repayment quite simply beyond the means of most emigrants to this start-from-scratch land.

In the fall of 1855, Brigham Young issued the following call as part of another general epistle to the Saints: "Let all . . . who can, gather up for Zion, and come while the way is open before them; let the poor also come . . . let them come on foot, with handcarts or wheel-barrows; let them gird up their loins and walk through."[384]

The human-powered handcart would become one of the most brilliant—and tragic—experiments in all western migration. From 1856 to

---

[383]Orson F. Whitney, *The Life of Heber C. Kimball*, p. 356.

[384]Thirteenth General Epistle, October 29, 1855.

1860, three thousand handcart pioneers in ten companies walked the 1,300 miles from Iowa City, the then-current end of the rail line, to Salt Lake City, pulling and pushing all that they owned, or more accurately, all that they *retained*, having discarded, sold, or bartered much along the way. These handcart companies were mostly comprised of poorer Saints from England, Wales, and Scandinavia, although some individuals of means were assigned to accompany them.

The handcart was a human-powered wagon, a wooden wheelbarrow of sorts. The standard handcart box measured 3 feet by 4 feet, with 8-inch-high walls, centered over a single axle with wagon-style wheels. From the front box of the handcart extended a crossbar against which the person pulling could lean into the load and pull. Some handcarts were covered with a bow-frame canvas assembly. Fully loaded, a handcart could hold around 500 pounds of provisions and possessions; of that total weight, adults were allowed 17 pounds of clothing and bedding, children 10 pounds.

The handcart experiment would go very well for a few months, enabling more than eight hundred people to cross the continent to Salt Lake City in relative safety.[385] But the two final companies of 1856, the James G. Willie and Edward Martin companies, comprised of 980 people pulling 233 handcarts, would blunder through a series of mishaps and unfortunate choices, most a result of leaving too late in the season.

Of the company leaders, only one, Levi Savage, warned of the serious consequences of attempting the 1,300-mile journey at such a late date and urged the Saints to postpone their departure until the following spring. He was outvoted. "What I have said [about danger] I know to be true," he said, "but seeing you are to go forward, I will go with you; will help you all I can; will work with you, will rest with you, will suffer with you, and if necessary, will die with you." He did all but the last. "No man," wrote John Chislett of the Willie Company, "worked harder than [Savage] to alleviate the suffering which he had foreseen, when he had to endure it."[386]

Still, in mid-Nebraska on September 12—500 miles from the valley—they were overtaken by a group of seventeen missionaries returning

---

[385]But not entirely without tragedy; perhaps twenty people died in these three companies (see Leroy and Ann Hafen, *Handcarts to Zion*, Bison Books, p. 193).

[386]See B. H. Roberts, *Comprehensive History of the Church*, Vol. 4, Ch. 98, pp. 89–91.

from England who recognized most of the walkers as converts from their own recent ministrations in that land. The missionaries, traveling in light wagons, expressed their concerns to the company captains and then hurried on to Salt Lake with the news for Brigham Young.

On Saturday, October 4, the British missionaries reached Salt Lake City, and Elder Franklin D. Richards went directly to Brigham Young. The handcarters were three days north and west of Fort Laramie, just approaching the Last Crossing of the Platte, about 400 trail miles from the City.

The following morning, Brigham Young spoke to several hundred Latter-day Saints, assembled for General Conference in the "old tabernacle" on Temple Square. It would be one of the most dynamic—and fortunate—discourses of his thirty-year tenure at the head of the church.

I will now give this people the subject and the text for the Elders who may speak to-day and during the Conference. It is this: on the 5th day of October, 1856, many of our brethren and sisters are on the Plains with hand-carts, and probably many are now seven hundred miles from this place, and they must be brought here, we must send assistance to them. The text will be: to get them here!

I want the brethren who may speak to understand that their text is the people on the Plains, and the subject matter for this community is to send for them and bring them in before the winter sets in.

That is my religion; that is the dictation of the Holy Ghost that I possess, it is to save the people. We must bring them in from the Plains. . . .

I shall call upon the Bishops this day, I shall not wait until tomorrow, nor until next day, for sixty good mule teams and twelve or fifteen wagons. I do not want to send oxen, I want good horses and mules. They are in this Territory, and we must have them; also twelve tons of flour and forty good teamsters, besides those that drive the teams . . . forty good young men who know how to drive teams . . . sixty or sixty-five good spans of mules, or horses . . . twenty-four thousand pounds of flour, which we have on hand.

I will tell you all that your faith, religion, and profession of religion, will never save one soul of you in the celestial kingdom of our God, unless you carry out just such principles as I am now teaching you. Go and bring in those people now on the Plains![387]

By Tuesday, October 7, the wagons and teams were on their way. They met Captain James Willie at South Pass, riding desperately ahead on a worn-out mule, on the evening of October 20. The snow was deep and still flying.

Captain Willie directed the rescuers to his own camp, where little James Kirkwood had still not been seen.

Eleven-year-old James came to America from Scotland with his widowed mother and three brothers, one of whom was crippled. James's primary job on the long journey was to care for his four-year-old brother, Joseph, while his mother and oldest brother pulled the cart that carried the crippled brother and all their belongings. By the time they reached the high plains of central Wyoming, it was late October. Snow was falling, and the rivers were beginning to freeze.

As they neared an area some 25 miles west of today's Jeffrey City, the preferred route of passage along the Sweetwater River was obliterated by drifting snow, leaving no certainty as to where solid ground ended and unreliable ice began. So, forced to abandon the river bottom, they turned north and began to inch their way over a deceptively brutal summit dubbed Rocky Ridge for its geologic propensity for ripping shoe leather to shreds. (I've walked it and ripped mine.)Leaving a trail of blood, the pioneers, many of whom had been wearing only cloth wrapped around their feet for days, pressed on.

When little Joseph could walk no more, eleven-year-old James put him on his back and stumbled onward. Eventually, they fell behind the main group. Approximately seventeen hours after arising in bitter cold, with little to eat all day long, James entered the camp, lowered his younger brother to the ground next to his mother's handcart, sat down beside him, and died.

The next morning, his mother and brothers—including little Joseph—scraped a shallow grave out of the frozen earth and laid his body to rest

---

[387]Brigham Young, *Journal of Discourses*, Vol. 4, pp. 113–114.

in a lonely place called Rock Creek Hollow. Fourteen other bodies were laid beside him.

The rescuers would arrive two days later. Then, pushing onward, George D. Grant, who weeks before in Florence had encouraged the journey, took a small group of rescuers and continued eastward 100 miles. He encamped in the granite shadows of an unusual rock outcropping jutting straight up out of the plains called Devil's Gate. There, several shanties of an abandoned traders' fort gave them a semblance of shelter. Three riders—Brigham Young's son Joseph (recently returned from England), Daniel W. Jones, and Abel Garr—continued onward. On October 28, they found the 576 still-living members of the Martin Handcart Company. Among them, Elizabeth Horrocks Jackson:

> My sister was the only relative I had to whom I could look for assistance in this trying ordeal, and she was sick. So severe was her affliction that she became deranged in her mind, and for several days she ate nothing but hard frozen snow. I could therefore appeal to the Lord alone—he who had promised to be a husband to the widow and a father to the fatherless. I appealed to him and he came to my aid.
>
> A few days after the death of my husband, the male members of the company had become reduced in number by death; and those who remained were so weak and emaciated by sickness, that on reaching the camping place at night, there were not sufficient men with strength enough to raise the poles and pitch the tents. The result was that we camped out with nothing but the vault of Heaven for a roof and the stars for companions. The snow lay several inches deep upon the ground. The night was bitterly cold. I sat down on a rock with one child in my lap and one on each side of me. In that condition I remained until morning.
>
> My sick sister, the first part of the night, climbed up hill to the place where some men had built a fire. She remained there until the people made down their beds and retired, to sleep, if they could. She then climbed or slid down the hill on the snow to where there was another fire which was kept alive by some persons who were watching the body of a man who had died that night. There she remained until daylight. It will be readily perceived that under such adverse circumstances I had become despondent. I was six or seven thousand miles from my native land, in a wild rocky mountain country, in a destitute

condition, the ground covered with snow, the waters covered with ice, and I with three fatherless children with scarcely anything to protect them from the merciless storms.

When I retired to bed that night, being the 27th of October, I had a stunning revelation. In my dream, my husband stood by me, and said, "Cheer up, Elizabeth, deliverance is at hand." The dream was fulfilled, for the next day (Oct. 28, 1856) Joseph A. Young, Daniel Jones and Abel Garr galloped unexpectedly into camp, amid tears and cheers and smiles and laughter of the emigrants. These three men were the first of the most advanced Relief Company sent out from Salt Lake City to meet the belated emigrants.[388]

It was a pitiful sight More than a week before, on encountering the first of seven eventual crossings of the Sweetwater River, the handcarters had begun to lighten their loads by discarding bedding. Now they were sorely in need of it. By the time the rescuers reached them, fifty-six members of the company had died.

The "Valley Boys," sensing impending annihilation, saw to it that the handcarters kept moving. Daniel Jones later wrote: "The train was strung out for three or four miles. There were old men pulling and tugging their carts, sometimes loaded with a sick wife or children—women pulling alongside sick husbands—little children six to eight years old struggling through the mud and snow. As night came on the mud would freeze on their clothes and feet. We gathered on to some of the most helpless with our riatas tied to the carts and helped as many as we could. . . . Several died that night."[389]

Over the next four days, Jones and his two companions pushed the pioneers onward another 55 miles to Devil's Gate. Upon seeing them, Grant sent a dispatch to Brigham Young, in which he wrote, "The sight is almost too much for the stoutest of us, but we go on doing all we can. I have never felt so much interest in any mission that I have been sent on."

With the arrival of several hundred freezing and starving people, however, the narrow shelter of Devil's Gate was entirely inadequate. On No-

---

[388]From "Leaves from the Life of Elizabeth Horrocks Jackson Kingsford," *Historical Archives*, The Church of Jesus Christ of Latter-day Saints.

[389]Daniel W. Jones, *Forty Years Among the Indians*, p. 68.

vember 3, they moved westward two miles to a broad break in the granite ridge that promised shelter and firewood. Reaching it would require one more crossing of the Sweetwater, now treacherous with floating blocks of ice. Upon realizing the exigencies of their course, it is recorded that "men who once had been strong sat on the frozen ground and wept."

The winds howled: the snow drifted around their rag-clothed legs. It seemed certain death to enter that river. It was equally suicidal to remain where they were. The shelter of the cove offered the only hope of survival.

Three teenaged Valley Boys[390] stepped forward and approached the river, the cries of the wounded, dying, and spent all around them. One by one, they loaded the exhausted handcarters onto their backs and carried them to the far side of the river, recrossing again and again for more. Although some later accounts credit the three boys with carrying "nearly every member" of the handcart company across (more than five hundred of them), that is unlikely. (Wrote twenty-six-year-old Daniel Jones, whose cumulative future exploits would make him a hero almost without peer in Mormon history, "Some writers have endeavored to make individual heroes of some of our company. I have no remembrance of anyone shirking his duty.")

What remains unquestioned is that each of the three teenagers carried an astonishing number of people across the river.

"When President Brigham Young heard of this heroic act," wrote another chronicler, "he wept like a child, and later declared publicly, 'that act alone will ensure C. Allen Huntington. George W. Grant [George D.'s son], and David P. Kimball [Heber C.'s son] an everlasting salvation in the Celestial Kingdom of God, worlds without end.' "[391]

Abandoning their wheelbarrows, but not their sufferings, the rescued and the rescuers would continue toward Salt Lake City, leaving approximately two hundred and twenty members of the two companies in shallow graves scattered across the rocky plains.

Wrote Elizabeth Jackson:

---

[390]Some accounts list all three as being eighteen-year-old. LDS Family History records, while sketchy, show that at least two of them—Grant and Kimball—were younger.

[391]Solomon F. Kimball, *Improvement Era*, Feb. 1914, p. 288. It is interesting to note that George W. Grant's father, George D., had nearly given his own life in a similar river rescue seventeen years before, only months before George W. was born. (See Sarah Rich Autobiography, typescript, *Brigham Young University Studies*, pp. 29–30.)

Though the sufferings after that still continued, yet the worst was over and the survivors of that ill-fated handcart company arrived in Salt Lake City Nov. 30, 1856 [survivors of the Willie Company had arrived on November 9].

I have a desire to leave a record of those scenes and events through which I have passed, that my children, down to my latest posterity, may read what their ancestors were willing to suffer, and did suffer, patiently for the gospel's sake. And I wish them to understand too, that what I now word is the history of hundreds of others, who have passed through like scenes for the same cause. I also desire them to know that it was in obedience to the commands of the true and living God, and with the assurance of an eternal reward—an exaltation in his kingdom—that we suffered these things. I hope, too, that it will inspire my posterity with fortitude to stand firm and faithful to the truth, and be willing to suffer, and sacrifice all things they may be required to pass through for the sake of the Kingdom of God.

Once again, the Saints were in meeting in the Old Tabernacle on Sunday, November 30, when messengers arrived to inform Brigham Young that the rescue party with members of the Martin Handcart Company was approaching the city down Emigration Canyon. As before, Brigham Young dismissed the congregation, giving them their charge:

When those persons arrive I do not want to see them put into houses by themselves. I want to have them distributed in this city among the families that have good, comfortable houses; and I wish the sisters now before me, and all who know how and can, to nurse and wait upon the newcomers, and prudently administer medicine and food to them.

The afternoon meeting will be omitted, for I wish the sisters to go home and prepare to give those who have just arrived a mouthful of something to eat, and to wash them, and nurse them up. Prayer is good, but when baked potatoes, and pudding, and milk are needed, prayer will not supply their place. Some you will find with their feet frozen to their ankles: some are frozen to their knees and some have their hands frosted. We want you to receive them as your own children, and to have the same feeling for them.[392]

---

[392]*Deseret News,* December 10, 1856.

Captain Willie's journal records the response of people in the city to his incoming flocks: "On our arrival there the Bishops of the different Wards took every person who was not provided with a home to comfortable quarters. Some had their hands and feet badly frozen; but everything which could be done to alleviate their sufferings, was done. . . . Hundreds of the Citizens flocked round the wagons on our way through the City, cordially welcoming their Brethren and Sisters to their mountain home."[393]

One hundred years later, the story of the Willie and Martin handcart companies would be revisited in reverent and masterful detail by one of America's great literary voices; but, like nearly everything else written by Wallace Stegner, it would never find much merit in the eyes of the media gatekeepers. Stegner's summation wrote: "Perhaps their suffering seems less dramatic because the handcart pioneers bore it meekly, praising God, instead of fighting for life with the ferocity of animals and eating their dead to keep their own life beating, as both the Fremont and Donner parties did. But if courage and endurance make a story, if humankindness and helpfulness and brotherly love in the midst of raw horror are worth recording, this half-forgotten episode of the Mormon migration is one of the great tales of the West and of America."[394]

Five more handcart companies would cross to Salt Lake in the next four years. None would experience similar tragedy.

From 1847, the year of their forced exodus from American soil, to 1869, when the east-west fingers of the transcontinental railroad joined hands in their own Utah territory, an estimated seventy thousand converts of The Church of Jesus Christ of Latter-day Saints crossed the plains to the refuge of the Rockies. In that time, roughly 340 ships brought forty-nine thousand of them from docks around the globe: Hamburg, Sydney, Wellington (New Zealand), Cape Town, Calcutta, Amsterdam, and certainly, London and Liverpool.

Quite unlike the majority of people crossing the American West in the mid 1800s—most of them men, seasoned in farming or in the trades—the Latter-day Saints were a polyglot lot that mostly defied definition: entire families, even extended families; single adults; orphaned

---

[393]James G. Willie, *Journal History*, November 9, 1856, p. 15.

[394]Wallace Stegner, "Ordeal by Handcart," in *Collier's*, July 6, 1956, pp. 78–85.

(but rapidly adopted) children; lawyers, doctors, piano builders, seamstresses, architects, masons, mathematicians; the rich and the poor. And their purpose in migrating was also far divergent from the larger stream of travelers. "These tens of thousands," wrote J. Reuben Clark in 1947, "were the warp and the woof of Brigham Young's great commonwealth . . . all gathered from the four corners of the earth . . . all to the glory of God and the up-building of his kingdom."[395]

Of the handcart episode specifically, and the whole Trail experience in general, author Arthur King Peters would sum up in his wonderful book *Seven Trails West*: "This heroic episode of Mormon history exemplifies many of the enduring qualities of nascent Mormonism itself: thorough organization, iron discipline, unswerving devotion to a cause, and limitless self-sacrifice. The true Mormon Trail was not on the prairie but in the spirit."[396]

No other words have ever described contemporary "Mormon" heritage better.

---

[395]J. Reuben Clark, Jr., Conference Report, October 1947, p. 159.

[396]Arthur King Peters, *Seven Trails West* (New York, NY.: Abbeville, 1996), p. 124.

CHAPTER 17

Give and Take

Established in their mountain refuge—alone at last—Church leaders began urging a "reformation," or recommitment to gospel principles in the fall of 1856. Influencing the episode, which would last for only a little more than a year and a half but inform church thought and discourse from there on out, were matters both internal and external, spiritual and temporal. In September 1856, the Utah settlements were about halfway into a three-year drought, accompanied by a devastating invasion of crop-eating insects. To the national press, already fattening its pages with rhetoric on the Rocky Mountain relic of barbarism, it appeared the "hand of God" was exacting retribution from these wayward western castoffs.

When the Saints expected sympathy, there was none. "In view of this alarming condition . . ." wrote Apostle John Taylor in one New York editorial, "we might reasonably expect to witness some manifeston of sympathy . . . On the contrary there are frequent manifestations of satisfaction that the problem of 'Mormonism' and its destiny is likely to be settled by the grasshoppers. What little comment we have noticed here and there has a tone of delighted chuckle that chills the blood. There is a spirit of murder in it, a suppressed shout of triumph of the persecutor over his victim, that is suppressed only because the triumph is not yet sure."[397]

From early, revivalistic speeches in the northern Utah communities, the prairie fires of spiritual passion spread to the south, with thousands being rebaptized as a sign of their recommitment. Church headquarters systematized the effort in the Salt Lake City area by assigning two "home missionaries" to each family in every congregation. The home missionaries would refresh the gospel sensibilities of the family with a twenty-seven-step catechism previous to the rebaptism.[398]

---

[397]*The Mormon,* September 22, 1855.

[398]The program would evolve over the decades, becoming the current "home teaching" program in 1963.

Soon the reformation effort was carried to settlements and missions throughout the world, and while specifics varied from location to location, rebaptism was strongly encouraged, especially by First Presidency first counselor Jedediah Grant. In some areas, like Britain, those who were unwilling to recommit through rebaptism were trimmed from the rolls of the church. From Mormon pulpits worldwide "fiery and at times intemperate sermons"[399] called the Saints to repentance, and the ordinance of the sacrament was even suspended for a time in Utah.[400]

It was in the midst of this reformation—an era of passionate reentrenchment of the principles that had thus far kept them (mostly) together, that circumstances once again conspired to tear them apart.

On Pioneer Day, July 24, 1857, Brigham Young received word that the U.S. Army was advancing on Utah. Young and most of the residents of the valley were near the mouth of Big Cottonwood Canyon having a celebration when three horsemen rode hastily into camp with the news: twenty-five hundred U.S. troops were en route from Fort Leavenworth, heavily provisioned and ready for war. And more were assembling.

Three years before, Congress had approved an act that would allow future incoming states and territories (there were thirty-one U.S. states in 1854) to choose by popular vote whether slavery would be permitted within their borders. Two years after that, a new political party, the Republican, announced its foundational opposition to the act. In attempting to illustrate what would happen should a geographic region be allowed such reckless autonomy, they pointed to Utah, where the other of the "twin relics of barbarism" (polygamy) was now being openly practiced.

Although the Republicans won a good deal of public sentiment with this comparison, their effort essentially backfired. They lost the election to an ardent southern Democrat named James Buchanan. The new president immediately set about trying to extract slavery from the nation's focus by inflaming the polygamy issue and announcing his plan to replace the western theocrat Brigham Young as governor of Utah Territory. Buchanan's secretary of war, John Floyd, who would within four years accept an appointment as brigadier general in the Confederate Army, saw the perfect opportunity for extracting a good portion of the U.S. Army from

---

[399] *Encyclopedia of Mormonism*, Vol. 2, s.v. "History of the Church."

[400] *Lion of the Lord: Essays on the Life and Service of Brigham Young*, pp. 252–253.

the nation itself (along with weapons and goods). At Floyd's recommendation, Buchanan dispatched the new governor, a Georgian named Alfred Cumming, to Utah under the "protection" of U.S. troops led by Albert Sidney Johnston. Troops and supplies began assembling at Fort Leavenworth on May 28.

The disastrous efforts of the next thirteen months would become known as "Buchanan's Blunder," a military mistake that would engage one-third of the entire U.S. infantry and cost upward of forty million dollars.[401]

Upon learning on July 24 that twenty-five hundred troops were on their way west, Brigham Young commented that he had asked for ten years of peace, and had gotten them—to the day. "Will [we] ask any odds of them? No, in the name of Israel's God, we will not; for as soon as we ask odds, we get ends—of bayonets. When we have asked them for bread, they have given us stones; and when we have asked them for meat, they have given us scorpions. What is the use in asking any more?"[402]

By mid-September, as the army was approaching the place where the Martin Handcart Company had frozen in place eleven months before, Brigham Young issued a proclamation to all the citizens of his territory, who were clearly living in fearful anticipation of the invasion.

September 15th, 1857.

Proclamation by the Governor

Citizens of Utah:

We are invaded by a hostile force who are evidently assailing us to accomplish our overthrow and destruction.

For the last twenty-five years we have trusted officials of the government, from constables and justices to judges, governors and presidents, only to be scorned, held in derision, insulted and betrayed. Our

---

[401]1. New York *Herald*, Feb, 7, 1858, cited in B. H. Roberts, *Comprehensive History of the Church*, Vol. 4, Ch. 113, p. 410; also rerun in *Deseret News*, April 7, 1858; 2. "Uncle Sam, the generous old gentleman, had to submit to his pocket being picked to the tune of about forty millions of dollars—the cost of the Utah expedition." (George Albert Smith, *Journal of Discourses*, Vol. 11, p. 181, October 8, 1865)

[402]*Journal of Discourses*, Vol. 5, p. 235, Brigham Young, September 13, 1857.

houses have been plundered and then burned, our fields laid waste, our principal men butchered while under the pledged faith of the government for their safety, and our families driven from their homes to find that shelter in the barren wilderness and that protection among hostile savages which were denied them in the boasted abodes of Christianity and civilization.

Our opponents have availed themselves of prejudice existing against us because of our religious faith, to send out a formidable host to accomplish our destruction. We have had no privilege, no opportunity of defending ourselves from the false, foul, and unjust aspersions against us before the nation. The government has not condescended to cause an investigating committee or other persons to be sent to inquire into and ascertain the truth, as is customary in such cases.

We are condemned unheard and forced to an issue with an armed, mercenary mob, which has been sent against us at the instigation of . . . corrupt officials who have brought false accusations against us to screen themselves in their own infamy; and of hireling priests and howling editors who prostitute the truth for filthy lucre's sake.

The issue which has been thus forced upon us compels us to resort to the great first law of self-preservation and stand in our own defense, a right guaranteed unto us by the genius of the institutions of our country, and upon which the government is based.

Our duty to ourselves, to our families, requires us not to tamely submit to be driven and slain, without an attempt to preserve ourselves. Our duty to our country, our holy religion, our God, to freedom and liberty, requires that we should not quietly stand still and see those fetters forging around, which are calculated to enslave and bring us in subjection to an unlawful military despotism such as can only emanate (in a country of constitutional law) from usurpation, tyranny and oppression.

Therefore, I, Brigham Young, governor, and superintendent of Indian affairs for the territory of Utah *[both by appointment of the U.S. president]*, in the name of the people of the United States in the territory of Utah,

1st—Forbid all armed forces, of every description, from coming into this territory under any pretense whatever.

2d—That all the forces in said territory hold themselves in readiness to march, at a moments' notice, to repel any and all such invasion.

3d—Martial law is hereby declared to exist in this territory, from and after the publication of this proclamation; and no person shall be allowed to pass or repass into, or through, or from this territory, without a permit from the proper officer.

Given under my hand and seal at Great Salt Lake City, territory of Utah, this fifteenth day of September, A.D., Eighteen Hundred and Fifty-seven, and of the Independence of the United States of America the eighty-second.

[Signed] *Brigham Young.*[403]

Plans were made, maps were consulted, spirits were cheered. As the army moved onto the Pacific side of the Continental Divide, small bands of Utah militiamen began burning supply trains, spoiling water sources, and stampeding livestock. But no blood was spilled.

The federal army suffered through a severe winter, losing more than half of their horses and stock animals "by fifties"[404] at a time. The daylight temperature on the high Wyoming plains hovered just above zero for weeks.

On February 25, 1858, a visitor arrived in Salt Lake City, Utah, having traveled from New York City to Panama, across the isthmus, north to California and up the "Mormon corridor" to the territorial capital. Introducing himself as "Dr. Osborne," a botanist, he was soon in the presence of Brigham Young, who recognized him immediately as the Saints' old friend from Iowa, Thomas Kane.

Kane was here, on his own and not feeling well. But he had come to serve his friends however he could, as a mediator with the army if accepted. President Buchanan had refused to accord him any official status, and in fact "could not at the present moment, in view of the hostile attitude they [the Latter-day Saints] have assumed against the United States, send any agent to visit them on behalf of the United States,"[405] but he furnished him with a signed letter, "commending him to the fa-

---

[403]House Executive Documents, 35th Congress, 1st Session, x, No. 71, pp. 34, 35.

[404]*Documentary Account of the Utah Expedition*, ed. LeRoy R. Hafen, pp. 170–173, including footnotes.

[405]Letter of President Buchanan, House Executive Documents, 35th Congress, 2nd Session, 1858–9, pp. 162–163.

vorable regard of all officers of the United States whom he might meet in the course of his travels and . . . render him all the aid and facilities in their power in expediting the journey he had undertaken of his own accord."[406]

Two weeks later, Brigham Young did what Buchanan wouldn't, and sent Kane off to the army camp with an escort of horsemen as an official representative of the Utah people. Kane's escort accompanied him into western Wyoming, within about 12 miles of the army base at Camp Scott. From there, he proceeded alone, arriving at the cold, disanimated, and disorganized military camp on the evening of March 12. Assured by Young that the Holy Spirit would guide him in his efforts, he was soon whisked to the tent of [Governor] Cumming, ignoring with some success General Johnston altogether. The two found themselves seeing things the same way: the army was being toyed with, and President Buchanan was the lead puppeteer.

Soon Kane approached General Johnston with a note from Brigham Young, who had heard the troops were low on provisions. Young offered Johnston's troops two hundred head of cattle and up to 20,000 pounds of flour, "to which they will be made perfectly welcome, or pay for, just as they choose."[407] Johnston replied curtly that Young was "not correctly informed with regard to the state of the supply of provisions of this army. There has been no deficiency," he declared, "nor is there any now. We have abundance."[408]

Eventually, Kane convinced Cumming to go to Salt Lake City without a military escort, and trust the people in receiving him as their governor. They would, but not without one significant hitch: many thought (incorrectly, they soon learned) "that he was not only a 'Missourian,' but one of the Jackson county mob."[409] A contemporary Utah campfire song went like this:

> Old Sam has sent I understand
> Du dah!

---

[406]Ibid.

[407]B. H. Roberts, *Comprehensive History of the Church*, Vol. 4, Ch. 110, p. 353.

[408]Johnston's letter to Brigham Young, April 15, 1855; House Executive Documents, 35th Congress, 2nd Session, vol. ii, pt. ii, p. 85.

[409]B. H. Roberts, *Comprehensive History of the Church*, Vol. 4, Ch. 112, p. 396

A Missouri ass to rule our land,
Du dah! Du dah day.[410]

On April 3, Governor Cumming informed Johnston he was leaving for Salt Lake City with Colonel Kane—no military escort needed, thank you—and two days later, he rode out of the camp, leaving the soldiers staring from the doorways of their wind-battered tents.

As the Wyoming snows began to give way, the army once again moved west, attempting to enter Utah through the long, narrow depths of Echo Canyon. Utah militiamen harassed them from the opposing heights of the steep canyon walls.[411]

When the ragged federal soldiers finally reached Salt Lake City on June 26, 1858, the city was all but vacant. Only a smattering of guards could be seen, with torches ready to ignite every straw-filled house, barn, store, and shop in the city. At Brigham Young's directive, more than thirty thousand Latter-day Saints had taken the "Big Move" 45 miles south to Provo. Should the army try to take the city, a Big Fire would consume everything in sight within minutes. The granite foundation of the Salt Lake temple, five years underway (and 35 years from completion) but just reaching ground level, was buried and plowed over as if it were a field ready for planting.

"Rather than see my wives and daughters ravished and polluted and the seeds of corruption sown in the hearts of my sons of a brutal soldiery," wrote Brigham Young to a friend, "I would leave my home in ashes, my gardens and orchards a waste and subsist upon roots and herbs, a wanderer through these mountains for the remainder of my natural life."[412]

When Johnston rode into Salt Lake City, no rebellion, however, was in sight. Court records were found to be perfectly stored and filed. Humiliated publicly, Buchanan's army was authorized to offer "amnesty"[413] to the Latter-day Saints in Utah. It was a moot frivolity. Then the army continued through the deserted city, where American flags waved from

---

[410]Ibid.

[411]See *LDS Biographical Encyclopedia*, Volume 1, s.v. "Robert Taylor Burton," and James R. Clark, *Messages of the First Presidency*, Vol. 4, p. 244.

[412]*Journal History*, January 6, 1858; P. Nibley, *Brigham Young*, p. 325.

[413]The entire text of the "pardon" is included in B. H. Roberts, *Comprehensive History of the Church*, Vol. 4, Ch. 114, pp. 422–426.

the windows, and set up base 40 miles to the southwest at Camp Floyd (named after the war secretary). There, soldiers would remain until called back east at the outbreak of the Civil War just two years later. "In their hasty departure," wrote James Talmage, "the soldiers disposed of everything outside of actual necessities in the way of accouterment and camp equipage. The army found the people in poverty, and left them in comparative wealth."[414]

Like soon-to-be-former U.S. War Secretary John Floyd, Albert Sidney Johnston would soon command troops for the Confederates.

On the day of Cumming's departure for Salt Lake City, the "district court" convened its spring term at Camp Scott, impaneling a "grand jury" that condemned the practice of polygamy in Utah Territory. This sagebrush indictment would be the first official move in a six-decade harassment of The Church of Jesus Christ of Latter-day Saints over polygamy. It would play into every effort the Latter-day Saints made for statehood over the next four decades (when they finally got it), and nearly every effort they made at self-representation for two decades after that.

Upon entering the Salt Lake valley in 1847, the contracting of plural marriages became a topic of much more open discussion and practice, although most Latter-day Saint men never took plural wives. While it was a principle of regulated and circumscribed practice, it was, nevertheless, one considered among the most sacred of covenants. Even at its height, only a minority of Latter-day Saints ever lived in a plural union.

With the biblical patriarchs as models, direct revelation as incentive, and the Second Amendment to the U.S. Constitution seemingly guaranteeing the effort, the Latter-day Saints lived the law of plural marriages largely unmolested until 1862, when congressional legislation first intervened. For another twenty years, the Latter-day Saints argued for recognition of the free exercise of religion clause in the Second Amendment all the way to the Supreme Court. But in 1882, the Edmunds Act, aimed clearly and overtly at the Latter-day Saints, barred persons living in plural marriages from jury service, public office, and voting.

Five years later, the Edmunds-Tucker Act disincorporated the church and authorized seizure of church real estate and tithing funds, placing into receivership even the church's most sacred buildings, the temples

---

[414]James E. Talmage, *The Story and Philosophy of "Mormonism,"* p. 82.

(of which there were then three completed and one, Salt Lake, nearing completion). Women, who had been voting in elections in the territory since 1870, were disenfranchised. More than thirteen hundred fathers, including many church leaders, were taken from their homes and imprisoned. A cloud of anxious fear brooded over the Utah Territory throughout the late 1880s.

Following Brigham Young's death from peritonitis in 1877, the practice continued, but third church president John Taylor—he who had survived the brutal assault in the Carthage jail—died of natural causes while living in exile in 1887. His successor, Wilford Woodruff, watched the funeral procession from behind the veiled windows of his church historian's office on South Temple Street.

Three years later, President Woodruff issued a press release, now know as "the Manifesto," declaring the church's official cessation of the practice of plural marriage. Five and a half years after that, Utah became the nation's forty-fifth state.

Many outside the faith continue to suggest that President Woodruff ended the polygamy era so that Utah could gain statehood. That's convenient, but it misses the point. As declared by President Woodruff some five weeks later, the future of the church, its very existence, was at stake.

> The Lord showed me by vision and revelation exactly what would take place if we did not stop this practice. If we had not stopped it . . . all [temple] ordinances would be stopped throughout the land of Zion. Confusion would reign . . . and many men would be made prisoners. This trouble would have come upon the whole church, and we should have been compelled to stop the practice. Now, the question is, whether it should be stopped in this manner, or in the way the Lord has manifested to us, and leave our Prophets and Apostles and fathers free men, and the temples in the hands of the people . . . I say to you that that is exactly the condition we as a people would have been in had we not taken the course we have. I saw exactly what would come to pass if there was not something done. But I want to say this: I should have let all the temples go out of our hands; I should have gone to prison myself, and let every other man go there, had not the God of heaven commanded me to do what I did do.[415]

---

[415]Doctrine and Covenants Official Declaration—1.

There were approximately twenty-five hundred plural families living in the Utah Territory in 1890 when the Manifesto was issued. Although the Edmunds-Tucker Act attempted to annul all such relationships, illegtimizing both children and wives, the Utah constitution benevolently avoided that. "The ordinance in our state constitution," wrote church historian B. H. Roberts some years later, "was adopted in such form and spirit that while future polygamous or plural marriages were forever prohibited, it contemplated leaving undisturbed the already existing plural marriage relations. Under these circumstances I do not hesitate to say that for Mormon men to abandon the wives they had taken in good faith, who had been induced to accept that relationship under religious persuasion and conviction, would be both cowardly and criminal in the eyes of God and all good and respectable men."[416]

With the natural passing of many polygamists, the number of plural unions began to drop rapidly, although some, contracted in the years before the Manifesto, lasted into the twentieth century. Since the Manifesto was issued, however, and particularly since 1904, when the First Presidency issued a second manifesto, any member of The Church of Jesus Christ of Latter-day Saints entering into or living in a polygamous union is excommunicated from the church.

There remain an estimated thirty thousand non–Latter-day Saint *polygs* and *cohabs*[417] in the western United States today. Calling themselves "Mormon fundamentalists," they feel they are the torchbearers, the brave faithful holding strong in the wake of church presidents who have, one after another since 1890, given in. Rather, the fundamental doctrine of Mormonism is, and always has been, that the true Church of Jesus Christ will be led by direct revelation of God to His *current* prophet. It is not plural marriage. As in the days of certain (not all) Old Testament prophets, that practice occurred when it occurred because the Lord said it should, and it stopped when he directed otherwise. His reasons for doing either are not entirely known to us.

And that's about all we can say about it.

---

[416] B. H. Roberts, *Defense of the Faith and the Saints*, Vol. 1, p. 106.

[417] This term (from *cohabitate*) was adopted by federal marshals in the 1880s seeking heads-of-houses to bust.

PART 4

Steaming Toward Kolob

How is it that hardly any major religion has looked at science and concluded, "This is better than we thought! The universe is much bigger than our prophets said; grander, more subtle, more elegant. God must be even greater than we dreamed"? A religion, old or new, that stressed the magnificence of the universe as revealed by modern science might be able to draw forth the reserves of reverence and awe hardly tapped by the conventional faiths. Sooner or later, such a religion will emerge."

CARL SAGAN
Pale Blue Dot: A Vision of the Human Future in Space, 1994

CHAPTER 18

From Zero to Sixty in 2.2

With the granting of statehood to Utah on January 4, 1896, the formative—i.e., pioneering—period of The Church of Jesus Christ of Latter-day Saints was essentially over. But it was an era that would never—will never—be extracted from the handbooks, the curricula, and the collective psyche of the Latter-day Saints anywhere in the world.

Some of it is natural. The president of the church in the year 2000 once explained: "My own grandfather [Ira Nathaniel Hinckley], barely out of his teens, became an expert blacksmith and wagon builder [in Nauvoo]. He would later build his own wagon and with his young wife and baby and his brother-in-law set off for the West. Somewhere on that long journey, his wife sickened and died and his brother-in-law died on the same day. He buried them both, tearfully said good-bye, tenderly picked up his child, and marched on to the valley of the Great Salt Lake."[418]

And some of it is calculated and purposeful: on the 167th anniversary of the church founding, that same church president, Gordon B. Hinckley, put it this way:

> I wish to go on record concerning the magnitude of what our forebears accomplished and what this means to us. It is a story so large in scope, so fraught with human suffering and the workings of faith, that it will never grow old or stale. Whether you are among the posterity of the pioneers or whether you were baptized only yesterday, each is the beneficiary of their great undertaking. What a wonderful thing it is to have behind us a great and noble body of progenitors! What a marvelous thing to be the recipients of a magnificent heritage that speaks of the guiding hand of the Lord, of the listening ear of His prophets, of the total dedication of a vast congregation of Saints who loved this cause more than life itself![419]

---

[418]Gordon B. Hinckley, in Conference Report, April 1997, 88–89.

[419]Gordon B. Hinckley, in Conference Report, April 1997, 87.

On one hand I can say, as I often have to pioneer-stock friends, "*My* ancestors are the reason *your* ancestors had to leave New York and Illinois in the first place." In fact, my ancestors kept missing the Mormons by about five years: My great great grandfather, Charles Carlton Newell, was born in the Finger Lakes region of western New York five years after the first LDS missionaries preached to Native Americans in that area (one of which he married twenty-one years later). My third great grandfather, James Allen Forgey settled his family on a farm in the area of Mount Pisgah, Iowa, just five years after the Latter-day Saints abandoned that temporary town on the plains for the Salt Lake valley. As far as I know, he ate corn they planted.

On the other hand, I feel and accept and claim that spiritual heritage bequeathed by the Mormon Pioneers as every bit my own. Like Ira Hinckley, both of us lone converts in our teens, we made ourselves a part of it by our voluntary immersion in its waters and its ways. He walked the plains and crossed the Rockies. I spent two years on a mission dodging bullets and beer bottles in Colombia.

More and more through the decades of the twentieth century, Latter-day Saint history would begin playing out in places like Adelaide and Johannesburg and Medellín. By the end of the nineteenth century, the call to gather to a central Zion was effectively suspended. Some of the reasoning was financial. The Perpetual Emigrating Fund, which had financed at least in part the migration of more than thirty-thousand people to Utah and received repayment by very few, was no longer perpetual by 1887. More importantly, though, the burdens imposed by the federal witch-hunt that preceded and accompanied the fight for statehood had placed the church at the verge of bankruptcy.

Lorenzo Snow assumed the church presidency in 1898 at the death of Wilford Woodruff, and he also assumed the debt, which soon threatened to bury *him*. Speaking to a conference of Latter-day Saints in southern Utah's St. George on May 8, 1899, he suddenly felt a clear and distinct impression to make them a promise. "The time has now come," he said, "for every Latter-day Saint, who calculates to be prepared for the future and to hold his feet strong upon a proper foundation, to do the will of the Lord and to pay his tithing in full. That is the word of the Lord to you, and it will be the word of the Lord to every settlement throughout the land of Zion. This is the answer to our financial problems. Even though as a Church we are heavily in debt, I say unto you that, if this people will pay a full and honest tithing, the shackles of indebtedness will be removed from us."[420]

The law of tithing—an Old Testament principle revealed anew to Joseph Smith in 1838—was a winnowing tool of faith: to donate one-tenth of one's income, either in commodities or in cash, to the church for its needs. The members throughout the territory responded, and the Church paid off its last indebtedness eight years later. But by then, President Snow had already been dead six years.

Succeeding President Snow after his brief thirty-seven-month presidency was Joseph F. Smith. "Joseph F." was born to a very sick mother while his father, the church patriarch, Hyrum, was incarcerated in Liberty Jail in western Missouri. With Hyrum's assassination five years later in Carthage Jail, Joseph F. was left fatherless. As a nine-year-old, he drove a team of oxen across the plains to the Rocky Mountains; as a fourteen-year-old, he was left an orphan at the death of his mother, and as a fifteen-year-old, he was sent on a four-year, no-expenses-paid mission to the Sandwich Islands, where he nearly died of some tropical fever.

Returning through southern California and finding Johnston's army converging on Utah and Latter-day Saint settlers in San Bernardino clearing out for the Valley, he was suddenly confronted by a band of

anti-Mormon toughs [who] rode into the camp on horseback, cursing and swearing and threatening what they would do to the "Mormons." Joseph F. was a little distance from the camp gathering wood for the fire, but he saw that the few members of his own party had cautiously gone into the brush down the creek, out of sight. When he saw that . . . the thought came into his mind, "Shall I run from these fellows? Why should I fear them?" With that he marched up with his arm full of wood to the campfire where one of the ruffians, still with his pistol in his hand, shouting and cursing about the "Mormons," in a loud voice said to Joseph F., "Are you a Mormon?"

And the answer came straight, "Yes, siree; dyed in the wool; true blue, through and through."

At that the ruffian grasped him by the hand and said, "Well, you

---

[420]Speech given May 8, 1899, reported in *Millennial Star,* May 18, 1899, 61:533.

are the pleasantest man I ever met! Shake, young fellow, I am glad to see a man that stands up for his convictions."[421]

As church president, Joseph F. was faced with moving the church into a new century and a new position in the eyes of the world. Within the first decade of the 1900s, Latter-day Saints worldwide were being counseled to build Zion where they were. A letter from President Smith to the editor of the *London Evening Times* in February 1911 would explain: "[Gathering to Utah] is not compulsory, and particularly under present conditions, is not urged, because it is desirable that our people shall remain in their native lands and form congregations of a permanent character to aid in the work of proselyting."[422]

That message would be repeated churchwide. (And reiterated numerous times, as recently as 1999.)

Clearly the most significant doctrinal contribution of his administration was his "Vision of the Redemption of the Dead," which he received just six weeks before his death.

In his words:

On the third of October, in the year nineteen hundred and eighteen, I sat in my room pondering over the Scriptures and reflecting upon the great atoning sacrifice that was made by the Son of God for the redemption of the world . . . As I pondered over these things which are written, the eyes of my understanding were opened, and the Spirit of the Lord rested upon me, and I saw the hosts of the dead, both small and great. And there were gathered together in one place an innumerable company of the spirits of the just, who had been faithful in the testimony of Jesus while they lived in mortality . . . I beheld that they were filled with joy and gladness, and were rejoicing together because the day of their deliverance was at hand. They were assembled awaiting the advent of the Son of God into the spirit world, to declare their redemption from the bands of death.

---

[421]As recounted by his son, Joseph Fielding Smith, in *Gospel Doctrine*, p. 518.

[422]See James R. Clark, *Messages of the First Presidency*, Vol. 4, p. 222.

As President Smith watched the vision, "the Son of God appeared, declaring liberty to the captives who had been faithful, and there he preached to them the everlasting gospel, the doctrine of the resurrection and the redemption of mankind from the fall, and from individual sins on conditions of repentance."

"But unto the wicked he did not go."

The Vision of Joseph F. Smith, son of Hyrum, would expand the doctrine of The Church of Jesus Christ of Latter-day Saints on the specifics of eternity perhaps more than any other thing since Joseph's 1832 vision of the three degrees of postmortal glory. Among the expansions: the existence of a sort of paradisiacal holding pen for the spirits of the just (of any religious persuasion); the personal visit to them of the Savior during his three-day absence from his Palestinian tomb; the organization of missionary labors among the unrighteous dead by "the faithful Elders of this dispensation" who were in the spirit world, among them Joseph and Hyrum Smith and Brigham Young.

Suffice it to say that the Vision was Big in the minds of Latter-day Saints, and it would get bigger. The doctrine was not new, but it was subrevolutionarily expansive, enlarging with great detail doctrine that Joseph had introduced nearly ninety years before. By the end of the month, the Vision had been accepted by the First Presidency and the Twelve as a revelation to the church. In 1976, it became an addendum to the scriptural *Pearl of Great Price*, and in 1979 it became *Doctrine and Covenants* Section 138, the latest addition to that standard work, illustrating as well as anything why Latter-day Saints don't typically speak of the "canon" (i.e. closed or limited) of scripture.

Heber J. Grant—born in Salt Lake City about the same time the survivors of the Willie Handcart Company were getting their socks thawed out—assumed the helm of the church in the late fall of 1918, just days after the end of World War I and upon the death of Joseph F. Smith. In more ways than one, Grant's administration would mark the end of the pioneer era. (Although he had taken three plural wives previous to the Manifesto, only one remained alive by the time of his church presidency.)

He would approve the construction of the first church temples outside the United States or even outside of Utah; one in Hawaii and another in Alberta, Canada. He would oversee the first radio broadcast of General Conference in 1924 (on a church-owned radio station) and the first broadcast of the Mormon Tabernacle Choir the following year (they would begin the weekly broadcast in 1929). He would carry the church through the Great Depression and launch the Church Welfare Program (initially the Security Program) and the youth seminary and institute program. Under his direction, the church's health code, the Word of Wisdom, would, after a hundred years, gain the stature of a binding component of faithfulness and temple worthiness. In many ways, he fathered the Church of Jesus Christ of Latter-day Saints that members and nonmembers would recognize for decades to come, "[helping] transform the Church from a sequestered, misunderstood, pioneer faith to an accepted, vibrant religion of twentieth-century America."[423]

His successor, George Albert Smith, would become known as a champion for the rising generation, but he would also acknowledge those that had preceded him. He oversaw the creation of scores of historic monuments and markers on the pioneer trail from Nauvoo, and he participated in the repurchase of a number of historic church properties in the eastern states, including the Joseph Smith farmstead in Manchester, New York. Taking the lead of the church just prior to the end of World War II, he authorized the distribution of thousands of tons of Utah-grown and packaged food, clothing, and medical supplies in Europe, an effort coordinated on the continent by Apostle Ezra Taft Benson. He saw the church reach the million-member mark during the centennial year of the Saints entry to the valley, which event he memorialized with a 75-foot-high granite and bronze monument in Pioneer Monument State Park (now called This Is the Place State Park).

David Oman McKay was sustained as church president in 1951 at seventy-seven years of age; altogether, he would serve as a General Authority for nearly sixty-four years, the longest to date of any church leader. During his administration, the church would nearly triple in size, and would change markedly its international makeup. In 1910, when McKay had been an apostle for four years, church membership totaled about 395,000, with 90 percent living in the United States. Fifty-eight percent of those resided in Utah, and a large part of the remainder lived in the contiguous western states. In 1955, after McKay had been president for four years, he dedicated the first non–North American temple—an emblem of church growth more than any other thing—in Zollikofen, Swit-

---

[423]*Encyclopedia of Mormonism*, Vol. 2, S.V. "Grant, Heber J."

zerland. Three years later, he dedicated another in England. When he died in January 1970, the church was nearing three million members, 70 percent of whom lived in the United States and Canada.

The LDS Church's tenth prophet-president was Joseph F.'s first son, Joseph Fielding Smith. Long an influential writer, church historian (or assistant historian) for sixty-four years, and for sixty years an apostle, "Joseph Fielding" had, in the minds of many Latter-day Saints, few peers when it came to church history and doctrine. His views as an apostle had not been without controversy, and he was often seen as a strict "literalist" in his interpretation of Scriptures on topics like the age of Earth, human origins, and the rights of the priesthood.

But he was equally strict in the management of his own life. He was known to travel miles out of his way (obeying the speed limit, I'm sure) just to patronize merchants who faithfully closed their businesses on the Sabbath, and he followed closely the Mormon health code's injunction to eat meat "sparingly." Any overt recognition by others of such actions would have likely been met by an honestly quizzical reply: "but this is nothing more nor less than what the Lord has asked us to do."

Joseph Fielding was intense. He was committed. He was probably disappointed when he died seventeen days short of his ninety-sixth birthday.

When Harold B. Lee assumed the presidency of the church on July 7, 1972, it was assumed he would be around for a long time. At seventy-three, he was considered a young man for the office. But he only occupied it for 538 days.

President Lee had a way of doing lots of things early. The first church president since Joseph F. to be born outside Utah (up the road, in Idaho), he began school earlier than did most children his age, and he was ordained a deacon before the official age of twelve. He was teaching school at seventeen and presiding over hundreds of missionaries and church members in Denver four years after that. At thirty-one, Lee became one of the youngest stake presidents in the church and was a founding force in the Church Security Program in 1936. When he was called to full-time church service as an apostle at forty-two years of age, he was affectionately referred to as "the kid" by his senior brethren. When he died the day after Christmas in 1973, he gave about one hour's notice.

The man who replaced Lee was the first Prophet I ever knew. Spencer W. Kimball was a small man with a huge heart. Kimball, who had long since lost most of his vocal cords to cancer, was heard in public only through the aid of microphones. His weak and raspy voice yet echoes strongly in the minds of most who heard him, including mine.

During Kimball's twelve-year presidency, more than 2.6 million people converted to The Church of Jesus Christ of Latter-day Saints. Perhaps I was the only seventeen-year-old Taoist mountain hippie among them, but at a certain point in the process, the mechanics of conversion operated at some level on nearly every one of us. Most of us are still hanging on. Others, like a friend I baptized four months later, lasted less than a year.

Meaning what?

This is a religion; it is a faith. It is not a club neither academic nor social. Although otherwise intelligent writers and scholars (within and without the church) continue to examine the corporate structure or the doctrinal basis or the historical record of the church as an institution, some of us continue to seek the God behind all of it. That's what we were looking for in the first place. And that's exactly what we found. The specifics of the experience are unique to each, and I can only speak for myself, but here's the common denominator of lasting conversion in the whole Mormon experience, learned by every nineteen-year-old missionary fresh from his mama's hearth: "Take our word for nothing. Go to God in prayer, and ask him if what we've told you is true."

Spencer W. Kimball would reinforce for the entire church exactly how fundamental a step that was in Latter-day Saint theology.

Since the 1840s, men of black African lineage had not been allowed to hold the lay priesthood in the church. Although a few had done so in the early years, the restriction appears to have become total by the time the Saints entered the Salt Lake valley in 1847. Many speakers and writers (within the church and without) have attempted to paint this issue with a brush much too large, claiming that the reasons for the ban were not clear, or that they changed over time, or that they were simply prejudicial. While I know where they're going with each of these theories (some with admirable intent), each of them is absolutely false.

There is a single reason the Latter-day Saints kept their black members from holding the priesthood, and that is because the Lord said through his prophets (twelve of them) that it would be so. The reasons behind the Lord's decision we can only wonder at, and that's exactly what many have done.

Prophet Number 12 would render all the reasoning irrelevant.

He would later tell a church audience in South Africa:

I remember very vividly that day after day I walked to the [Salt Lake City] temple and ascended to the fourth floor where we have our solemn assemblies and where we have our meetings of the Twelve and the First Presidency. After everybody had gone out of the temple, I knelt and prayed. I prayed with much fervency. I knew that something was before us that was extremely important to many of the children of God. Day after day I went alone and with great solemnity and seriousness in the upper rooms of the temple, and there I offered my soul and offered my efforts . . . I wanted to do what he wanted. I talked about it to him and said, "Lord, I want only what is right. We are not making any plans to be spectacularly moving. We want only the thing that thou dost want, and we want it when you want it and not until."

We met with the Council of the Twelve Apostles, time after time in the holy room where there is a picture of the Savior in many different moods and also pictures of all the Presidents of the Church. Finally we had the feeling and the impression from the Lord, who made it very clear to us, that this was the thing to do to make the gospel universal to all worthy people.[424]

On June 8, 1978, a statement signed by the Kimball presidency would be read and then distributed to journalists gathered in a press briefing room on the twenty-fifth floor of the Church Office Building in Salt Lake City: "The long-promised day has come when every faithful, worthy man in the Church may receive the holy priesthood, with power to exercise its divine authority, and enjoy with his loved ones every blessing that flows therefrom, including the blessings of the temple. Accordingly, all worthy male members of the Church may be ordained to the priesthood without regard for race or color."[425]

It was, without exception, the most momentous occasion in church history since the Manifesto on polygamy eighty-eight years before. The shock waves ran through the United States and international media and throughout the church, with most members—including me—hearing it on the evening news.

---

[424]Johannesburg, South Africa, Area Conference, October 23, 1978, cited in *The Teachings of Spencer W. Kimball*, p. 451.

[425]From the official press release; see also *Doctrine and Covenants*, Official Declaration No. 2.

As in the aftermath of the Manifesto, a few church members struggled for a time to come to grips with the doctrine—right before their eyes—of a living prophet leading the church. Most were overjoyed.

In all, Spencer Kimball's twelve-year tenure as church president (following thirty years as an apostle) was one of the most productive in church history. At the time of his death in November 1985, one-half of the church's six million members had known no other Prophet.

Unlike Kimball, a small-town Arizona insurance agent at the time of his call to the Twelve in 1943, Ezra Taft Benson was known by millions of Americans both inside and outside the church. An agricultural economist of some note before his call to full-time church service (also in 1943), Benson was installed as president of the church mission in Europe and given a charge to help rebuild that land at the close of World War II. In 1946, he visited more than a hundred cities in thirteen countries, overseeing the distribution of ninety-two boxcar loads of food, clothing, bedding, and medical supplies donated by the church. The effort became the cornerstone of an international humanitarian relief program that would eventually reach full bloom in the 1990s.[426]

In 1952, following the counsel of Church President David O. McKay, Benson accepted a cabinet position as secretary of agriculture for eight years in the Eisenhower administration. During those years, his strident views on American patriotism and strict constitutional loyalty (according to a decidedly Republican point of view) were often exercised. While Benson's personal views, then and later, tended to range somewhat beyond the requirements of his faith, they were, nonetheless, extrapolated from them: the "American-ness" (meaning United States)[427] of Latter-day Saint doctrine is at once both explicit and unintentional.

Church materials and speakers make numerous efforts to state that the restoration of the Church of Jesus Christ could not have happened in the political and social clime of any other nation than the United States of America; that Columbus was led here to this undiscovered country by

---

[426]The Church Welfare Program, formally launched during the depths of the Great Depression in 1936, would rise to laudable heights of service long before the humanitarian effort would.

[427]My frequent clarification of "United States/America" phraseology stems from having lived two years in a South American nation whose residents often reminded me that they were American, too.

God; that the revolutionary severing from England and the founding of the United States were in fact essential steps in the restoration process. At the foundation of this doctrine lies the following scripture from *Doctrine and Covenants:* "And for this purpose have I [God] established the constitution of this land, by the hands of wise men whom I raised up unto this very purpose."⁴²⁸

Regarding those "wise men," the following account is deemed sacred by all Latter-day Saints. On August 21, 1877, while serving as president of the temple in St. George in southern Utah, Wilford Woodruff was visited by the disembodied spirits of a number of American patriots. A few weeks later he told the story:

> I will here say, before closing, that two weeks before I left St. George, the spirits of the dead gathered around me, wanting to know why we did not redeem them. Said they, "You have had the use of the Endowment House for a number of years, and yet nothing has ever been done for us. We laid the foundation of the government you now enjoy, and we never apostatized from it, but we remained true to it and were faithful to God." These were the signers of the Declaration of Independence, and they waited on me for two days and two nights. I straightway went into the baptismal font and called upon brother [J. D. T.] McCallister [who was also present] to baptize me for the signers of the Declaration of Independence, and fifty other eminent men, making one hundred in all, including John Wesley, Columbus, and others; I then baptized him for every President of the United States, except three [Martin Van Buren, James Buchanan and Ulysses Grant, who was still living]; and when their cause is just, somebody will do the work for them.⁴²⁹ [The proxy work for all three was later completed.]

Twenty-two years later, and twenty-two days before he died, Woodruff again spoke of the St. George visit. "I am going to bear my testimony to this assembly, if I never do it again in my life, that those men who laid the foundation of this American Government and signed the Declaration of Independence were the best spirits the God of heaven could

---

⁴²⁸*Doctrine and Covenants* 101:77–80.

⁴²⁹*Journal of Discourses*, Vol. 19, p. 230, Wilford Woodruff, September 16, 1877.

find on the face of the earth. They were choice spirits, not wicked men. George Washington and all the men that labored for the purpose were inspired of the Lord."[430]

Perhaps no church leader in history has referred to this episode as frequently as did Ezra Taft Benson. On the other hand, the church in Benson's day was rapidly becoming an international growth phenomenon. Of the 2.7 million people who converted to the church during his eight-and-a-half-year administration, only a little more than half a million— about 17 percent—came from the United States, and the non-U.S. growth rate was far exceeding that of the U.S. rate.

More fundamentally, though, The Church of Jesus Christ of Latter-day Saints in each nation is run by members of the church from that nation. It is a lay clergy worldwide: Austrians run their congregations in Austria; Colombians in Colombia; Koreans in Korea.

Having traveled and counseled Latter-day Saints around the world, Ezra Taft Benson, as church president, knew this very well. His administration would therefore be marked as one of Latter-day Saint fundamentals: Christ as Savior, the Apostasy and Restoration, and the Book of Mormon.

His successor, Howard W. Hunter, was an uncommonly gentle soul, one so quiet and self-effacing, in fact, that most figured his would be a very uneventful presidency. Few could name the subject of any talk he had given in nearly thirty-five years as an apostle. But when he died less than nine months later—the shortest administration in church history— President Hunter had reinvigorated Latter-day Saints worldwide with his plea to focus on the Savior, to do what the Savior would do, to honor the Savior in everything we did.

His successor, Gordon B. Hinckley, would inherit a membership nearing ten million, but in many ways it was as if they had inherited him. No one in church history, including Brigham Young, was so fully expected and instantly accepted as Gordon B. Hinckley.

Installed as a third counselor to President Kimball in 1981 (after twenty years in the Quorum of the Twelve) due to failing health of the other counselors in the First Presidency, he was made second counselor a year and a half later, following the death of Nathan Eldon Tanner. Ezra Taft Benson called Hinckley as first counselor in his presidency three

---

[430]Wilford Woodruff, General Conference address, April 10, 1898.

years later, and Howard Hunter called him to the same position nine years after that. But much of the time, Hinckley in fact carried the lion's share of the First Presidency's load, as one after another the aging counselors and presidents struggled mightily with their health.

At the time of his sustaining as fifteenth president of the church on March 12, 1995, at eighty-four years of age, Hinckley had either dedicated or rededicated (following renovation) twenty-six of the forty-seven operating temples of the church. He was healthy, reminding a Salt Lake City reporter in his opening press conference that he had never spent a night in the hospital until he was seventy-five, adding "that doesn't mean I'm ready to run a hundred-yard dash!" But most of all, he was consummately ready.

Having completed a bachelor's degree in English and served a mission to Great Britain—both rare accomplishments in the midst of the Great Depression—he was hired by the church to create missionary and publicity materials in 1935. Over the next two decades, he became a veritable production house, with products in film, print, and radio, all directed to non-LDS audiences. Named a General Authority in 1958, and an apostle in 1961, he would become the senior apostle and president of the church at a time when knowledge of the media and skill with such audience would be near essential.

In the first years of his presidency, Hinckley would break new ground with the national and international media. Counselors and apostles would at first recommend he do otherwise—and then follow his lead.

In February 1996, on Gordon B. Hinckley's watch, church membership would "cross over" from mostly North American (U.S. and Canada, where it was the seventh largest religious body) to mostly not.[431] Twenty-one months later, the total would reach ten million, increasing at a rate that made news stories all over the globe.

"That the Mormons have overtaken such prominent . . . faiths [in the United States] as the Congregationalists, Presbyterians, Episcopalians and even the Lutherans must be one of the most unremarked cultural watersheds in American history," wrote non-Mormon sociologist Rodney Stark in the *Review of Religious Research* in 1984.[432] On the heels of Stark's published research findings, however, the growth of The Church of Jesus

---

[431]This was the second such crossover; in the early 1850s, church membership in Great Britain had exceeded that in the United States. Then most emigrated.

[432]*Review of Religious Research*, vol. 26: 18–24

Christ of Latter-day Saints has become a topic of frequent remark in national and international circles, both among editors and pastors. (And according to Stark, LDS membership statistics are "extremely reliable. Is there another denomination that actually sends out auditors to check local figures?"[433]) Yet the Saints' "rapid growth had occurred in the face of much greater hostility than has been directed toward any Protestant sect and is thereby all the more remarkable."

Stark's early research found the church growing at a rate exceeding 30 percent, and frequently 40 percent, a decade in its first century. Growth rates in the 1950s (52 percent), 1960s (73 percent), and 1970s (58 percent) were phenomenal. Using a straight-line projection ("it's done this in the past, it should do this in the future") through the conservative decades, Stark estimated there would be sixty-three million Mormons in the year 2080. He was eaten alive by critics and colleagues.

Following receipt of "an amazing amount of counseling concerning the pitfalls of straight-line projections,"[434] Stark reworked his figures and added a decade and a half of the latest growth figures (up to and including 1994) to his calculations. The critics were right: LDS growth was in fact varying from the 30 percent straight-line. It was more closely approximating a 50 percent line. In fact, Stark's 50-percent-a-decade ten million members wasn't supposed to happen until late 1999. It happened in November 1997.

Additionally, he found that "Mormon growth is stimulated rather than curtailed by modernization," presaging a comparable rise into the future. The revised straight-line shows 60 million Latter-day Saints in the year 2050—2.2 centuries after the church's founding—and 268 million by the year 2080.

But the Latter-day Saints, among those eschatological religionists one British journalist painted as believing they are "living at the end of the world,"[435] trust that the year 2050, let alone 2080, will never happen, right?

It's time we moved this story into the future.

---

[433]Ibid.

[434]"The Rise of a New World Faith, Postscript" p. 22; in James T. Duke, ed., *Latter-day Saint Social Life*, Religious Studies Center, Brigham Young University, 1998.

[435]*Living at the End of the World*, Marina Benjamin, Picador UK, 1998. Cool title, strange book. My name in the acknowledgments should not be construed as having anything to do with how the chapter on the Latter-day Saints turned out.

CHAPTER 19

The Biggest Heaven and the Littlest Hell

Just what is the Latter-day Saints' timetable for the end of the world?

We don't know. We're not the guys in the sandwich placards walking through city park. We've never projected a date; we've never held an end-of-the-world assembly or symposium; we don't mark our calendars.

The Savior said, "Of that day and hour knoweth no man, no, not the angels of heaven, but my Father only" (Matt. 24:36). Any supposition to the contrary is misguided and arrogant.

But we do know it's coming. It has been part of the plan all along: mortality—earth life—is but a small moment in the eternal round. This was the day of our probation, preceded by one existence and to be followed by yet another. It *will* come to an end.

All we claim to know of the date is that it will follow certain "signs" given on the earth and in the heavens, which the righteous will recognize. Among the signs of the last days promised by the Savior and recorded, most concentratedly, in Matt. 24 are these: "wars and rumours of wars"; "famines, and pestilences, and earthquakes, in divers places across the earth"; "many false prophets shall rise, and shall deceive many"; "because iniquity shall abound, the love of many shall wax cold"; "this gospel of the kingdom shall be preached in all the world for a witness unto all nations."

"And then shall the end come."[436]

These particular signs do appear to be adding up. But Matt. 24 does not contain the entire catalog of end-of-planet augury. Isaiah prophesied that the Lord would set his hand to gather the scattered Israelites (Is. 11: 11); Malachi foresaw the return to earth of the great prophet Elijah "before the coming of the great and dreadful day of the Lord" (Mal. 4:5); Peter testified of the "restitution of all things" (Acts 3:21) in the last days.

The Israelites are gathering. Elijah has come. Peter has returned to restore—with Elijah, Moses, Adam, Elias, and John the Baptist—all the

---

[436]All from Matt. 24, KJV.

doctrine, priesthood authority, and structure of the full Church of Jesus Christ. That is our claim. We also claim that he named it, "even The Church of Jesus Christ *of Latter-day* Saints."[437]

So yes, we buy into the "last days" discourse. The term is used twenty-eight times in *Doctrine and Covenants*, compared with five in the New Testament. But just what is Mormon doctrine in regard to it? If we're right on the verge, what's next?

Mark's account of the Savior's instruction regarding the aforementioned signs of the last days reports that he concluded with these words: "So . . . when ye shall see these things come to pass, know that it [the End] is nigh, even at the doors."[438]

This "end" is not the end of the earth, but the end of Fallen Earth, with its attendant abundance of misery and misfortune. Of the signs given in Matthew, to which the entire Christian world at large is paying attention, Latter-day Saints probably chat about the preaching of the gospel "in all the world" more than the others. At the turn of the second millennium A.D., we have church "units" (branches or wards) in 162 nations and territories and full-time missionaries in just under 140. Using U.S. State Department figures as a yardstick,[439] this means the Latter-day Saints have no official presence in twenty-nine nations, including China (population 1.1. billion), Iran (50 million), or Cuba (10 million). We've been in Russia since 1989 (our second try) and India for a bit longer, but count fewer than eleven thousand members in those two nations, which host 1.3 billion people.

It would appear that the Latter-day Saints trust in several more decades passing before the gospel has been preached in all the world. Wouldn't it? Not necessarily.[440] We do not claim to know all that the Lord may be doing at the hands of other ministers. First, there is the apostle John, he who was translated without tasting death, whose desire[441]

---

[437]*Doctrine and Covenants* 115:4, April 1838.

[438]Mark 13:29.

[439]This is the particular yardstick used by church statisticians. Various entities recognize a widely divergent number of nations and territories. In 1995, for instance, the *Guinness Book of World Records* listed 256, the U.N. 185, and the World Bank 166.

[440]That possibility remains just that, however: some interpretations of before-the-end chronology contend official church congregations and temple-endowed members will lead Latter-day Saints in all nations, requiring, at present view, a good chunk of time.

[441]The account of this discussion given in the New Testament is brief and ambiguous; a revelation given to Joseph Smith amplifies the event: "And the Lord said unto me: John,

(granted) was to remain on the earth and preach the gospel in many nations. Additionally, three Books of Mormon disciples made the same request and received the same promise.[442] Where are they, and how effective, after two thousand years of practice, have they been?

How about an idea somewhat more conventional: missionaries of other faiths have entered nations where Latter-day Saints have not been, and may never get, testifying of Jesus as Savior and teaching truths as they understand them from the Bible. To these we say, "God bless you," and wish them all success, we really do. Building on their foundation of faith, we can clarify and add to later on. We've done it for 170 years, and the huge majority of our converts are graduates from other Christian faiths.[443]

On the other hand, we don't expect to baptize all or even most of them. We have no expectations about the growth of the church other than it will likely continue to grow, and grow rapidly. But sixty million? Two hundred and sixty-eight million? We don't know. Professor Stark's figures, impressive and self-adulatory as they are, have been promulgated only by the church Public Affairs office, not the First Presidency's office.

In any case, all we know about the end of the world is what the Savior told the Prophet Joseph Smith: "Therefore, the keys of this dispensation are committed into your hands; and by this ye may know that the great and dreadful day of the Lord is near, even at the doors."[444]

That dreadful day, of course, is the Second Coming.

"In Jewish and Christian thought there are two basic ways of viewing the coming of the messiah," wrote Gerald N. Lund in 1989.

Some consider promises of a Messiah and a millennial era symbolic of a time when men will finally learn to live in peace and harmony and

---

my beloved, what desirest thou? For if you shall ask what you will, it shall be granted unto you. And I said unto him: Lord, give unto me power over death, that I may live and bring souls unto thee. And the Lord said unto me: Verily, verily, I say unto thee, because thou desirest this thou shalt tarry until I come in my glory, and shalt prophesy before nations, kindreds, tongues and people." (*Doctrine and Covenants* 7:1–3)

[442]The "Three Nephites."

[443]The huge majority of church members are converts. By 1998, a total of 67 percent of all living members of the church were first-generation converts.

[444]*Doctrine and Covenants* 110:16.

the world will enter a new age of enlightenment and progress; no one individual nor any one specific event will usher in this age. The Church of Jesus Christ of Latter-day Saints opposes this view and agrees with the many other Jewish and Christian groups who affirm that there is an actual Messiah, that he will come at some future time to the earth, and that only through his coming and the events associated therewith will a millennial age of peace, harmony, and joy begin. Jews look for the first coming of the Messiah; Latter-day Saints and other Christians for the second coming of Jesus Christ.[445]

The days preceding the triumphant return to earth of the Savior of man will not be easy days. Children will be shooting children, or their own parents; parents will turn on their own children; wars of unprecedented proportions will rage across the earth; persistent and aggressive diseases unknown before will reach plague levels; economic systems will collapse; abuses physical and psychological will rage; natural disasters will sweep and rock and shatter the land; evil will stalk children at home, at school, and in much that they see and hear; people's hearts will fail them for fear.

As the end of the earth nears, the planet itself will be in commotion; enormous and vicious storms will lash the land, destroying crops and plunging whole nations or continents into famine; "the earth [will] tremble and . . . reel to and fro as a drunken man" as the continents are driven back into one land as they were before the flood. All governments will fail and collapse; the sun will be darkened in the sky and the moon will turn blood red [weather patterns? volcanic eruptions? nuclear holocaust?]; the stars will appear to fall en masse from the sky "even as a fig tree casteth her untimely figs, when she is shaken of a might wind."[446]

Finally, in a valley some sixty miles north of Jerusalem, below the site of the ancient city of Har Megiddo (or Armageddon), the armies of the earth will face each other down on the plain of Esdraelon. Though battles will rage across the earth, this valley of Jezreel will form the apex of the most destructive and violent battle ever known.

Then, at the height of battle, "the curtain of heaven [will] be un-

---

[445]In *Encyclopedia of Mormonism*, Vol. 2, s.v. "Jesus Christ."

[446]Rev. 6:12–13.

folded . . . and the face of the Lord shall be unveiled."[447] Jesus Christ will step out of the heavens, clothed in red, in such a manner that "all flesh shall see [Him] together."[448] This time he will not be a helpless, anonymous baby in a dirty Judean stable, but the Lord of Lords and King of Kings, the very Creator of the earth, the Savior of all mankind, come to assume leadership and control of that which is his. "So great shall be the glory of his presence that the sun shall hide his face in shame,"[449] says one modern revelation; the presence of the earth's very God shall be so great that the elements will "melt with fervent heat"[450] and "the mountains shall flow down at [his] presence."[451]

Both the righteous living and the righteous dead (but not the merely lukewarm of either) will be lifted into the sky to greet the descending Lord, whose triumphal touchdown on the Mount of Olives will split it asunder, "and there shall be a very great valley; and half of the mountain shall remove toward the north, and half of it toward the south."[452]

"And then shall the Jews look upon me and say: What are these wounds in thine hands and in thy feet? Then shall they know that I am the Lord; for I will say unto them: These wounds are the wounds with which I was wounded in the house of my friends. I am he who was lifted up. I am Jesus that was crucified. I am the Son of God. And then shall they weep because of their iniquities; then shall they lament because they persecuted their king."[453]

And then there will be peace.

Latter-day Saint doctrine teaches, as does most sectarian Christian doctrine, that the subsequent thousand years, known as the Millennium, will be an era of peace, presided over by the Prince of Peace himself. This is the era of which the biblical Isaiah spoke, during which men "shall beat their swords into plowshares, and their spears into pruninghooks: nation shall not lift up sword against nation, neither shall they learn war

---

[447]*Doctrine and Covenants* 88:95.

[448]Ibid. 101:23.

[449]Ibid. 133:49.

[450]Ibid. 101:25.

[451]Ibid. 133:44.

[452]Zech. 14:4.

[453]*Doctrine and Covenants* 45:51–53.

any more."[454] This is when the post-Eden enmities within the animal kingdom as well will cease, finding the wolf lying with the lamb, and the lion eating straw like the ox. (See Is. 11.) Given such parameters, it is inconceivable to think that people will yet be puncturing the brains of cattle and breaking the necks of minks.

But LDS doctrine expands upon or adds to several components of the common Christian concept of the millennial era.

1. In fact, the commotions surrounding the Second Coming of the Savior will include a complete renewing of the earth, a refreshing, a magnificent chemical and physical transformation of the orb to its paradisaical state known during the first days of Adam. So complete will be this transfiguration that the former earth "shall not be remembered, nor come into mind." (Is. 65:17)

2. Like in that Adamic era, the globe will host a single contiguous landmass.

3. Upon that single yet extensive continent, the Savior will establish equal seats of government in each of the two hemispheres it will reach into: one in Jackson County, Missouri—to which the Latter-day Saints will have been called to once again gather just previous to the Millennium—and the other in a rebuilt, restored, and beautified Jerusalem. ("For out of Zion shall go forth the law, and the word of the Lord from Jerusalem"—Isa. 2:3).

4. Although the Savior will reign over the earth, he will likely not occupy it continuously nor personally direct all matters of government, but leave much in the hands of the righteous who remain.

5. Saints of former days—Adam, Eve, Noah, Abraham, Moses, and Joseph Smith among them—will visit the earth and instruct, as will the immortal spirits of righteous and inspired men and women of great skill or ingenuity in fields of government, science, and the arts.

---

[454]Isa. 2:4.

6. Although "all that do wickedly" will have been consumed at or previous to the Lord's Second Coming, millions of decent folks among all sects, parties, and denominations (or allied with none at all) including Catholics, Buddhists, and Hindus—will yet live on the earth.

7. For a while, an unprecedented missionary effort by the Latter-day Saints, combined with a very apparent awareness of just whose priesthood has been duly recognized by the Savior, will soon convert most. Those who don't convert will be ushered into the postmortal realm where they can think about it a while longer.

8. In many ways, life will be normal (albeit gloriously safe and peaceful): "And they shall build houses, and inhabit them; and they shall plant vineyards, and eat the fruit of them" wrote Isaiah (65:21–22). Death will still be the portal between mortality and immortality, but the righteous who die after the beginning of the Millennium "shall not sleep . . . in the earth, but shall be changed [resurrected] in the twinkling of an eye," and children born in this era "shall grow up until they become old," defined by modern revelation "as the age of a tree."[455]

9. Satan will be bound, literally restrained, from peddling his prurience on the earth. For a thousand years, children will grow up without sin.

The millennial era will be a time of extensive labor, not laziness. In addition to the teaching of true and valid gospel principles to those good enough to have survived the "end of the world," temples will be built in great numbers, and essential ordinance work for all the "dead" since the time of Adam and Eve will move forward rapidly.

But time is not over yet. Nor is the cleansing. Toward the end of the thousand years, Satan "shall be loosed for a little season" and people will again begin to deny their God, even as he reigns in their midst. "And Michael . . . even the archangel, shall gather together his armies, even the hosts of heaven. And the devil shall gather together his armies; even the hosts of hell, and shall come up to battle against Michael and his armies.

---

[455]*Doctrine and Covenants* 101:30.

And then cometh the battle of the great God; and the devil and his armies shall be cast away into their own place, that they shall not have power over the saints any more at all."[456]

Ever.

"And then shall the angels be crowned with the glory of his [Christ's] might, and the saints shall be filled with his glory, and receive their inheritance *and be made equal with him* [italics mine]."[457]

And the earth will be their home. "This earth, in its sanctified and immortal state," taught the Prophet Joseph Smith, "will be made like unto crystal," a "sea of glass" according to John the Revelator,[458] a brilliant, translucent planet like unto the very abode of God, nigh unto Kolob, that great and leading star of the universe. Its own inhabitants will be the heirs of the heavenly glory so long promised, the meek who have in fact inherited the earth; a new earth, a celestial orb of unsurpassed majesty, one who has fulfilled "the measure of its creation"[459] from the very beginning.

But what of the others?

Hell? Purgatory? Endless suffering amidst hellfire and brimstone?

This is the point, theologically, at which I opted out of cultural Christianity at about the age of fourteen, and checked into strict vegetarianism, Carlos Castañeda, and Henry David Thoreau. Having been raised with no religious faith at all, it was nevertheless the faith of my culture, my nation, and I harbored within me my own little spark of that innate desire given to all children of God: to know where I came from, what it was all about, what was life's meaning. So I tried.

What I found were the Crusades (in the name of the Christian God?!), the Inquisition, the Mexican conquest, and the plundering of Peru. I tried to learn Christianity, as a local preacher told me I was going to hell for not "confessing Jesus" and threatened to kill my Siamese cat for walking through his tulips. I worked on it while I lifted my good Christian buddy up and out of his own vomit following the rapid ingestion of eight cans of beer. I watched TV reports of Mississippi Christians bashing the heads of blacks (and thanked my lucky stars I was growing up in Colorado).

---

[456]*Doctrine and Covenants* 88:11–114.

[457]Ibid. 88:107.

[458]Rev. 15:2.

[459]*Doctrine and Covenants* 88:25.

Unfortunately, I didn't know Jesus, so Thoreau it was. For a while.

When I heard the LDS missionaries four years later, though, it was an entirely different Christianity than what I'd been exposed to. (The sects who despise us maintained this is exactly why they despise us; those million individuals who join us every three years say it's exactly why they joined us.)

What I found out is that the Latter-day Saints don't despise anyone, short of the patently evil among mankind, nor consign them to hell. Nor does their God. And *that* was incredibly refreshing. To my teenage ears it sounded . . . well, so Christian. It sounded like a God I wanted to know.

Here's the Latter-day Saint view of where he sends us. Let's start with these verses from the Book of Mormon[460]:

> Now, concerning the state of the soul between death and the resurrection—Behold, it has been made known unto me by an angel, that the spirits of all men, as soon as they are departed from this mortal body, yea, the spirits of all men, whether they be good or evil, are taken home to that God who gave them life.
>
> And then shall it come to pass, that the spirits of those who are righteous are received into a state of happiness, which is called paradise, a state of rest, a state of peace, where they shall rest from all their troubles and from all care, and sorrow.
>
> And then shall it come to pass, that the spirits of the wicked, yea, who are evil . . . these shall be cast out into outer darkness; there shall be weeping, and wailing, and gnashing of teeth, and this because of their own iniquity, being led captive by the will of the devil.

Thus a separation, a judgment, the righteous going to one world known as "paradise" and the wicked to another: spirit prison. End of story? Not at all. The Book of Mormon prophet continues: "Now this is the state of the souls of the wicked, yea, in darkness, and a state of awful, fearful looking for the fiery indignation of the wrath of God upon them; thus they remain in this state, as well as the righteous in paradise, *until the time of their resurrection.* [italics mine]."

The moment of death, at which the spirit leaves the physical body, initiates a preliminary judgment only, a very general, broad-stroke kind of

---

[460]Alma 40:11–14.

move. As previously discussed, this paradise—not heaven, but a proximate place of rest and refuge and beauty—will welcome even those such as the man hung on the cross contiguous to Christ: a convicted thief receiving, in his own words, "the due reward"[461] of his actions. (And possibly his companion as well; the Bible account does not exclude him and neither will we.) As seen in the Vision of Joseph F. Smith this Paradise will give time and opportunity to "a vast multitude," an "innumerable company" to hear the gospel and either accept or reject its principles before a final judgment.

The early stages of this process occur now and have been occurring since the first human being died. An initial judgment places one in Paradise or the spirit prison. Then, those among the dead who hold valid priesthood authority received while on the earth minister among the others as missionaries, as teachers. Their proselytory ministration takes them throughout the realm of Paradise, but it then extends into the darkened corridors of the spirit prison, where even the wicked are offered the full range of gospel teaching and capability.

Offered. Although every soul among the dead in either realm will someday hear with their ears and acknowledge with absolute clarity that Jesus is the Christ, the Redeemer who died for them, none will be forced to accept his teachings or his actions on their behalf. The immutable law of eternity—free agency—will prevail. For those who accept the teachings and ordinances prescribed by their Savior, essential ordinances of salvation performed for them vicariously in earthly temples will have saving power. For those who do not, they will merely have been paperwork, names on a list: conscientious rejectors.

But our ages-ago acceptance of this sojourn on earth had two primary purposes. One was to determine our level of valiance—now being evaluated—and the other was to receive a physical body. At some point in our spirit interlude, we will get it back.

The Resurrection was initiated two thousand years ago, when the Son of God broke the bands of death and became "the firstfruits of them that slept,"[462] his spirit rejoining his immortalized body, never again to separate from it. The righteous dead living previous to Christ rose with

---

[461]Luke 23:41.

[462]I Cor. 15:20.

him, and continued on with their eternal—and now glorified—progress. The righteous who have died since Christ (minus four already resurrected that we know of: Peter, James, John the Baptist, and Moroni) will rise to greet Christ at his Coming. Those righteous who die during the Millennium will not "taste of death" but resurrect instantly. Those in the spirit world who fully accept the gospel there (the great majority of them in Paradise but, conceivably, a few even from the rolls of the spirit prison) will be given some time to "prove it," then be clothed upon once again with their bodies. All these are considered participants in the First Resurrection, the "resurrection of the just."[463]

Those from the beginning of earth time who have wasted the days of their probation, chosen to do wickedly even with the knowledge to do right, will all await the Second Resurrection. They won't wait in peace. "These are they who are liars, and sorcerers, and adulterers, and whoremongers, and whosoever loves and makes a lie. These are they who are cast down to hell and suffer the wrath of Almighty God, until the fulness of times, when Christ shall have subdued all enemies under his feet, and shall have perfected his work."[464]

Having rejected the Atonement of Christ, but not entirely the whisperings of the spirit that make one at least human and not a total monster, they in effect atone for their own sins throughout the long day of the Millennium. And yet they wait some more.

When the thousand years are ended, when the "little season" and the great war have ended, having suffered the torments of the damned and faced the full and vivid and searing consciousness of their conduct on the earth, they will remember it all, and they will wish the mountains could fall upon them and snuff them out in their shame.

They will suffer, but there they can yet repent. "As rapidly as they can . . . gain light, believe truth, acquire intelligence, cast off sin, and break the chains of hell," wrote Elder Bruce R. McConkie, "they can leave the hell that imprisons them and dwell with the righteous in the peace of paradise."[465] Hell, for most, will have an end.

These will rise in the Second Resurrection, the completion of the

---

[463]Luke 14:14.

[464]*Doctrine and Covenants* 76: 103–106.

[465]Bruce R. McConkie, Mormon Doctrine, p. 755, s.v. "Spirit Prison."

placing in immortal bodies the spirits of all who have ever been born on the earth. As "gender is an essential characteristic of individual premortal, mortal, and eternal identity and purpose,"[466] the Resurrection (all phases of it) will assure that males will reacquire their human male bodies, females their female bodies, dogs will be dogs, and so on.

Modern revelation tells us that "the dead [look] upon the long absence of their spirits from their bodies as a bondage,"[467] and that "spirit and element [body], inseparably connected, receive a fulness of joy, and when separated, man cannot receive a fulness of joy."[468] Following the Resurrection, each of us will look like ourselves, except that flaws, including potbellies, warts, deformities, and the like, will be gone, and a perfected physical figure—the very figure of our premortal spirit now clothed upon with immortal matter—will be ours.

And then comes the Final Judgment. This is the event seen by John the Revelator in vision on Patmos, of which he wrote: "And I saw the dead, small and great, stand before God; and the books were opened: and another book was opened, which is the book of life: and the dead were judged out of those things which were written in the books, according to their works . . . and they were judged every man according to their works."[469] The Book of Mormon adds "and our thoughts will also condemn us"[470] should they have been impure ones.

Three sets of records will be used by the Lord in making this final judgment: the records kept in heaven, the records kept on earth, and the record written on our own soul, the perfect postmortal memory and conscience of each individual. And here a miracle within the purview and power of only a God will come into play, a miracle experienced thousands of times by millions of individuals on the earth but now driven home with perfect clarity: some things will have been erased from the heavenly record. Repentance—sincere, complete, total—undertaken either while on earth or while awaiting the Resurrection will have struck entire entries, even vile ones, from our

---

[466]From paragraph two: "The Family: A Proclamation to the World," First Presidency and Quorum of the Twelve, September 23, 1995.

[467]*Doctrine and Covenants* 138:50.

[468]Ibid. 93:33.

[469]Rev. 20:12–13.

[470]Alma 12:14.

ledger, dropping us to our knees in tears and beatific acknowledgment of a Savior just and true. That is why he came and suffered. That was the whole purpose of the Atonement. We cannot expect that the suffering in Gethsemane, "which suffering caused myself, even God, the greatest of all, to tremble because of pain, and to bleed at every pore, and to suffer both body and spirit,"[471] was expended lightly nor that it will be distributed so.

To Latter-day Saints, the Atonement of Jesus Christ is the very epicenter of our faith, the focus of our effort both inward and outward. It stands as the most important event in universal history, the fulcrum of time and eternity. We do not send our young sons and daughters to the far reaches of the planet at great and personal expense so that we can become a big church; we send them to save souls. In the Final Judgment, the package comes full circle: we lived together as spirit brothers and sisters, sons and daughters of God, in a premortal world. We all agreed to come to earth to gain a body and be tested as to our true valiancy of soul when out of our Father's presence. Some of us agreed to be born in nations, or in homes, or in eras where wars would rage and poverty prevail; or to take upon ourselves a body or mind (in mortality only) bereft of full form or capacities. Some of us agreed to come to earth when or where gospel light and knowledge was unknown or unavailable, and some of us agreed to be the messengers who would bring it.

In our earthly sojourn, all (but one) will fall short of the glory of our Father. None (but one) will complete the journey entirely clean. But we can show valiance nonetheless, or repent and change even well after death.[472] There will be many "noble and great ones," some of whom would find and follow that premortal Firstborn Son while yet in mortality and others who would find and acknowledge and obey him—to full salvation—in the postmortal world, including many among the faithful disciples of Buddha, Muhammed, Brahma, and Zarathustra, and many who belong to no church at all.

Eventually, "We must [all] come forth and stand before him in his

---

[471]*Doctrine and Covenants* 19:18.

[472]This idea of postmortal progression is not to be taken lightly: "Ye cannot say, when ye are brought to . . . crisis, that I will repent, that I will return to my God. Nay, ye cannot say this; for that same spirit which doth possess your bodies at the time that ye go out of this life, that same spirit will have power to possess your body in that eternal world." (Book of Mormon, Alma 34:34) Those truly wanting to follow the Savior will move forward; those expecting to cheat will not pass Go.

glory, and in his power, and in his might, majesty, and dominion, and [either] acknowledge to our everlasting shame that all his judgments are just"[473] and "fain be glad if we could command the rocks and the mountains to fall upon us to hide us from his presence,"[474] or else hear those words from His own mouth, "Come unto me, ye blessed, there is a place prepared for you in the mansions of my Father."[475]

"And then shall the wicked [those who refused to repent even in the face of God and eternity] be cast out, and they shall have cause to howl, and weep, and wail, and gnash their teeth; and this because they would not hearken unto the voice of the Lord; therefore the Lord redeemeth them not."[476] These are they for whom "there is no forgiveness in this world nor in the world to come, having denied the Holy Spirit after having received it, and having denied the Only Begotten Son of the Father, having crucified him unto themselves and put him to an open shame."[477] These are the ungodly[478], those who no longer reflect even a shadow of their heritage as children of God.

Embodied, resurrected beings, albeit with bodies having no glory, they will prevail in hell over Lucifer, but that is all. Their eternity will be bitter. "And the end thereof, neither the place thereof, nor their torment, no man knows; neither was it revealed, neither is, neither will be revealed unto man, except to them who are made partakers thereof."[479]

Such will likely be few. Hell, in the end, will be a tiny, forgotten corner of the universe. The great God will find no solace in the path these few have chosen. They were his children. Yet all has been offered: light, strength, repentance, help, knowledge, and a grace sufficient to cover all sins should each of them merely have sought forgiveness and a better way. They simply weren't interested. None of them would be happy in heaven, anyway, and perhaps their self-selected misery is their only reward for having tried mortality.

---

[473]Alma 12:15.

[474]Ibid., 12:14.

[475]Enos 1:27.

[476]Ibid., Mosiah 16:2.

[477]*Doctrine and Covenants* 76:34–35.

[478]Ibid., 49.

[479]Ibid., 45–46.

It is considered the darkest hue of lie and blasphemy by many "Christian" faiths to suggest that Muslims will inherit heaven, or Buddhists or Pagans or Hindus or, heaven forbid, Mormons! Having not "confessed Christ" while in mortality, they are doomed to suffer eternal damnation along with a billion little children and babies, and good riddance anyway.

I, for one, thank God for a different God.

The Latter-day Saints teach the most expansive concept of heaven, short of a free-for-all, that there is. And here it is, right from the Bible: "There are also celestial bodies, and bodies terrestrial: but the glory of the celestial is one, and the glory of the terrestrial is another. There is one glory of the sun, and another glory of the moon, and another glory of the stars: for one star differeth from another star in glory. So also is the resurrection of the dead."[480]

Three degrees of "glory," said the Apostle Paul. You will note there are only two listed in the first sentence of that quote, but three in the second. The Prophet Joseph Smith corrected the parallelism in his retranslation. Three degrees of glory, corresponding in their magnificence with the sun, the moon, and the stars.

But Latter-day Saint doctrine on heaven neither rests with Paul and the other Bible writers (even with the corrections) nor derives from him. Almost nothing in Latter-day Saint doctrine does. The few exceptions are primarily the day-to-day accounts from Christ's life in Palestine. We're grateful for all of it. We teach it in our Sunday School classes. We accept it all as Scripture, and proclaim that more Scripture, the sacred records of other people unknown to us now, will yet expand our expandable canon. But we don't depend upon it.

Here's where our doctrine on the afterlife comes from. On February 16, 1832, while retranslating a portion of the New Testament, Joseph Smith and Sidney Rigdon found themselves in the blinding presence of the Savior himself, who opened their eyes to a vision of the eternal worlds and personally narrated the tour.

Church Historian B. H. Roberts would later comment on the Vision by setting it in contrast to the view of heaven common in (non-LDS) Christian thought: "[that] view of man's future is that there are two states in one or the other of which man will spend eternity—in heaven or in

---

[480]1 Cor. 15:40.

hell. If one shall gain heaven, even by ever so small a margin, he will enter immediately upon a complete possession of all its unspeakable joys, equally with the angels and the holiest of saints. On the other hand, if one shall miss heaven, even by ever so small a margin, he is doomed to everlasting torment equally with the wickedest of men and vilest of devils, and there is no deliverance for him through all the countless ages of eternity!"[481] In contrast, wrote Roberts, the "Vision, the like of which, for beauty, for reasonableness, for value as doctrine, for comforting influence, for vindication of the mercy and justice of God—stands unsurpassed even in sacred literature."[482]

The guided tour began in hell, a brief and baleful glimpse of that inexplicably horrible world, then quickly moved to the top, walking the Prophet and his companion through a successive gradation of glories, corresponding in magnitude and splendor with the stars, the moon, and the sun (and the analogy is only an analogy). It is among the most revered of revelations in Latter-day Saint theology.

Highest of all glories is the Celestial Kingdom, where the Father and the Son dwell. This is heaven. Of it, Joseph Smith would write: "I saw the transcendent beauty of the gate through which the heirs of that kingdom will enter, which was like unto circling flames of fire; also the blazing throne of God, whereon was seated the Father and the Son. I saw the beautiful streets of that kingdom, which had the appearance of being paved with gold"[483] set against "a globe like a sea of glass and fire, where all things . . . are manifest, past, present, and future, and are continually before the Lord."[484]

Even in the celestial glory, there are three heavens or degrees, however, and in order to obtain the highest degree, a man and woman must have been sealed in the eternal marriage covenant in one of the church's holy temples by someone holding the authority restored to earth by Elijah, either during their mortal probation or through the efforts of those acting on their behalf vicariously. And they must have continued entirely faithful since.

---

[481]*History of the Church*, Vol. 4, Introduction, p. 34.

[482]B. H. Roberts, *Comprehensive History of the Church*, Vol. 1, Ch. 22, p. 272.

[483]*Doctrine and Covenants* 137:1–4.

[484]Ibid., 130:7

A sealing is not a marriage. A Latter-day Saint can be married in a Las Vegas roadhouse or a Botswanian hut, and the church will recognize any legitimate ceremony as legally binding. For mortality only. Like everyone else, at death do they part. A sealing (whatsoever is bound on earth shall be bound in heaven) is a specific ordinance performed in one of the church's temples. It can happen in conjunction with a wedding or subsequent to one performed elsewhere. It requires a significant effort in personal faithfulness.

Due to our beliefs in eternal progression, postmortal ministry, and a just and beneficent God, those who have never married in this life can yet enjoy that eternal relationship, as can those of any other earthly faith (or no faith at all) who accept the plenary gospel in the afterlife. Ordinances will be performed in their name on the earth; they can accept or reject them. Those who accept will continue on their eternal progression, someday to become as God their Father, to create worlds, people them with spirit children "innumerable as the sands of the seashore," and enjoy eternal increase of all things.

That is the potential, the full heritage of the children of God: "And if children, then heirs; heirs of God, and joint-heirs with Christ," (Rom. 8:16–17).

Those who reject the eternal marriage covenant, though perfectly righteous in all other ways, will take up residence in a lesser sphere of the celestial kingdom where they will serve as "ministering servants . . . for those who are worthy of a far more, and an exceeding, and an eternal weight of glory. For these angels did not abide my [complete] law; therefore, they cannot be enlarged, but remain separately and singly, without exaltation, in their saved condition, to all eternity; and from henceforth are not gods, but are angels of God forever and ever."[485]

However, "all who have died without a knowledge of this gospel, who would have received it if they had been permitted to tarry, shall be heirs of the celestial kingdom of God" as will "all children who die before they arrive at the years of accountability, for I, the Lord, will judge all men according to their works, according to the desire of their hearts."[486]

Those who died as babies and children will be raised to maturity by

---

[485]Ibid., 132:16–17.

[486]Ibid., 137:7–10.

their exalted parents, in family chains that extend back to Adam and forward forever.

Babies in heaven. Billions who spent mortality as faithful Buddhists, Baptists, Quakers, and Anglicans, all of whom (minus the babies) came to know the truth through the spirit-world ministrations of authorized servants of the Christ and accepted it there, all of whom (minus the babies) needed the essential ordinances of salvation performed for them on the earth but who benefited instead from work for the dead performed in their behalf by others.

The babies—righteous spirits without flaw—needed none of it; only a body.

And then Joseph saw the vision of the terrestrial kingdom, a lesser realm in which the analogous light of glory, like the moon, is a reflected light from a higher source. The bodies are different, and so are the potentialities.

Here eternity will be spent by those who heard the gospel on the earth but rejected it, accepting it finally in the spirit world: otherwise honorable men and women who are nevertheless lukewarm in their commitment to the full gospel standard and worship of their Savior, "wherefore, they obtain not the crown over the kingdom of our God."[487]

Unlike the celestial kingdom, this realm offers a limit to progress. It is fixed, circumscribed. The beings who inhabit this world will have no capacity for reproduction, and family units will not exist. Although rewarded a kingdom of glory in many ways beyond explication, its inhabitants will suffer from the clear knowledge that much more could have been theirs, if only . . .

In his Vision, expanded and clarified by subsequent prophets, Joseph Smith saw one more kingdom of glory, a lesser kingdom, the telestial. But before we go there, please understand one thing: the Latter-day Saint view of God—our God, your God, the real God—is that he is our Father, literally and eternally. He loves his children with a depth and a capacity that none among us can even comprehend. By the time of the Final Judgment, those children of God who inherit the terrestrial and telestial kingdoms will have been offered a chance to repent and accept the plan of salvation, their Savior, and their Father again and again and again. And they simply won't

---

[487]Ibid., 76:74–79.

choose to go along. In their heart of hearts, they just won't have an authentic disposition to do so. "While there is one soul of this race *willing* . . . to accept and obey the laws of redemption," wrote Charles W. Penrose, "Christ's work will be incomplete until that being is brought up from death and hell and placed in a position of progress, upward and onward."[488]

All will choose to be exactly where they end up: "For what doth it profit a man if a gift is bestowed upon him, and he receive not the gift? Behold, he rejoices not in that which is given unto him, neither rejoices in him who is the giver of the gift."[489]

"And again, we saw the glory of the telestial," recorded Joseph Smith, "which glory is that of the lesser, even as the glory of the stars differs from that of the glory of the moon in the firmament. These are they who received not the gospel of Christ, neither the testimony of Jesus. These are they who deny not the Holy Spirit. These are they who are thrust down to hell. These are they who shall not be redeemed from the devil until the last resurrection, until the Lord, even Christ the Lamb, shall have finished his work."[490]

These will be innumerable, even as the sands upon the seashore, and as one star differs from another star in brightness, so will these. There will be "numerous, perhaps numberless, gradations"[491] of beings in this realm. Yet they will be heirs of salvation, and inheritors of glory, a glory "which surpasses all understanding."[492]

While soliloquistic surmising among rank-and-file Latter-day Saints often intimates that this tertiary heaven will thus be the final abode of the greatest portion of our heavenly Father's children—and the celestial home to the minority few—the doctrine does not so enumerate. Better reason would suggest that the offspring of God—"if children, then heirs"—will in fact merit "all that [the] father hath"[493] in great numbers. Certainly, the millions upon millions of children of God who have died in their mortal in-

---

[488]Charles W. Penrose, "Mormon Doctrine," p. 72.

[489]*Doctrine and Covenants* 88:33.

[490]bid., 76:81–85.

[491]James E. Talmage, *Articles of Faith*, Ch. 4, p. 95.

[492]*Doctrine and Covenants* 76:89.

[493]Ibid., 84:38.

fancy, so righteous from the preexistence that they only needed come for a body and then return, will swell the ranks of the celestial host.

And there eternity lies.

In the fullest sense of the word, only the celestial kingdom is considered "heaven" by Latter-day Saints. But these lesser realms are known—because prophets have seen them—to be worlds of such glory and stature that the mortal mind cannot even comprehend them, let alone describe them to others. "Could you gaze into heaven five minutes," said Joseph Smith, "you would know more than you would by reading all that ever was written on the subject."[494]

The record shows that Joseph Smith gazed into heaven numerous times—speaking with its inhabitants—for much longer than five minutes. And in each instance but the first, he had witnesses with him, witnesses who never denied their testimony of the occurrences and of open discourse with the God of this universe. Subsequent prophets have recorded similar visitations.

This is the Latter-day Saint faith. It honors the Bible, uses the Bible, believes the Bible—but it does not *depend* on the Bible. We descend from no Bible church and no biblical record. We rely, first and exclusively, on few Bible doctrines. We descend from living prophets and rely on continuing revelation, and "any doctrine that does not bear the label 'revelation' is not our doctrine and is unworthy of our faith."[495] We descend from a personal visitation of God the Father and his Son Jesus Christ to a fourteen-year-old farm boy in the western woods of New York who didn't intend to start anything. He just wanted to know.

And all we can say, after all, is what he said: "And now, after the many testimonies which have been given of Jesus Christ, this is the testimony, last of all which we give of him: That he lives! For we saw him, even on the right hand of God; and we heard the voice bearing record that he is the Only Begotten of the Father—That by him, and through him, and of him, the worlds are and were created, and the inhabitants thereof are begotten sons and daughters unto God.[496]

And thus, the story of the Latter-day Saints.

---

[494]*History of the Church*, Vol. 6, p. 50.

[495]Joseph F. McConkie, *Here We Stand*, p. 129.

[496]*Doctrine and Covenants* 76:22–24.

Epilogue

In his book *How the Irish Saved Civilization,* Thomas Cahill asserts that "Jehovah's Witnesses or Mormonism" are academically anemic faiths, "full of assertions, but . . . yield[ing] no intellectual system to nourish a great intellect."[497]

Yale's more celebrated Harold Bloom speaks of Joseph Smith's "religious genius" ("or daemon") but attributes his "uncanny recovery" of Whittier's ancient religion to mere "charismatic accuracy."[498]

Other bona fide religion scholars hold meetings to address the rising tide of Mormon membership (much of it from among their own flocks) and scholarship, warning that the scholarship is "frankly, intimidating." Wrote two of them in 1997: "In recent years the sophistication and erudition of LDS apologetics has risen considerably while evangelical responses have not. We [evangelical Christians] are losing the battle and we do not know it."[499]

Two responses:

1. I have never made the count, but I harbor high and fairly confident suspicions that the depth and page count of LDS scholarship, doctrinal discourse, curricula, and general publication approaches that of any other single religious faith in the world. (One can see a good portion of it on the 98 miles of shelving at the Harold B. Lee Library at Brigham Young University.)

---

[497]*How the Irish Saved Civilization,* Thomas Cahill, p. 49. Great book about my *other* heritage, the one that helped run the Latter-day Saints across the American continent and, as far as I know, from the Emerald Isle itself. While Latter-day Saints would take exception to a number of Cahill's religious assumptions, one line most would quite enjoy is this: "If we are to be saved, it will not be by Romans but by saints" (p. 218).

[498]Harold Bloom, *The American Religion,* p. 101.

[499]Both quotes from Carl Mosser and Paul Owen, "Mormon Apologetic, Scholarship and Evangelical Neglect: Losing the Battle and Not Knowing It?" 1997 Evangelical Theological Society, Far West Annual Meeting, April 25, 1997.

2. Institutionally, we are not about to try proving our faith to anyone. It is a faith. It is known, accepted, and embraced in other ways. While personal gospel scholarship is highly encouraged among Latter-day Saints, it has never been recommended as a route to conversion or spiritual solidity. Instead, our approach is fairly basic, tending to serve both the erudite, the illiterate, and everyone else in between:

Teach the basic message.
Ask the person to pray about it.

Okay, there are nuances to effective application of these two steps, but they are merely nuances. The fruit of this approach is represented by three hundred thousand converts a year,[500] most the product of sixty thousand nineteen-year-olds—trained mostly at their parents' knees—serving voluntary pay-their-own-way missions around the world and armed with very little in the way of traditional "scholarship."[501]

I've been on both ends of the process. On the receiving end, I found three things formed the core of my conversion, and all three converged on me that cold March night at ten thousand feet in Colorado. You've met two of them already in the preceding narrative:

1. A generous plan of salvation, represented for me by more than anything else that strange question of Paul's: "Else what shall they do which are baptized for the dead, if the dead rise not at all? why are they then baptized for the dead?" (I Cor. 15:29) Even the dead

---

[500]Lest you think I am fudging on the numbers, I'll give you some exact figures; remember, our numbers are independently audited): *Convert baptisms* in 1994: 300,730; 1995: 304,330; 1996: 321,385; 1997: 317,798; 1998: 299,134. *Internal growth* (the number of children the already baptized are adding to overall church membership), is about 75,000 per year. These numbers are entirely separate and distinct.

[501]One note about education and religiosity in general is important, however. Latter-day Saints in the United States, where the only real research on the subject has been attempted, tend to have a higher educational attainment profile than the average American, and they tend to be more religiously committed the higher their educational level. This is the reverse of most other religions. See Albrecht and Heaton, *Review of Religious Research* 26:43–48.

(who yet live in another realm) would have full opportunity to be saved.

2. The Book of Mormon, representing a living religion with all its accoutrements: living prophets, modern and continuous revelation, authority straight from God.

But the third and final thing I found was the most overwhelming of all.

As the missionaries closed our first meeting that night, one of them asked me to pray, right there, with them in the room. I had never prayed before nor heard it done. But on the heels of all else I had experienced that night, the missionaries shared with me the basic steps of Mormon prayer: talk to God out of your own heart. All I really knew of God was what they had just told me Joseph Smith found out about him that spring day in 1820.

But I wanted to know him, too, so I knelt down and got ready.

And then all question fled. Suddenly I knew God was real. I knew he loved me. And I knew what I had just been taught was the truth. I converted, right then and there. All the way.

From the perspective of both sides of the experience, even the best Latter-day Saint missionaries do not convert anyone. Their God does.[502] Our God. Our Father whom we left so long ago. Only he, through the whispering ministration of his agent, the Holy Ghost, could get a religion so radically unique, with a history so young and tempestuous to work— smoothly—in 165 nations, attracting everyone from Adventists to Zoroastrians. Only he can speak to that ancient, engraved code, the premortal identity, the DNA of deity.

Thus, we teach of families that can be forever, and whet appetites by showing families that work here and now. We teach a concept of salvation generous enough to find a place for Jews and Gentiles, babies and Buddhists, sinners and saints, preachers and practicers. We remind burdened, abandoned, disconsolate humans of who they are, where they've been, and where they can possibly go. And then we explain it in

---

[502]Perfectly One in purpose with his Son, the Savior, and his Son, the Holy Ghost.

an entirely new light, a light that goes all the way back. All the way to the beginning.

We tell them God is really alive, that we are his children, that he loves us and wants us back. And then we back off and leave it up to the person to determine how badly he or she wants to know if what we've said is true.

That's all anyone ever asked of me.

Appendix

Important Doctrines and Policies of The Church of Jesus Christ of Latter-day Saints

BAPTISM (SEE ALSO INFANT BAPTISM, BAPTISM FOR THE DEAD)

Baptism by complete bodily immersion in water by one holding authority is a requirement for entry into The Church of Jesus Christ of Latter-day Saints and an essential ordinance for salvation. When Joseph Smith queried the Lord in 1830 regarding some who wanted to join the new faith relying on the merits of their previous baptism in other Christian denominations, he recorded the following answer: "Although a man should be baptized an hundred times it availeth him nothing, for you cannot enter in at the strait gate by the law of Moses, neither by your dead works. For it is because of your dead works that I have caused this last covenant and this church to be built up unto me, even as in days of old. Wherefore, enter ye in at the gate, as I have commanded, and seek not to counsel your God." (*Doctrine and Covenants* 22:2–4)

It was the last time Joseph asked that particular question.

BAPTISM FOR THE DEAD

"Else what shall they do which are baptized for the dead, if the dead rise not at all? why are they then baptized for the dead?" (1 Cor. 15:29) No other Christian denomination to my knowledge performs baptisms for the dead, and many claim it is not a biblical doctrine in the first place. That Paul would mention it in the verse quoted above would seem to belie such contentions. But it's much simpler than that. The Lord revealed to his restoration Prophet that baptism was an essential ordinance of salvation, even for the deceased, and such ordinances have been carried out by the Latter-day Saints since the 1840s, since late 1841 only in temples.

This is likely the most misunderstood doctrine of Mormonism. We do not "baptize our dead," as even reputable and otherwise intelligent writers continue to phrase it. We baptize living people acting as proxies for—in the name of—a deceased person, males for males, females for females. I have been baptized for my deceased grandpa, my wife for my deceased grandma, and so on. Nor do we do it to "make them Mormon," as other writers insist. We do it because it's an essential ordinance of salvation, an ordinance that permits the deceased, disembodied spirit to accept Christ—not Mormon, not Joseph Smith—in the manner Christ ordained. Should they in the spirit world accept the ordinance performed on their behalf in an earthly temple, it makes them Christian.

BIBLE (SEE REVELATION/SCRIPTURE)

"We believe the Bible [New and Old Testaments] to be the word of God as far as it is translated correctly." (Articles of Faith 1:8) The Bible is one of our "standard works," and its contents are honored as scripture. And while preexistence, baptism for the dead, prophets, continuing revelation and scripture, temples, degrees of glory, and marriage and families in the afterlife can be supported in some measure with Bible verses, we rely on none of them. We are not a Bible-only church. We do not preach a reinterpretation of old Scripture, that mind-scratching process that spawned the fourth-century church and its twenty thousand protesting offspring. We take the given scripture where it is and move forward, with new Scripture, new prophets, and new personal visitations from God and other heavenly messengers.

Here's how the Book of Mormon puts it:

Know ye not that there are more nations than one? Know ye not that I, the Lord your God, have created all men, and that I remember those who are upon the isles of the sea; and that I rule in the heavens above and in the earth beneath; and I bring forth my word unto the children of men, yea, even upon all the nations of the earth?

Wherefore murmur ye, because that ye shall receive more of my word? Know ye not that the testimony of two nations is a witness unto you that I am God, that I remember one nation like unto another? Wherefore, I speak the same words unto one nation like unto another. And when the two nations shall run together the testimony of the two nations shall run together also.

And because that I have spoken one word ye need not suppose that I cannot speak another; for my work is not yet finished; neither shall it

be until the end of man, neither from that time henceforth and forever.
(2 Nephi 29:7–9)

Thus, to contentions of other Christians (continual, incessant, and sililoquial) that the Bible is all, and no more is either needed or allowed, we can only answer: "Good news! The Lord has spoken again!" And who are we to tell him what he surely meant or try to shut him up?

CHRIST, NAME OF

Latter-day Saints use names of the Savior (Christ, Lord, Jesus) quite sparingly, believing it a matter of reverence to avoid frequent or casual usage. (When my wife worked as a freelance writer and contributing editor for a large Christian publishing group, she had to force herself to speak their lingo. She also had to keep it a secret that she was LDS, but that's covered under the next entry.) We are frequently maligned for not "praising the Lord" more vociferously.

Further, we take very seriously the third Mosaic commandment to not take the name of the Lord in vain. Habitual usage of terms using *God, Christ,* or *Jesus Christ* in any context besides reverent discourse or prayer is grounds for ecclesiastical counseling and even disciplinary action. In addition, faithful Latter-day Saints refrain from using the common cusswords of the day.

CHRISTIAN

Members of The Church of Jesus Christ of Latter-day Saints center their faith on Jesus Christ and on him alone. We can say it no plainer, yet certain Christian groups continue to reject our claim and our fellowship.

We honor those of other faiths—including non-Christian ones—in all their efforts to make the world a better place and its inhabitants better persons. (See "Other Religions.") Individually and institutionally, we subscribe to newsletters of organizations who prefer not to have us as customers. We listen to recording artists who wouldn't give ours the time of day. We fund causes that only grudgingly list us as donors (and sometimes "forget to"). We wish them all well and pray for their success. We wish they'd do the same for us in our efforts to make the world a better place.

CLOTHING/DRESS

Certain audiences continue to believe that Mormons dress like the Amish, who, after all, only dress the way Americans did 150 years ago. Latter-day Saints dress no different than do the contiguous populations of the nations in which they live, and they never have. When most American men had beards, Mormon men—including our prophets—had beards; when the common style changed, we changed. In recent decades, beginning with the long hair of the sixties, we have tended to favor, in fact promote, the more conservative path, but for the most part we look like our neighbors. (Hopefully, fewer of our kids shave their heads and pierce their nipples.)

All Latter-day Saints are encouraged to choose modest styles of dress and grooming, but for those who have been through the temple, it becomes a bit more imperative. First, temple covenants require one to live a "higher law" in all aspects of one's life; second, those who have received their "endowment" in the temple throw away their Fruit of the Looms forever: the sacred temple garment replaces secular undergarments from then on. The garment has been the focus of much curiosity among Mormon-watchers. Three points: (1) it is white, not red (2) it does not go to the ankles and wrists but fits comfortably beneath a short-sleeved shirt or blouse and knee-length shorts; (3) it is a sacred article of clothing given to the faithful, and those who understand this have little more to say about it.

While instances of the wearer being shielded from physical harm in threatening circumstances due to the garment's protection are myriad, its primary purpose is to serve as a reminder, a token of the promises made in the House of the Lord. Thus, those who wear the garment faithfully will not be seen in "revealing attire" (including halter tops, miniskirts, sleeveless shirts, etc.) except during activities—swimming, strenuous sports, a visit to the doctor—that compromise the sacred, private nature of the garment.

CROSS, THE

Latter-day Saints do not use the cross in either dress or architectural ornamentation, suggesting to the usual detractors that we are not Christians. It's not that we don't believe in the cross, or that there is any official proscription on such personal ornamentation; it's simply a reflection of our belief that the cross was not the important component in that Calvaric drama—the man upon it was. And he has risen and returned. The cross is merely history.

ENVIRONMENT/ENVIRONMENTALISM

The number of parallels between ancient Israel and the nineteenth-century Church of Jesus Christ of Latter-day Saints are impressive. Among them are the parallels surrounding the concept of exodus: (1) a mass escape from foreign or adverse domination, (2) flight into the wilderness accompanied by (3) miraculous feedings, (4) the parting (or freezing over) of a prohibitory body of water, and (5) leadership by one strong-willed and manifestly visionary man. Like the ancient Israelites, the Latter-day Saints fled to the desert wilderness for their own survival as a people and as a church. Yet to make that transition work, the Latter-day Saints, for their part, had to change the desert—in biblical terms frequently referred to, to make it "blossom as the rose." (See Isa. 35:1.)

Throughout most of the decades following the Mormon hegira to Utah and the subsequent colonization effort in the West, a determined focus on turning the desert into a garden has prevailed in the minds of intermountain Latter-day Saints and their leaders, called from among the people. Most current leaders of the church (a lay clergy) descend from this paradigm: their dads and granddads were sheepherders, farmers, and merchants, not Princeton humanities professors. Thus, in the perspective of this died-in-the-wool Colorado tree hugger, Utah is a bastion of belligerence when it comes to second-millennium environmentalism.

Fortunately, Latter-day Saints doctrine regarding care of the planet and its systems is much more expansive and generous than (Utah) Latter-day Saints practice regarding care of the planet and its systems. The doctrine teaches that the planet is a living entity with a purposeful creation, both as an abode for humans and other creatures and as a provider. Once it has fulfilled "the measure of its creation" it will "be renewed and receive its paradisiacal glory." (Articles of Faith 1:10) Humanity's responsibility toward the earth is to serve as stewards, as loving and committed caregivers. As stated by LDS theologian Hugh Nibley, "Man's dominion [as charged in the book of Genesis] is a call to service, not a license to exterminate."

The winds of change in this regard are becoming more and more apparent, even in Utah. The doctrine will win out.

FAMILY

The exaltation (admittance to the highest heaven) of families is a foundational effort of all Latter-day Saint ministry and doctrine. Due to a number of theological factors, LDS families tend to be larger than those of their neighbors, but there is no requirement as to the number of children that qualifies a family as faithful. Divorce is allowed but not encouraged; rather, the healing and strengthening of family relationships are paramount.

GENDER

"Gender is an essential characteristic of individual premortal, mortal, and eternal identity and purpose." ("The Family: A Proclamation to the World") There are human males and human females and disoriented individuals. There are even some with physical abnormalities and challenges, but there is no third sex.

"Our hearts reach out to those who struggle with feelings of affinity for the same gender. We remember you before the Lord, we sympathize with you, we regard you as our brothers and sisters. However, we cannot condone immoral practices on your part any more than we can condone immoral practices on the part of others. To be morally clean, a person must refrain from adultery and fornication, from homosexual or lesbian relations, and from every other unholy, unnatural, or impure practice." (From a Public Affairs Shelf Item, approved by the First Presidency and the Quorum of the Twelve, April 18, 1996)

We draw a distinction between homosexual feelings and homosexual activity; individuals with such an affinity who keep it in check continue in full fellowship in the church, including (for men) the exercise of their priesthood and (for both sexes) attendance at the temple. Those who don't—just like heterosexuals who stray beyond the bounds of faithful chastity—are subject to church discipline, including excommunication.

SAME-SEX MARRIAGE   Public discussion of same-sex marriage has often contended (for the defense) that the purpose of the marital union is the procreation of children, to which the plaintiffs have often countered, so what about those who can't have kids? Should their union be denied as well?

All of which misses the point(s) entirely.

1. God and God's nature ordained that man and woman should be marriage partners; no other combination is valid in his eyes, whether mortal politics agrees or not.

2. Families are not mortal creations; families were designed to be eternal, and homosexual unions will have no validity in the afterlife. All who fall short of the highest degree of the celestial kingdom will remain single through all eternity.

HEALTH CODE (MEAT, CAFFEINE, TOBACCO, ALCOHOL, ETC.)

Along with polygamy, which is not practiced, the Latter-day Saint health code—or rather its proscription of certain substances like tea, coffee, tobacco, and alcohol—is likely the most-known aspect of modern Mormonism.

The Word of Wisdom, a revelation given in 1833 and enforced as policy beginning about a hundred years later, prohibits the ingestion of tobacco products, alcoholic beverages, caffeinated coffee and tea, and illegal drugs. Members using them do not hold a temple recommend and may be subject to disciplinary action (disfellowshipment or excommunication, although the latter would be rare).

It has a positive side, too, however. The foundation of the health code is the knowledge that our physical body is the temple of our immortal spirit and should be treated accordingly. Thus, the eating of fruits, vegetables, and whole grains—particularly wheat—and the sparing use of meat are all recommended in the revelation.

INDIANS (NATIVE AMERICANS)

Latter-day Saint doctrine holds that many (not all) Native Americans (on both continents) and Pacific Islanders are descendants of Book of Mormon peoples who migrated by boat to the Americas from the land of Israel in three disparate journeys: one in about 2200 B.C. and two others around 600 B.C. Contrary to the common non-LDS contention and in fact the pedestrian beliefs of most Latter-day Saints, we do not profess that all native peoples on either continent exude from these progenitors, nor do we reject the reality of others crossing the Bering land bridge. We only claim that some did (and their own record, by the way, says they brought horses with them). And we believe we are under covenant to seek them out and offer them the gospel blessings their ancient fathers once knew.

The primary populations followed in the Book of Mormon—those known as Nephites and Lamanites—are descendants of Joseph, son of Jacob, who was sold into Egypt. And that Joseph "saw our day . . . and he obtained a promise of the Lord, that out of the fruit of his loins the Lord God would raise up a righteous branch unto the house of Israel; not the Messiah, but a branch which was to be broken off [and taken far away] . . . to be remembered in the covenants of the Lord that the Messiah should be made manifest unto them in the latter days . . . unto the bringing of them out of darkness unto light—yea, out of hidden darkness and out of captivity unto freedom." (2 Nephi 3:5) One of the primary purposes of the Book of Mormon, in fact, "is to show unto the remnant of the House of Israel what great things the Lord hath done for their fathers; and that they may know the covenants of the Lord, that they are not cast off forever, and . . . that Jesus is the Christ, the Eternal God, manifesting himself unto all nations." (Book of Mormon, title page)

Many Native Americans have heard and clearly accepted that the Book of Mormon is their own book. Modern church growth rates are phenomenal among Latin Americans (183,000 convert baptisms in a typical recent year) and among the native peoples of the Pacific Islands (one in every fifteen Tahitians, one in every four Samoans).

Infant Baptism

I'll let the penultimate Book of Mormon prophet, Mormon himself, explain this one.

Listen to the words of Christ, your Redeemer, your Lord and your God. Behold, I came into the world not to call the righteous but sinners to repentance; the whole need no physician, but they that are sick; wherefore, little children are whole, for they are not capable of committing sin. . . . It is solemn mockery before God, that ye should baptize little children. . . . Little children need no repentance, neither baptism. Behold, baptism is unto repentance to the fulfilling the commandments unto the remission of sins. But little children are alive in Christ, even from the foundation of the world; if not so, God is a partial God, and also a changeable God, and a respector to persons; for how many little children have died without baptism! Wherefore, if little children could not be saved without baptism, these must have gone to an endless hell. Behold I say unto you, that he that supposeth that little children need baptism is in the gall of bitterness and in the bonds of iniquity, for he hath neither faith, hope, nor charity; wherefore, should he be cut off while in the thought, he must go down to hell." (Moroni 8:8–14)

DEATH OF THE UNBAPTIZED/LITTLE CHILDREN: "All who have died without a knowledge of this Gospel, who would have received it if they had been permitted to tarry, shall be heirs of the celestial kingdom of God; also all that shall die henceforth without a knowledge of it, who would have received it with all their hearts, shall be heirs of that kingdom, for I, the Lord, will judge all men according to their works, according to the desire of their hearts. . . . all children who die before they arrive at the years of accountability are saved in the celestial kingdom of heaven." (*Doctrine and Covenants* 137:7–10) The "years of accountability" have been established by revelation as eight years old.

LAY CLERGY

With but a few qualifications, The Church of Jesus Christ of Latter-day Saints has no professional clergy. Instead, there are congregational "pastors" (bishops or branch presidents); women's (Relief Society), children's (Primary), and youth (Young Men/Women) auxiliary leaders; Sunday-school teachers; speakers in meetings; stake (diocese) leaders; Area Authorities. All serve without pay, and none have been "trained" in traditional theological schools. Those men known as "General Authorities" (currently around 115) who have been called to suspend all other employment and serve full-time in the church at its highest levels are paid a modest (and uniform) living stipend. None lives in a mansion.

MARRIAGE/DIVORCE

"We . . . solemnly proclaim that marriage between a man and a woman is ordained of God and that the family is central to the Creator's plan for the eternal destiny of His children." (The Family: A Proclamation to the World) We do not support—in fact, we vigorously fight legally—same-sex marriage (see "Gender"). We *do* allow divorce, yet it is only rarely seen as the best option.

MEN AND WOMEN, ROLE OF

The Church of Jesus Christ of Latter-day Saints supports and doctrinally defends the traditional "roles" of men and women, fathers and mothers. "By divine design, fathers are to preside over their families in love and righteousness and are responsible to provide the necessities of life and protection for their families. Mothers are primarily responsible for the nurture of their children. In these sacred responsibilities, fathers and mothers are obligated to help one another as equal partners. Disability, death, or other circumstances may necessitate individual adaptation."

This said, Utah has a higher proportion of mothers with children under the age of six employed in the full-time work force than any other state. Why?

Reasons suggested by the pundits include Utah's economy coupled with the size of LDS families and the per capita income. Reasons typically offered by the working moms and their supportive husbands include wanting "a better life" for their children and claiming a change in church policy. The scholars have data, although it is still somewhat inconclusive. The working moms/supportive spouses are merely taking license with the "individual adaptation" clause.

Church policy has not changed, as that would require a change in the inherent and eternal natures and purposes of men and women. However, the growth of the church is altering the demography of the faith, flooding congregations with many circumstantial refugees. Thus, church leaders have wisely and beneficently acknowledged this shift, welcoming to the path of hope a whole host of folks bearing a whole host of challenges that were seen but infrequently in the past.

Perhaps the clearest recent statement on the resultant "big picture" is the following from Apostle Richard G. Scott in 1993: "You [mothers] in these unusual circumstances qualify for additional inspiration and strength from the Lord. Those who leave the home for lesser reasons will not." (Conference Report, Apr. 1993, 42–43; or *Ensign*, May 1993, 34)

OTHER RELIGIONS

"I respect the religion of every man and woman, and honor them in their desire to live it," said Church President Gordon B. Hinckley. (General Conference, Oct. 1998) We say it, and we mean it. Church missionaries who follow the plan in their teaching efforts are taught to build upon the foundations of faith already established, whether those foundations are Buddhist, Christian, or nominal existentialism.

In matters of humanitarian service or certain sociopolitical causes deemed matters of fundamental moral concern (e.g., pornography, gambling, same-sex marriage), we ally ourselves vigorously with other associations and churches. With religious interfaith councils, however, we have little to do, particularly with those endeavoring to carve out some "middle ground" commonality in regard to doctrine and practice. There we stand apart.

REVELATION/SCRIPTURE

Revelation is the standard and regular channel of communication between God in his heaven and humans on the earth. It has operated continuously since Adam. "Surely the Lord God will do nothing, but he revealeth his secret unto his servants the prophets." (Amos 3:7) The position of The Church of Jesus Christ of Latter-day Saints is that the Lord is still revealing his will to his prophets, and in fact to every person who exercises faith and seeks such answers, including those not of our church. Each receives revelation for his or her own area of legitimacy—the LDS Church prophet for the church and the world; a father or mother for their own family, work, and concerns; etc. We reject outright and without compromise that the age of revelation ceased with the apostles or with the biblical record.

"We believe all that God has revealed, all that He does now reveal, and we believe that He will yet reveal many great and important things pertaining to the Kingdom of God." (Articles of Faith 1:9) Revelations "pertaining to the Kingdom of God" are recorded in the Scriptures—in the Bible, the Book of Mormon, *Doctrine and Covenants*, the *Pearl of Great Price*; in the General Conference talks given by General Authorities every six months; and in various other documents and official records of the church.

SEXUAL RELATIONS

Sexual relations outside of marriage are grounds for disciplinary action. In other words, both premarital and extramarital sexual relations are closely circumscribed. LDS youth are held to strict standards of morality, and most observe them. For individuals who have made marital covenants in the temple, extramarital activity may be grounds for excommunication.

SELECTED BIBLIOGRAPHY

The Book of Mormon. Translated by Joseph Smith, Jr. Salt Lake City: The Church of Jesus Christ of Latter-day Saints, 1981.

Brigham Young University Studies. Provo, Utah: Brigham Young University Press, 1959–1999.

The Doctrine and Covenants of The Church of Jesus Christ of Latter-day Saints. Salt Lake City. The Church of Jesus Christ of Latter-day Saints, 1981.

Brown, S. Kent; Cannon, Donald Q.; and Jackson, Richard H. Historical Atlas of Mormonism. New York: Simon & Schuster, 1994.

The Holy Bible, Authorized King James Version.

Jenson, Andrew. Latter-day Saint Biographical Encyclopedia. A Compilation of Biographical Sketches of Prominent Men and Women in the Church of Jesus Christ of Latter-day Saints. Excerpts, 4 vols. Salt Lake City: A. Jenson History, 1901–1936.

Journal of Discourses. Edited by George D. Watt, et al. 26 vols. Liverpool: F. D. Richards, et al., 1854–1886.

Ludlow, Daniel H, ed. The Encyclopedia of Mormonism. 4 vols. New York: Macmillan Publishing, 1992.

McConkie, Bruce R. Doctrinal New Testament Commentary: Vols. 1–3. Salt Lake City: Bookcraft, 1966, 1971, 1973.

McConkie, Bruce R. The Messiah Series, vols. 1–6. Salt Lake City: Deseret Book, 1978–1982.

The Pearl of Great Price. Salt Lake City: Church of Jesus Christ of Latter-day Saints, 1981.

Roberts, B. H. Comprehensive History of The Church of Jesus Christ of Latter-day Saints. 6 Vols. 1930. Reprint. Orem, Utah: Sonos Publishing, Inc., 1991.

Smith, Joseph Fielding. Answers to Gospel Questions. vols. 1–4. Salt Lake City: Deseret Book, 1957–1963.

Smith, Joseph Fielding. Doctrines of Salvation: Sermons and Writings of Joseph Fielding Smith. 3 vols. Edited by Bruce R. McConkie. Salt Lake City: Bookcraft, 1954–1956.

Smith, Joseph. History of The Church of Jesus Christ of Latter-day Saints. Edited by B. H. Roberts. 2nd ed., rev. 7 vols. Salt Lake City: Deseret Book, 1980.

Talmage, James E. Jesus the Christ. 15th ed., rev. Salt Lake City: The Church of Jesus Christ of Latter-day Saints, 1977.

Times and Seasons. Edited by Ebenezer Robinson, et al. 6 vols. Commerce, Illinois, and Nauvoo, Illinois, 1839–1846. (132 issues)

Young, Brigham. Discourses of Brigham Young. Compiled by John A. Widtsoe. Salt Lake City: Deseret Book, 1978.

Acknowledgment is given to the excellent staff of the Church Historical department Library and to the fabulous Collector's Library software produced by Infobases, Inc.

INDEX